D0461497

CALLING THE SHOTS

KELLY HRUDEY

CALLING THE SHOTS

Ups, Downs and Rebounds—My Life in the Great Game of Hockey

With

KIRSTIE McLELLAN DAY

HarperCollins*Publishers*Ltd

Calling the Shots
Copyright © 2017 by Kelly Hrudey and Kirstie McLellan Day.
All rights reserved.

Published by HarperCollins Publishers Ltd

First edition

Unless otherwise noted, photographs in this book
appear courtesy of the author.

No part of this book may be used or reproduced in any manner
whatsoever without the prior written permission of the publisher, except
in the case of brief quotations embodied in reviews.

HarperCollins books may be purchased for educational, business, or sales
promotional use through our Special Markets Department.

HarperCollins Publishers Ltd
2 Bloor Street East, 20th Floor
Toronto, Ontario, Canada
M4W 1A8

www.harpercollins.ca

Library and Archives Canada Cataloguing in Publication
information is available upon request.

ISBN 978-1-44345-224-3

Printed and bound in the United States

LSC/H 9 8 7 6 5 4 3 2 1

I'm the luckiest guy alive to have four strong, smart and beautiful women in my life—Donna, Jessica, Megan and Kaitlin—and I dedicate this book to them.

Contents

Foreword

THE GAME OF HOCKEY IS SUCH a unique sport. So many of us come together from all over the world with the hope that one day we'll be able to play in the National Hockey League.

It's fairly well known that goaltenders are a little different from forwards and defencemen. But for some reason, I was lucky enough to play with some great goalies who were not like that at all. Guys like Grant Fuhr, Mike Richter and, of course, Kelly Hrudey, just to name a few.

I first got to know Kelly during the 1987 Canada Cup. I was with the Oilers and he was with the Islanders. I remember that he was immediately one of the most well liked players at training camp. Besides taking shots day in and day out, he was always the last guy off the ice. On top of that, he gave his input at the penalty-kill and power-play meetings. Seeing those plays through a goalie's eyes really helped us.

A few years later, when Kelly was traded to the L.A. Kings, he gave us a real boost of energy on the ice. And he was like a captain off the ice, never shy to get into another player's face, whether it was me, Rob Blake or a fourth-line centre. But he always did it in a classy way.

Kelly wanted what was best for the team, and in the 1993 playoffs, that came through loud and clear. Early on, during rounds one and two, Kelly, who was our number one goalie, split some of the games with our backup, Robb Stauber. But Kelly didn't make a big deal out of it. His focus didn't change one bit. When he wasn't playing, he still practised harder than anyone and showed the same strong leadership he always did.

When it came to round three, where we faced Toronto, he never faltered. He took the bull by the horns and helped us win the series in seven games. That meant we were going to the Stanley Cup Final. In my opinion, there was no one more deserving than he was.

Unlike a lot of goalies who like to keep to themselves, Kelly had great flair. The L.A. fans loved him. He was a huge fan favourite. They loved the rebel, the defiant player whose trademark was a ripped piece of blue underwear that he wrapped around his head to keep the sweat out of his eyes. I always got a kick out of seeing the fans in the stands wearing blue bandanas.

We were all proud to be Kelly's teammates, and I'm sure he will give all you fans a wonderful insight into hockey and the lessons he learned in his everyday life.

Enjoy the book,
Wayne D. Gretzky

Prologue

I'VE ALWAYS LOVED THE GAME of hockey, from when I was young. I spent hours and hours in our basement with my older brother, Ken, playing ball hockey. And I was glued to the television watching *Hockey Night in Canada* on Saturday nights. I had trading cards back then—all the Toronto Maple Leafs and all the Montreal Canadiens. I put those players on a pedestal. They were my idols. Guys like Jean Béliveau.

When I played for the Islanders, and then the Kings, and then the Sharks, I'd see him up in the stands at the Montreal Forum. I remember thinking, "Wow, wouldn't it be something to become a man like Jean Béliveau?" He was a great presence. So elegant-looking in his beautiful tailored suits with that head of perfectly combed thick white hair. People throw around the words "hockey royalty" all the time, but he really was the king, and here he was, watching me play. I mean, how cool is that?

And Bobby Orr. He became an agent once he was done playing, and I had just gotten into broadcasting when I saw him standing at the Zamboni entrance in Florida. The Panthers were

1

on the ice for a morning skate and he was all by himself. It took a lot of courage for me to go up and introduce myself. Much to my surprise, he knew my name! It was like, "Oh my God, Bobby Orr knows who I am." A thrilling moment. We had a really nice chat, but I can't recall exactly what we talked about because I was so in awe. He reminded me of some of the greats by how humble he was.

Today, I am part of a brotherhood that started with guys like Orr and Béliveau and those before his time, like Georges Vézina. These are the guys who laid the foundation.

I never expected to play in the National Hockey League. Ever. And yet I had the privilege of playing in New York under Al Arbour, one of the greatest coaches in the league, and in Los Angeles with Wayne Gretzky, the greatest player ever to play the game. I played with some of the smartest, funniest most talented teammates at a time when I think hockey was at its most exciting.

I always read the game-day press notes. I'd look at how many years a player had under his belt, and I'd say, "How can a guy play twelve years or more in this league?" And then one time, I was in the dressing room getting ready for a game in L.A.— I'd been in the league around eight years—and I recall going, "You know what? I think I'm gonna be one of those guys. One day the press notes are going to list my name, my age and how many years I've played in the NHL, and it's going be north of ten years." Well, it turned out to be a fifteen-year ride.

Fifteen years of hard work, dedication, will and passion. Fifteen years full of love, support and loyalty. Fifteen years of ups, downs and rebounds. The highest of highs and the lowest of lows. That wave of emotion after a game is something most people never get to experience—anger, jubilation, frustration, satisfaction. But there was always one constant—pride. Every time I pulled on my jersey, I was proud to be a player in the NHL. I still am.

Chapter 1

Just a Warrior

FIRST TIME I MET ISLANDERS COACH Al Arbour, I was petrified. You know that feeling when you touch a bad plug? Electricity zips around your cells and somehow ends up leaving this awful feeling in your teeth. I was nineteen years old and intimidated for sure.

Al was old-school hockey. A very tall man. I was about five foot ten and still growing, and he was about six feet. But he had so much presence he looked about eight feet tall. He was a big and powerful guy. He wore thick black-rimmed glasses, which made him unique. When he was thinking, he'd pull them off and run his hand through his thick black hair. He'd put his glasses back on and you'd see these Brylcreem fingerprints.

Early on in the league, coaches were dictatorial. There was one way, and either you did it that way or you were on the bus to the minors. Simple as that. Prior to 1967–68, there were only six teams and an abundance of players, which meant fewer jobs and a lot of guys chasing them. Whether or not players liked what the coach was telling them wasn't really a factor.

Al was like a stern father figure who knew when to give you a kick in the butt and when to pat you on the back. He knew what you needed wasn't always what you expected. Sometimes you thought you were going to get one and you'd get the other. He kept you off guard. He wouldn't tell you that he used psychology, but he did.

Geezus, I'm getting emotional just thinking about him. I loved the man. He was the first guy I met in hockey who really cared about people. I mean at that pro level. No, I gotta take that back because my Indianapolis Checkers coach, Fred Creighton, was a beautiful man to me in the minors. Fred cared just as much about developing guys for the NHL as he did about winning the league championship.

Al tried to make a real connection with all of us. He did that by treating us all differently. Of course, there were some players he never reached. It doesn't work out every time. But he went beyond just the X's and O's. As an example, the way he treated Denis Potvin was a lot different than the way he treated me. When Potvin first joined the Islanders, Al Arbour was tough on him. Denis was drafted number one overall, and he performed magnificently right from the first day he stepped into the league. He was a guy that all the New York press praised, saying how great he was. As a result, many times Al had to drive home the point to Denis to get his ego get out of the way.

There's that famous story about Denis in his first season with the Islanders. Al was a stickler about being on time. If he said the bus was leaving at 10 a.m., you'd better be there at 9:45. The team would meet at the practice rink at Cantiague Park in Hicksville on Long Island. One blizzardy Sunday morning in the middle of December 1973, the guys were heading out for a night game at the Spectrum in Philly. About fifteen minutes before the bus was scheduled to leave that morning, Bobby Nystrom called Denis and woke him up. Denis hopped in his car and showed up literally five minutes late, but the bus was gone.

Now, here's what was crazy. There was a gas shortage in America at that time. OPEC had proclaimed an oil embargo and because it was a Sunday, the gas pumps on Long Island were closed. Denis was already driving on fumes, which meant he wouldn't make it all the way to Philadelphia.

Remember, Denis was only twenty years old and there was no internet, no such thing as cell phones. He may have looked cool with his long burns and handlebar 'stache, but in truth, he started out like the rest of us. An unsophisticated kid from a small place. He came from Hull-Ottawa and grew up on a street he called in his book *Power on Ice* "a Gallic Archie Bunker's street." He had no idea what to do, so he went home and waited for a call.

As soon as the bus hit Philly, his older brother Jean, who was also a defenceman on the Islanders, called him and told him to get his ass on a train. But Al grabbed the phone and said, "Don't bother. My lineup is made up and you missed the bus. I'll see you back on Long Island tomorrow at 10 a.m. for practice." So the Islanders' big number-one star missed the game and they lost 4–0.

Next morning, Denis came in at 9 a.m. and got dressed. He skated around a bit and saw Al come in at ten o'clock. Alone. Al pulled out his whistle and bag skated Denis for over an hour. Afterward, GM Bill Torrey fined Denis and advised him to apologize to the team. Denis was totally embarrassed, and it didn't help when the press ran with it. The incident made an impression on everybody. Especially Denis.

SEVEN YEARS LATER, IN 1980, I was drafted by the Islanders—second round, thirty-eighth overall. Listen, it was a different world back then. The draft was almost always in Montreal, and unless you were going to be a first rounder, you didn't go. I didn't have an agent, because no agent bothered to call me. Why would they? I was not a very good player growing up. I always got cut. I never even made a rep team until I was sixteen years old, and that was only after I was released by another team earlier that September. The idea of me going second round never occurred to anyone, least of all me.

The only indication I had that there might be any interest was a year earlier, in 1979–80. I started hearing my name mentioned at the end of my second season with the Medicine Hat Tigers, a junior team in the Western Hockey League. You know how it goes—"Hey, rumour has it the scouts are coming to see you." I would shrug it off. "They must have it wrong." And then, as the season went on into my draft year, the scouts actually started saying hi to me after games. And finally, there was this hockey publication—I think it was called *Hockey Prospects* or something. I used to pick it up every week from the news-stand. It would say who the potential 1980 draft guys were, and I was rated in the top four goalies along with Don Beaupre, Rick LaFerrière and Darrell May. I remember seeing that and I was shocked. Just frickin' bowled over.

Anyway, the day of the 1980 draft, I was at home in Edmonton, playing ball hockey with my brother, Ken, who is four years older, in my parents' undeveloped basement. We did that all the time. The phone rang around one thirty in the afternoon, and I ran upstairs. It was a guy who said, "Is Kelly there?"

"Speaking."

The man identified himself as Jimmy Devellano, and of course I knew who he was in the hockey world—the head scout of the New York Islanders.

Jimmy has a real quirky-sounding voice. You'd expect a rough kind of eff-you-mother-effer growl, but instead it's high. Not sharp like Foster Hewitt's, but just as nasal, and he has a real down-home way about him. Like he's leaning over the fence, talking about the weather, and he uses the word *okay* a lot. He explained who he was and then he said, "Kelly, okay, I'd like to let you know that we've drafted you in the second round, okay?" I don't recall much of the conversation after that. Just this rush of adrenaline that whooshed right through me. I was being drafted onto the team that had just won the Stanley Cup.

Later, Jimmy D told me that they didn't have me rated until the third round, maybe even the fourth, and that they'd rated an Ontario Hockey League goalie, Don Beaupre, even with me. But they were caught off guard when the Minnesota North Stars chose Beaupre with their second pick, thirty-seventh overall—one ahead of the Islanders. I guess the Islanders management huddled at the draft table and made the decision to pick me next.

I went down into the basement and told Ken, "I just got drafted by the New York Islanders." He said, "Cool." And we went back to playing ball hockey.

Training camp was a blur to me because I was meeting all these Stanley Cup winners like Denis Potvin and Mike Bossy and Billy Smith and then practising with them, which was amazing. The scrimmage rosters were posted on a wall around the corner from the dressing room, and I'd often do two shifts because I was the young guy, and at that time the collective bargaining agreement had no limits. I made nothing other than meal money, which I thought was outstanding. Breakfast, lunch and supper at the Burger King next to the Holiday Inn.

From what I gather, it was Jimmy D more than anyone else who wanted me. In fact, I was surprised when I read his book, *The Road to Hockeytown: Jimmy Devellano's Forty Years in the NHL*, where he says that the two best goaltenders he ever drafted were Chris Osgood and me. I mean, that's pretty amazing considering Jimmy D drafted a couple of dozen of them.

The very first exhibition game (that's what we always called them—now most say "preseason" games) was versus the Chicago Black Hawks. We took a commercial flight to Chicago, and I will never forget sitting in the middle seat between Bryan Trottier and Mike Bossy.

No question, management put me between those two superstars so I could learn the right way to behave like a pro. There was familiarity with Trots, because we'd played in the same general area of Canada—western junior. He was raised in Val Marie, Saskatchewan, and in 1974–75 had played for my old rivals, the Lethbridge Broncos. I liked the way he looked at the world through his own lens. To this day, if you call Bryan a contrarian, he'll say, "No I'm not, I'm a counter-contrarian because I don't always agree with everything that everybody disagrees with."

Al Arbour used to call him stubborn, but Trots would say, "I'm not stubborn, I'm bull-headed." If we were sitting in a room with twelve people, he'd disagree with all twelve, and if anyone agreed with him, he'd look for a different point of view. That's the way he's built. I don't think it's a bad thing. He didn't like to be predictable. And he didn't like for people to know his business. That strategy worked well on the ice. He didn't give away what he was going to do next.

Trottier could do so much offensively and defensively. He was, still is and always will be the best and easiest centre for a defenceman to play with. His stick was always available. If a guy was in trouble, he was always right there from a positional standpoint. I would come to find him just a pleasure to play with. He showed quality leadership.

Bossy had the most outstanding arms you've ever seen. Coconuts for biceps, and his wrists were like fire logs. His arms were the most stunning sight I've ever seen on a male body. Sitting next to him, I could feel his power. When I was growing up, the articles in *The Hockey News* and other magazines indicated that he was a slight guy. But in truth, he was six feet and 205 pounds of sheer muscle, a lot like Gordie Howe and Bobby Hull. Mike worked out a lot with a machine we used for shoulder rehabilitation called a UBE, or upper body ergometer. It was basically a bike that pedalled your arms. As I sat there on that flight, pretending to read my magazine, I was secretly stealing glances at those big arms and thinking, "Whoa!"

Mike had to be selfish. He knew that in order for our team to be successful, he had to put up a lot of points. Bossy was very deceptive. To put it in proper context, he was a better natural goal scorer than Alex Ovechkin. He often showed you the puck in a regular, perpendicular way, and then he'd pull it closer to his feet and change the angle, and while you were trying to readjust your position he'd do it again. He might open up the blade, he might cup the shot. Oftentimes he would fool you by making it look as though he was going for the high short side, but instead he would change his follow-through, because his favourite target was the five-hole. Through the legs. He scored a ton of goals five-hole.

He was an amazing player. There was this hunger that I

admired and respected. He was a guy who wanted to excel, and I love people who have that kind of competitiveness. I think Bryan Trottier gets the credit he deserves, and so do Denis Potvin and Billy Smith to a certain degree, but I don't think people recognize how great Mike Bossy was. I almost wish he were playing in today's world, which has so much media coverage, because he would be recognized as a player at a much higher level. He was a true star.

He scored on me from the blue line during that training camp. Skated up, took a slapshot and beat me—five-hole. Honestly, I'd never seen a shot that hard in my life. And it was accurate, not lucky. I thought, "Oh my God, I am so far away from being a legit NHL player."

For the most part, he was distant and not all that warm, but when I made the Islanders in 1983, Mike Bossy was the first guy on the team to invite me over to his house for dinner. He and his wife, Lucy, were very nice to me that night.

I ran into him on the concourse at the Denver airport about three years after I retired. I was with one of my *Hockey Night in Canada* producers, Sherali Najak. It was a very awkward meeting. Typically, when you see a guy you've played with, there's this special closeness that comes flooding back. It's like how you bond when you room with a guy in college, or go through boot camp with a guy in the military, and then you see each other twenty years later and you pick right back up.

Guys like that are brothers—not blood brothers, but brothers just the same. In hockey, you build emotional bonds when your teammate comes to the rink and plays his heart out every night, or throws himself in front of an Al MacInnis slapshot, or digs so deep he scores a game winner on broken bones. But with Mike it was different. He was just a warrior. A guy that played.

At that first training camp, we landed in Chicago and Al Arbour came up to me that morning. He said, "You're starting tonight." My first time on NHL ice and it was at Chicago Stadium. One of the most historic buildings in the National Hockey League. It was a weird building. You had to go down twenty-one stairs from ice level to the visitors' dressing room, which was unusually small and where the floor wasn't carpeted or rubber, it was linoleum. I think the Black Hawks did that on purpose to dull our edges. You could get away with that kind of stuff in that era. Legend has it teams used to put sand on the floor in the visitors' dressing room. I kid you not.

I was stretching in the net and I looked down at the other end of the ice, where I saw one of my heroes. A future Hall of Famer in his big red Black Hawks jersey with number 35 on the shoulders. He was skating back and forth in the crease, shaving the ice with his blades. Intense, like a caged polar bear, and totally focused on his job that night. All I could think was, "Oh my God, I'm on the same ice as Tony Esposito."

Second period, a former Medicine Hat Tiger, Tom Lysiak, scored on me. He had a two-on-one break and was coming down on my right. I came out, trying to play the angle. He took a slapshot and banked one in off the far post about eighteen inches off the ice on my glove side. It was so easy, he barely raised his arms, like, "Thank you for giving me all that room, kid." I thought, "Holy crap, I'm still a long way from being an NHL goalie."

I think I faced thirty-six shots. I let in five after two periods. You won't have any longevity in the NHL with that kind of performance, but if it's your first NHL game, it's not the worst.

You know what? Instead of looking down on me because I was just a recent draft choice, Clark Gillies, Bob Nystrom, Bob Bourne and a number of the other guys took me out to Pizzeria Uno in downtown Chicago. What a bunch of great guys. We flew home the next day, and a day or two later I was sent back to junior, which wasn't unexpected, but I took it hard anyway. Nobody likes getting cut.

Chapter 2

I Hate the Shake

YOU'VE GOT TO REMEMBER THAT BACK then there were only twenty-one starting goalies and twenty-one backups. Just forty-two jobs for goalies in the entire league, that's it. In 2016–17, ninety-five goalies were in net for at least a portion of a game. When I looked at the Islanders roster in 1980–81, I was thinking, "Holy cow, I've gotta leapfrog a lot of guys if I am ever going to make this team." I went back to the Medicine Hat Tigers with the attitude that I had a lot of work to do.

But it was a tumultuous year for the Tigers. We should've been a top team. We had so many good players returning for their last year—Ken Solheim, Rod Buskas—and great rookies like Murray Craven. Unfortunately, our coach, Pat Ginnell, totally derailed our season. I know Patty had greatness in his past, especially in the mid-'60s when he coached Bobby Clarke and Reggie Leach, and I'm not trying to take that away from his legacy—he died in 2003—but that year, Patty didn't show up very often. In fact, he came to only about a third of our practices. Steve Tsujiura, our captain, ran most of them. Whenever Patty was behind the bench, he was terrible, a tyrant, and frankly he might as well have stayed home. I learned nothing from him about the game, but I built inner strength because I had to persevere. He coached by fear, and I thought there was more to coaching than that.

Brent Sutter was drafted to the Islanders the same year as I was. We didn't know each other except as competitors. In 1980–81 he was in Lethbridge with the Broncos, and we played against each other a lot. Our team was older. A lot of us were in our last year of junior. We had the talent and experience to win the league championship and go to the Memorial Cup. A year earlier we went to the Eastern Conference final, two steps away, and we still had the same group of guys who were now a year better. The Broncos were a young team. Several of their players moved from the Red Deer Rustlers along with their coach, John Chapman. They had a good team—Brent, his brothers Ronnie and Richie, the Sutter twins, and Mike and Randy Moller. But we were better.

The Broncos started to play really well. There were nights I was stopping fifty to sixty shots, and a lot of them were Brent's. He put up 108 points that year.

Our team was in a terrible situation because we had little to no direction. There was a six- or seven-game road trip to the West Coast near the end of the season where we should have been building for the playoffs, but Patty was absent. He only showed up to one game on that trip.

Near the end of the season, we played an afternoon game in Lethbridge. It was an important game. We were all really excited because we won and it was huge. We got on the bus, ready to head back to Medicine Hat, all pretty hungry. What we usually did was spend our three-dollar per diem at McDonald's on a Big Mac, fries and a drink. That was the most food you could find for three bucks. Patty got on the bus and said, "Look, it's only a two-hour drive home. How about we don't eat? We'll drive straight from Lethbridge to Medicine Hat, and then you can have a nice warm meal at your billets'. It'll be better for you."

We were all like, "Yeah, sounds good!"

And then I said, "Okay, Patty, but you need to give us our money. We still get our three bucks." Oh, he was so mad at me. Twenty players times three—that's a decent night at the bar for just one guy. He was furious, but he did walk around and hand over the money.

We ended up playing the Broncos in the first round of the playoffs that year. And they beat us. It was hard losing to our bitter rivals. When the game was over, they lined up at centre ice to shake hands. But Patty ordered us to the dressing room. He wouldn't let us shake hands.

Now, I can't stand the handshake. Never did like it. I've never said anything nice to anybody on the other team, and I don't recall anybody ever saying anything nice to me. I don't find any value in it. I think it's bullshit. I think it's fake.

The problem with the handshake is that it's not in the spirit of how I played the game. I wanted to win, and if I won, I deserved it, and if you won, you deserved it. I never felt consoled by another guy's handshake.

I played in a state of hate. I didn't just dislike my opponents. I hated each and every one of them. Two minutes after the horn, that hatred hadn't gone away. It took a little longer than that. So when Patty told us not to shake with Lethbridge, we all went off the ice, and I was fine with it. But once we were in the tunnel, eight of us looked at each other and said, "That's not right," and we headed back out to shake their hands.

It was a very up-and-down season. I don't think the Tigers got the best out of me. If I'm being honest about that year, I had outgrown junior. I was now looking for the next big challenge.

Chapter 3

It's All in the DNA

I DIDN'T START PLAYING HOCKEY UNTIL I was twelve years old. It's my understanding that's pretty rare for a guy who made the NHL. The only other guy I knew who started nearly that late was Ed Jovanovski, who went on to play eighteen years in the league. Most NHLers started skating when they were three or four and were playing organized hockey by kindergarten. I wasn't just a late bloomer. Even in those days, I was a very, very late starter.

When I was eleven I went to my parents and asked them if I could join a hockey team. My dad knew the only reason I was asking was I wanted to be around my friends. He said, "Okay, but first you have to spend a year learning how to skate." Hockey's not like a lot of other sports. A little kid can grab a ball and glove and run out onto a baseball field, but you have to be able to get around the ice on skates to play hockey, and my dad recognized that. I was athletic and I loved all sports. In elementary school, I was voted best athlete in the school. I played everything except basketball. My vertical is only about three inches, so shooting hoops was not for me. I was lousy in hockey too, but I just loved the game.

In my teens, I was always cut, even at the community-league level. I rarely had AA on my jacket—mostly "Peewee C" or "Bantam C." I made a Peewee A team once, but only because Clint Malarchuk moved up. Clint was incredible and went on to become a great goalie in the NHL. He's famous now for a terrible incident when an opposing forward's skate sliced his jugular vein and he nearly bled to death on the ice—on live television. It's amazing how good he was despite his struggle with mental health issues. He was very open about all he went through in a documentary I was interviewed for called *Goalie: Life and Death in the Crease*, where he talks about how he actually shot himself in the head to get rid of all the paranoid thoughts he was suffering. Thank God he survived and got help.

Clint was an amazing goalie and I was nowhere near his level back then, but at around fifteen I started to break through. By the time I was sixteen, I finally made a rep team.

That team, Canadian Athletic Club Inland Cement, made a coaching change halfway through the year. We got this guy, a well-respected coach in Edmonton hockey by the name of Al Lymer. All of a sudden, we were doing tons of skating, drills and anaerobic fitness, and we ended up beating Calgary for the provincial championship. It was a two-game, total-goal series.

Mike Vernon, who went on to win Stanley Cups with the Flames and the Red Wings, was their goalie. The whole time we played them, I was thinking, "Wow, that guy is amazing," never dreaming that we would end up playing against each other in junior, and then again in the pros, and finally playing together in San Jose with the Sharks. I mean, what are the odds?

Going into that summer, there was no WCHL (renamed that season to WHL) draft. Instead, you got letters. I got one from the New Westminster Bruins and another from the Medicine Hat Tigers, inviting me to training camp. New West was a really good team and Medicine Hat wasn't. I thought I'd have a better chance of making the Tigers, and even more important, it was closer to home.

I didn't think I was nearly good enough, but I drove to Medicine Hat for training camp with my best friend, Jeff Marshall. We stayed at the Cecil Hotel, which was rundown and full of beer stink. We also had the pleasure of sharing a bathroom with everybody on the same floor. I didn't know enough to bring flip-flops back then, and I remember my feet sticking to the grime on the bathroom tile.

Vic Stasiuk was my coach. I was amazed by Vic. He was on the Bruins' famous Uke Line with Johnny Bucyk and Bronco Horvath in the late '50s. Vic was the ultimate gentleman and you could trust him. When you looked him in the eye, you could see sincerity. On the second day of training camp, Vic called me into his office after my skate. I was thinking, "It's bye-bye time," which was a reasonable assumption.

I sat down, ready for the speech, and he said to me, "Kelly, you have made the Medicine Hat Tigers. You've made the team." I never did find out why. But I remember blurting out, "Well, we've got a real problem. I only brought one pair of jeans and two T-shirts because I was expecting to get cut." I also told him that I couldn't commit to playing for him until I cleared it with my parents. Jeff and his dad and I headed home to Edmonton. Jeff had made the team too, but his parents wanted him to stay in Edmonton, finish school and play for the Junior A St. Albert Saints.

The Medicine Hat Tigers seemed to really want me. Their general manager, Doug Smeaton, drove up to my house to meet with our family in our living room. Doug was a real kind-hearted guy. He told us the Tigers saw me as a goalie who wasn't going to sit back. At tryouts, when I was done my turn in goal, I'd take off my helmet and grab a stick and join a two-on-one to shoot. He said they were impressed by that kind of work ethic and attitude. He also told my family that if I left home and joined the Tigers, I would come back a different person, more responsible and mature. I was seventeen.

First of all, we were all shocked that the Tigers wanted to take this leap of faith with me. We were a very close family—my mom, Pauline, my dad, Steve, Ken and me. We did everything together. That was the beautiful thing about my upbringing.

We had no money, so our vacations were the best. My dad was a very proud man. I lost him recently, so this is tough, but here goes. We could only afford a very small fold-down travel trailer. Hard shell. Dad hitched it up to our brown, fake-wood-panel Plymouth station wagon, and we hauled that thing through Banff and Jasper, which has some of the world's most breathtaking scenery. Dad liked to explore in the car. We'd crawl up the edge of a gravel mountain road. It was like driving along a steel girder at the top of the Empire State Building. Stones and rocks would spit out from under our tires and tumble down the mountainside, bouncing off the rocks like decapitated heads. It was all very exciting.

Mom was a little nervous, but Ken and I felt perfectly safe with Dad behind the wheel. We'd find a campground spot and get the fire going. I remember the smell of bacon cooking on the old cast-iron skillet, and the taste of fresh bread with cold butter and jam. At night, it was Ukrainian ham sausage, kobasa, and of course, roasted marshmallows for dessert.

Dad worked for Prairie Rose Bottling. He would bring home these one-gallon jugs of Orange Crush syrup and dilute it with tap water. Delicious. Ken and I would have drunk it morning, noon and night, but my mom restricted us to one pop every Friday night.

Both my dad's folks and my mom's parents were Ukrainian. From what I can make of the records I've found, my dad's dad, John Hrudey, was from Ukraine, but remember that Ukraine didn't declare itself an independent state until 1991. In those days, Ukrainians came from Austria-Hungary or Romania. My *gido* (grandfather) was from Galicia, an Austro-Hungarian province. On October 22, 1909, he crossed the Atlantic on a ship called the *Empress of Britain*, landing in Quebec. We think he was around thirteen or fourteen at the time. And all by himself. But because they wouldn't let kids sail alone, he was listed as being nineteen. I've talked to other friends whose grandparents and great-grandparents came to Canada by themselves at that age. When I look at my own girls, or think about what I was like at that age, I have real trouble wrapping my head around this kid landing in Quebec and making his way west and ending up in a rooming house in Victoria, Alberta.

He lived there with a large group of other immigrants. My gido basically raised himself, working as a labourer. He travelled around, working construction sites and for the Canadian Pacific Railway, doing whatever he could to save enough money to homestead and send for a girl from the old country to marry.

Ukrainian immigrants were assigned the worst land. Always in the wilderness, outside townships. My grandfather settled in a place they called Zawale, ten miles southwest of the railway town of Andrew, Alberta. It's not even on the map anymore. He built a modest two-room clapboard house, and then in the late 1920s he sent back home for a girl named Maria Cheborak. I knew her as *Baba*, the Ukrainian name for "grandmother." They married and had two children—Steve, my dad, born in 1929, and Irene, who was four years younger.

My mom's family settled outside Smoky Lake. Her father, Dmytro Karpo, came over in the 1920s travelling through Romania and bought some cheap land about six miles from town. But at the time, Smoky Lake consisted of just a little post office and store north of the North Saskatchewan River. In 1926, he sent for his twenty-three-year-old bride-to-be, Mary Yaremco.

It was incredibly hard living. My mom, Pauline, remembers her parents worrying about how they were going to make their government payments for the land. She remembers harvest, standing in the middle of a field in her little cotton dress, barefoot with a pitchfork in her hands, trying to help out. When she was three years old she remembers losing her older sister to pneumonia, and the death of her twin baby brother and sister.

She remembers her mother as a woman who was so very proud. Their home was simple—wooden floors impossible to keep clean, and handmade cotton quilts stuffed with sheep's wool to keep them warm on winter nights when the temperature would dip to forty below. Boona made their home beautiful by hand-embroidering everything from bedding to the kids' clothing to the cotton shelf liners.

My mom also remembers her dad, Metro, as quiet and distant. More like a visiting farmhand than a father. On the other side of the family, John Hrudey was the same. It turns out both grandfathers were hiding the same terrible secret.

Okay, I am going to get a little hot under the collar here. While researching this book, I was horrified to learn that in World War I, members of my family, including my gido, were wrongfully arrested for being enemy aliens.

A quick bit of history here. In 1914, Archduke Franz Ferdinand, the heir to the Austro-Hungarian throne, was assassinated by Serbian nationalists. As a result, Austria-Hungary declared war on Serbia in July. And because Russia had a treaty with Serbia, that brought them into it.

On the other side, Germany had a treaty with Austria-Hungary, so on August 1, it declared war on Russia. France came in because it also had a treaty with Russia, and Britain was on the side of France, so *it* got involved. Now, bound to Britain were Australia, Canada, India, New Zealand and the Union of South Africa. Bottom line, Canada was at war with my grandfather's homeland, Austria-Hungary.

In August 1914, under the War Measures Act, Canada declared thousands of Canadians, people who didn't homestead or own a house, to be enemy aliens. Most of them, including 1,500 Albertans, were Ukrainian immigrants. The next year, 1915, there was a new law in Canada that an enemy alien could be interned (in a camp) whether he was employed or unemployed—or for competing with a British subject for a job. So, unless you were dead or in school, you could be arrested.

By October of 1917, my gido, John Hrudey, had been in Canada for eight years. He was twenty-two years old and saving every dime for his future. He was rounded up along with eight other Ukrainian men on a construction site and arrested for failing to register as an enemy alien. He was ordered to appear in court on Hallowe'en before Police Magistrate Philip Carteret Hill Primrose, a former superintendent in the Royal Northwest Mounted Police and a future lieutenant-governor of Alberta. Today, some historians consider Primose the "hanging judge" of the wartime era in Alberta because he was one of the top three convictors of Ukrainians.

John Hrudey was fined twelve dollars and paid court costs of $2.75. An interpreter was paid one dollar out of the court costs, and here's where I get really pissed off about the whole thing— Primose made $1.75 per conviction. Remember, this was at a time when my grandpa might have made a dollar a day if he was lucky.

On April 3, 1918, my great-uncle Wasyl Karpo, my grandfather Metro's brother, appeared in Blairmore court before Justice of the Peace Pinkley for failing to have the police endorse his alien enemy registration card when he neglected to get permission to leave Fernie after working in a coal mine. He was fined $15 plus costs of $5.50. He was arrested along with a friend, and the RNWMP officers, Roofe and Grant, made $7.50 off each of them while Pinkley took home $4.

As a result of their arrests and convictions, both my gido and my great-uncle had criminal records for the rest of their lives. I can only imagine the shame and disappointment these proud men felt. Neither family ever spoke of it. Whenever I think about Primose, Pinkley and those two cops, I think, "I hope those pricks enjoyed their new suits and the steak dinners they ate off the sweat on my family's backs."

Chapter 4

Living Large

WHEN MY PARENTS MARRIED, THEY DECIDED their kids would not grow up having to do without, like they had. When I left for Medicine Hat my mom gave me her car, a cool little second-hand Mustang, and she took the bus to work. That's the kind of parents they were.

We were so close, I know it killed them when I left home so young. My brother, Ken, later told me it was literally like a loss in the family. Especially that first year. I called home every day for the first three months. Mom and Dad didn't have a lot of money. She worked at a children's clothing store as a shoe specialist, and like I said, Dad repaired Pepsi machines for a living. He was a smart guy. He could fix anything. It didn't bother him to take something apart. He was fearless that way. He used to invent stuff all the time. For instance, before they were commonplace, he built an air compressor that we used to inflate our bicycle tires. Then he took a night course to learn how to fix TVs. This was in the good old days of tube TVs. He fixed them after work and on weekends, I guess to pay for all those long-distance phone charges I racked up calling them from Medicine Hat when I got homesick. The phone bills came to three or four hundred bucks a month. It was a fortune to my parents. But they never said a word.

Around November, we played a Saturday night game and got beat pretty badly. I was disgusted with myself and tossed and turned all night. I called home first thing Sunday morning and said, "Mom, I want to come home. It was just awful last night." You would expect the answer on the other end of the line to be, "Yeah, come home." But instead my mom said, "Well, if you feel you want to, fine, but first go to practice this morning. When you get back, give me a call. If you still want to come home, then come home."

I went to practice, had a great time, and called back and told my mom, "It's okay, everything's fine. I'll stay."

We were a terrible team that first year, 1978–79. I played the majority of the games. Fifty-seven out of seventy-two. Our first weekend in Brandon, Manitoba, we lost something like 14–2. Vic Stasiuk quit at the halfway mark. He was a rancher in southern Alberta, and it was becoming impossible to do both jobs at the same time. He was replaced by a young coach named Sheldon Ferguson. Sheldon's still a scout in the National Hockey League, with Carolina. Sheldon was a great communicator. One time in practice, we had three-on-zero drills where guys come down on the goalie without any defencemen in the play. And I guess I must have been doing well, because at the end of the drill Sheldon came over to me and said, "Wow, nobody scored on you. I can't frickin' believe it! Three-on-zeros!"

I skated over to the bench to grab some water and thought, "Wow, nobody's ever said anything positive about my game like that to me before." I was having some good games. We played a team in Portland on a West Coast trip and got beat like 12–2. But I faced what seemed like 120 shots and was the first star. That kind of reinforcement got me to the next level.

Mom and Dad couldn't come watch me play very often because they couldn't afford it. They did attend the awards ceremony at the end of the year. We ended the season 15–50–7. I was named MVP and rookie of the year even though I had a goals-against average of 6.17. There's not a regular NHL goalie in the league today with a GAA over 3.55, and the top ten are under 2.28 in the regular season. To this day, I joke with the kids I talk to, "Hey, if I can make it to the NHL with a GAA of 6.17, so can you."

The next year, 1979–80, was my draft year, and I progressed again. This time our whole team did really well. We went to the East Division finals. Pat Ginnell coached us and pushed us hard, which was great. It was his first year and he was more committed.

My last season in junior, 1980–81, I was named to the second all-star team. Grant Fuhr was the first-team goalie. The next year, I went on to the pros. The minors, that is. My first year as a pro, 1981–82, was with the Indianapolis Checkers of the Central Hockey League. We won the league championship, and this time I was named playoff MVP and a first-team all-star. After that win, I naively went back to the next training camp hoping to make the Islanders but was sent down to Indianapolis again, and it was a real kick in the teeth. Now, when I look at it, I take my young self by the shoulders and say, "Get serious, Kelly. The Islanders had Billy Smith and Rollie Melanson and they had just won their third Stanley Cup." There wasn't room for me yet. But I had moved up to the third spot on the depth chart. I was getting closer.

Second year in the minors, '82–83, I was league MVP, we won the championship again and I was a first-team all-star. That fall, in training camp, the Islanders had just won their fourth Stanley Cup, and I finally made the team. On the last day of camp, there were five of us rookies left. That's how it was done back then. They'd make cuts all throughout training camp, and on the final day there'd be five guys banging on the door. Monty Trottier was one of them, Bryan's younger brother. There was also Garth MacGuigan, Kevin Devine and Darcy Regier. Darcy would go on to become the long-time general manager of the Buffalo Sabres. So, that last day of training camp, they were making the final cuts. We five were outside GM Bill Torrey's office, and we were called in one at a time. I was last. The four guys ahead of me were all told they were going back to Indianapolis, which was devastating. Nobody's goal in life is to make the minors.

I thought I was next on the chopping block. They already had two good goalies, Billy Smith and Rollie Melanson. Rollie was their third-round draft choice a year earlier than me. Rollie had already established himself as a top minor-league goaltender and he was moving up. He won three Stanley Cups as Billy Smith's backup after Chico Resch was traded to Colorado.

So when Bill Torrey told me I'd made the team, I was shocked and super excited. The most excited I'd ever been in my life. Nobody ever knows that he's going to make the National Hockey League. In fact, nobody really expects it when a life-long dream comes true, but now I had to go back out there and tell my friends, the four guys who had just been cut. For me, that was a bit of a problem. How dare I share such good news with them at a time when they were hurting so bad? So I didn't. I lied to them. I said, "I'm here for a bit, I don't know. I guess I'm sticking around for a few days. They have to make some decisions."

If you've ever been to Nassau Coliseum, you know that there's a big open parking lot next to the Marriott Hotel where I was staying. After I said goodbye to the guys, I was like Sylvester Stallone in *Rocky*, where he's running up the stairs. I raised my arms in the air and just flew down the steps. I was beside myself with joy, going, "Fuck yes! Fuck! Fuck! Fuck!"

I got a $40,000 signing bonus, so I put $20,000 into an annuity and then I splurged. I bought a five-hundred-dollar stereo for that car my mom and dad had bought me my second year with the Tigers. Oh, yeah. I was living large.

It's funny, but I don't think all that fondly of my first regular-season NHL game because I played a relief role, which wasn't all that thrilling. I had been a starter for the past five years—two in the minors, three years before that in junior. It happened against the Capitals on October 8, 1983. Walking into the Capital Centre wasn't like walking into Madison Square Garden or an iconic rink like that. The building was really dark inside. The paint above the stands was black, which made it look cavernous.

Our team was carrying three goalies—Billy, Rollie and me—which was unusual. Later in the season, Billy and Rollie made it known publicly that they weren't thrilled about the situation, even though the three of us got along really well.

Rollie was the starter in the Washington game, while I was the backup. But as I sat there, I could see the game was getting a little out of hand in favour of the other team and the situation warranted a change. Having said that, I didn't know if Al trusted me enough to throw me in.

At the start of the third period, we went down 6–3 and Al told me to get ready. He was going to take a chance on me. He pulled Rollie, and I felt somewhat awkward because Rollie hadn't got off to a great start that year and I knew that might have been because of my presence. I went in, and we started to come back. It was my first experience with a real powerhouse team. They just took over the game and Washington had no answer for the next three goals. But Washington scored a late goal on a fluky play. One of their right wingers, Bengt-Ake

Gustafsson—who was a great player, by the way—threw the puck across the crease on a two-on-one, and Bob Bourne, who was backchecking, accidently deflected a pass into our own net. That was the go-ahead goal, and I thought to myself, "Aw no, what a terrible way to lose the game."

But then Bob Nystrom scored late in the game, tying the score. And as luck would have it, Bob Bourne scored the game winner. Instant karma. I thought it was very cool that he had a chance to redeem himself like that.

I was grateful for the win, and it was significant because it made me their first goalie to be credited with a regular-season overtime win since 1942, but like I said, it didn't mean a ton to me. In fact, I've always wished I didn't have that as my first game on my resumé. Nobody dreams of going to the NHL and getting their first action in a backup position because the other guy didn't do very well.

Chapter 5

Agent Orange

LOCKER-ROOM JABBER, IT'S GOT A LIFE of its own. To be good at it, you have to be constantly manoeuvring and coming up with fresh stuff every day. On the Islanders, one of our left wingers, Greg Gilbert, was really, really clever. He was a guy who could stand up in front of everyone and tell stories without embarrassment. The stories weren't always wonderful. Sometimes they were boring and not funny. He'd get booed and guys would laugh and tell him to sit down or whatever. That was all part of it.

We had so many great experiences with the older players. We learned how to win from them. Twenty-two guys on the 1983–84 team were on the Stanley Cup team a year earlier. Despite the fact I was the only guy who made the team out of training camp, in the next few months a new group of younger guys came in. The old regime was kind of moving on.

They knew they were going to be replaced and their time was coming to an end, and yet they weren't bitter or jealous. I'd heard stories about painting guys head to toe with shoe polish and pulling out the razor to shave a golf green on the top of a rookie's head, but by the time I got there, I saw none of that stuff. The guys were just great to the rookies.

As those guys started to filter out, it was our job to carry it through from there. You take your whacks early in your career and that entitles you to give them later. Eventually, I learned to take a back seat to nobody when it came to giving jabs. I wish I could remember more of them. Unfortunately, they don't stick. If you're in the locker room, you don't dare write them down. What are you going to say, "Oh man, let me get this, I'm gonna write a book one day"? It's all done in good humour, not to embarrass anybody. It was fun to grow a thick skin and not to let things get to you. But even more important, you had to have the one-liners to fire back. You had to be lethal and quick.

We were such a close group. Gilbert, Brent Sutter, Paul Boutilier, Gord Dineen and I were part of that younger group that came in. Gilbert and Brent got there one and two seasons before me respectively. One night on the road in St. Louis, they were in their room when they heard a knock at the door. Gilbert opened the door and there stood two naked guys with paper bags over their heads with the eyes cut out. Gilbert called back to Brent, "It's just Clarkie and Bobby Bourne."

Clark Gillies was, and remains to this day, maybe the funniest teammate I've ever been around. He cracks jokes all the time, he's always in a good mood and he brings joy wherever he goes. A lot of us gravitated towards Clarkie. If you asked him, "Where are you from?" he'd say, "Well, I'm from Moose Jaw."

"Where's Moose Jaw?"

"Six feet from the moose's ass."

He had all these one-liners, and all of us guys—Bob Nystrom, Bob Bourne, Bryan Trottier, Duane Sutter, Brent Sutter, Greg Gilbert—we'd laugh our asses off. Because Clarkie is a talker, he's the life of the party, and that was just great for team morale. I only recall him getting mad at a teammate once. Rollie pushed him a little too far. Clarkie was getting more and more annoyed and Rollie kept going at him, and then it became very clear Clark had had enough.

Clark Gillies was a fantastic hockey player. You might even say a perfect hockey player. He could skate, score, shoot and pass, and he was tough, tough, tough—the whole package. I would even say he was a better hockey player than 90 per cent of the guys on the team.

But because of his size, his strength and his power, the responsibility of looking after his teammates fell onto him. I think he was forced into that role, sort of a reluctant warrior. He certainly wasn't a bully. Unfortunately for him, he was a good fighter. When he got angry, he could annihilate people. He fought with one of Boston's toughest enforcers ever, Terry O'Reilly. They went at it several times during a particularly tough playoff series with Boston in 1980. In that playoff year, Clark ended up with sixty-three penalty minutes in twenty-one games.

Recently, Terry told me that when they were on the ice together, he saw Clark change from the Clarkie we all knew into a big, scary monster. From a normal, pleasant-looking human being to a guy prepared to kill you. It's true, Clark got this look. His eyebrows would go inward and down, and the ends would wing up, like one of those cartoon drawings of a devil. And then his top lip would curl up over those big white teeth, stretching his bushy moustache into a mean, pencil-thin line. Geezus, he looked scary when he was mad. And it happened like, *snap*! Those fights were a big turning point for the Islanders. The Big Bad Bruins had a reputation. They were a very, very tough team, and the Islanders outmatched them in the physical part of the game.

THERE WAS THIS LITTLE DINER NEXT to our rink in Cantiague Park. The counter was always jammed with regulars. I remember the cook at the grill. He wore this used-to-be-white-about-ten-years-earlier apron with a butt hanging off his bottom lip. We'd watch the ash bounce around as he'd ask us, "How's it going?" Guys on our team would grab a runny egg and two pieces of greasy bacon on a bagel before practice, but I didn't because Al always had a morning weigh-in and I never wanted to be over. I was so jealous of Brent Sutter, who'd have to have three milkshakes a day to keep weight on.

Next door was a rundown, dingy pub. Terrible. The guys occasionally took me there after practice during training camp for a few beers. Hoisting a few was part of the glue that made a lot of teams stick together.

We drank together on the road too. My very first road trip with the team, we went to Quebec City and then Montreal for back-to-back games, and then to Washington to play the Capitals. In those days, the hotels didn't have computers so they sometimes messed up. It wasn't like today, where you breeze in and a concierge basically whisks you to your room.

We got into Washington late one night, and because I was the only rookie on the team, it meant I was last in line for a hotel key. Clark passed by me and said, "Hey rook, if you have a problem with your room and they're not set up, come on up. Bourney [Bob Bourne] and I, we'll call for a cot." Of course, I was praying that the hotel would screw up so I'd get to go hang with them. Well, I got my wish. I made my way up to Clark and Bob's room, and it was brilliant. The bathtub was already over-flowing with beer and ice. It was like magic how they had that set up so fast. I grabbed a cool one and flopped down on my cot, thinking, "This is the best frickin' night of my life."

Now, what didn't hotel rooms have back in 1983? TV remotes. So I was the remote for that night. "Rook, change the channel! Find us some football. Whoa, whoa, stop! Rook, don't you know better than to flip past *The Dukes of Hazzard*?" And I loved it. When I was fourteen years old I had a Clark Gillies New York Islanders NHL jersey. First jersey I ever bought. I started to tell Clark about it, and he was like, "That's enough. You make me feel old, kid."

Whenever we'd get off the bus in another city, Bob Nystrom and Billy Smith would go, "Rook, put your bag in your room and meet us in the lobby in five minutes." And they'd take me out for a few beers. They never let me buy. It was just, "Repay the favour by taking care of the young guys when you make the money." We formed this unbreakable bond. I still think of them as fantastic friends or big brothers. They were ultra-nice to me.

There was friction too. Here was a team that was tremendously successful—four-time Stanley Cup winners—and so everybody deserved their due. But that kind of success also caused words between three of our top players, Mike Bossy, Bryan Trottier and John Tonelli. We were all money-driven, but John wasn't getting paid what the other two were making.

Our GM, Bill Torrey, the team architect, would call you into his office and he'd show you a pie graph and tell you where you fit in. I think it was his way of trying to let people know he wasn't demeaning their talents, but that he only had so much money. Remember, the Islanders were only a little over a decade old, so even with the Cup wins, they were still a developing team. Not like the New York Rangers or Montreal Canadiens or Toronto Maple Leafs, teams that were well established and financially successful. Mr. Torrey was shrewd and he was ruthless. He was given a budget by the owners, and he prided himself on making that budget.

Of course, as a player, you understand that the more successful you are, the more money you are supposed to make. The next season, on December 31, 1984, we were on the road in Minnesota, staying at a little hotel near the arena, the old Met Center. The walls were paper thin. Okay, that's an understatement. They were so thin that if a guy passed gas three doors down, you could smell it. I was in a room close to Bossy and Trottier, who were the best of friends. Mike was tougher and stronger than people thought he was, and Trots was always telling him to keep that a secret from our opponents. He'd say, "Let them think you're weak, and that you can't check, and then when you do, you'll knock them on their asses." Bossy and Trots were always having a laugh together.

Bossy had a hundred nicknames in the locker room, and believe it or not, he answered to all of them. I think the most popular one was "La Machine." Every week, somebody tried to hang one on Bryan, even the newspaper writers, but nothing stuck except "Trots." Together, Mike and Bryan were known as "Bread and Butter" because they were tight. That name was given to them by retired Islanders tough guy Garry Howatt. But if anyone ever called out, "Bread and Butter!" Bryan wouldn't turn his head because he wasn't going to give anyone the pleasure of knowing they'd gotten to him.

Anyway, John Tonelli was in the room next to them that New Year's Eve, and the three of them got into it over money. I could hear Bossy and Trots yelling, "Look at the pie! Look at the goddamn pie! There's only so much left for you, John." I think John was traded to the Calgary Flames in 1986 for Steve Konroyd and Richard Kromm strictly over the issue of money. I mean, why else would you let go a guy like that? He was such a great player in his own right. I'm not saying it was a lop-sided trade. Konroyd and Kromm were younger but established players, and both were an important part of the rebuilding program Mr. Torrey was trying to carry out.

You hear that guys don't have that drinking-buddy mentality anymore, but I can tell you a quick story that surprised me. I'm a TV colour analyst for the Flames now—just finished my third year. Prior to taking this job, I was told that certain players on the team didn't drink. And my first year, I believed it.

And then, partway through my second year, we were in Philadelphia and I walked into the bar of this nice restaurant across from the hotel. A group of guys from the Flames were all sitting there, sharing a bottle of wine. I sat at a table nearby and had a couple beers, and they spotted me and invited me over. I rarely drink with players. In fact, I can only remember three times in three years with the team that I even shared a table with a player. Even though I really like the guys, I don't join them. I stay away. I don't want to cross the line. I'm not your friend, I'm not your teammate. I'm a broadcaster, and I want to do my job with a clean conscience. I can't be objective if I make a habit of hanging out with them. I mean, how am I going to comment fairly—maybe even say something harsh—if I'm worried about hurting a friendship?

But that night, I joined them for a drink and I said, "I have a question for you. I was told you guys never drink during the season."

And one of the guys said, "You know what, Kelly? We rarely drink, but if we do, we pick our spots. But Bob Hartley [who was the Flames' coach at the time] thinks if you have one beer all year, you're an alcoholic. So we're careful that stories don't get back to Bob." It was good to see these guys were real team guys and all that, but man, going back to my time, you learned how to play hurt, banged up and guilty. And boy, were we guilty.

People talk about cocaine. It was excessive in the '70s and early '80s. However, I didn't see any of it in the '90s, and I lived in L.A. Now I hear it's back to some degree. Mind you, other drugs like steroids have been around for a long time too. Steroids have been banned by the NHL since 2005, but before that they were fairly common.

The first time I ever even heard about anybody taking steroids was early in my career. You'd go for your physical during training camp. Usually you had privacy, but one year I was kind of shocked to find that there were five individual stalls in our dressing room, with curtains between so that you couldn't see the guy next to you, but you could hear the discussions he was having with the doctor right beside you. No secrets. It was very unprofessional. I mean, what happens if you have an STD? There was a player on the table, behind the curtain, right beside me. And one of our many team doctors stepped in to see him, and I heard, "Hi, how was your summer?"

The guy went, "Great."

This doctor, a very nice, quiet, understated man, said, "All right, take off your shirt." And then he said, "What the hell? How long have you been doing steroids?" And even though steroids weren't a banned substance in sports yet, he proceeded to tell the player about the dangers of using. I remember him saying they could hurt you later in life.

Next, the doctor whipped open my curtain and came into my stall. He said, "Okay, take off your shirt." And I went, "No one on steroids here, Doc. I'm a goalie."

There was something else that was commonplace just before I retired. It was a post-recovery drink called Ultimate Orange. We called it, prophetically, "Agent Orange." It tasted like a Creamsicle—delicious. I tried it once, wasn't for me. Lots of guys lived on it. I think it was kind of jokingly nicknamed after the actual Agent Orange herbicide that was dropped by the Americans in Vietnam, poisoning thousands of Vietnamese and giving cancer to thousands of American soldiers later in life. Well, in 2001, after I retired, I read in the *Los Angeles Times* about how Ultimate Orange contained a drug called ephedra, and that the U.S. Food and Drug Administration had received complaints alleging that people who took the drug had suffered heart attacks and strokes. Doctors even said that, in extreme cases, supplements containing ephedra, combined with rigorous exercise, could cause death.

Chapter 6

In All His Naked Glory

AL ARBOUR WAS FROM A LONG line of hockey players. Three of his great-uncles played in the NHL, including Amos Arbour, who was on the Montreal Canadiens in 1916, the first Canadiens team to win the Stanley Cup. But Al was never boastful. In fact, he always kind of talked badly about himself. Al played in sixteen NHL seasons over a stretch of eighteen years in the NHL. He played for Detroit in the mid-'50s with greats like Gordie Howe and Ted Lindsay and Glenn Hall. They won the Stanley Cup his first year, in 1954. And then he was claimed by the Chicago Black Hawks and helped win a Stanley Cup in 1961 along with Bobby Hull and Stan Mikita. Next, he was part of two Cup-winning teams with the Toronto Maple Leafs in 1962 and '64. He spent six seasons up and down between Rochester of the American Hockey League and Toronto, where his teammates included guys like Frank Mahovlich and Dave Keon, Red

Kelly and Tim Horton. Finally, he was selected in the 1967 expansion draft by St. Louis and wound up as a player/coach under Scotty Bowman.

When Al talked about his playing days, he'd say, "I was either the fourth guy, the fifth guy or I was out." Oftentimes, it would be, "I was a lousy player, but you guys are fantastic. You guys are great players . . ." He'd build us up like that. I wasn't buying it, by the way, because here was a guy who played in sixteen NHL seasons and won four Stanley Cups as a player in the "Original Six" era, and another four as a coach.

I don't think Al ever forgot what it was like to be a player. Never. He never forgot the emotions that we have. He didn't go above us and sit in an exalted position—"I am the big cheese because I am the coach." No, he always remembered what it was like to be a player.

And he had his own analytics before there were analytics. Say a guy was on a line with Bossy and Trottier. Al would say, "Don't dump the puck in. You put pucks on their sticks and you create and generate." But if you were on the fourth line, Al's analytics would be, "If you ever carry that puck over the blue line again, you won't see any more ice tonight. Dump it in."

This was all before the age of computers. What he would do was assign the equipment trainers to time our skaters' shifts. I believe Al was one of the first coaches to recognize that shorter shifts were better. He'd also have the trainers write down the other team's lines and matchups. Let's say we played the Canadiens. If we put out Bossy's line, who would their coach,

Jean Perron, put out for the Habs? Only a couple of coaches were doing that at the time, maybe just Al and Scotty Bowman. Today it's easy—you go to NHL.com and there are more stats there than you know what to do with. It gives you the match-ups too. Al was way ahead of his time.

When I came in, I heard one of the great Al Arbour stories of all time. It happened coming out of the 1980 playoffs. After Game Two of the semifinals against Buffalo, the boys took a charter flight back home landing at two in the morning at Republic Airport in East Farmingdale on Long Island.

The guys had parked in a small parking lot adjacent to the runway. They got off the plane, hopped in their cars and headed home. The following morning, they showed up at practice, and in walks Al with sunglasses on and his arm in a sling. Doesn't say a word, he just walks through, goes into his coach's office and shuts the door. Everybody's looking at each other, going, "What in the heck happened here?" They came to find out that Al had been one of the last to leave the parking lot that night. He pulled his car up to the gate to exit, but he hadn't pulled up close enough to the button to press it, so he half stepped out to reach it, and when he took his foot off the brake, the car took off without him. There were a couple of smaller airplanes tethered with wire to the side fence. It was dark out, and as Al chased his car across the parking lot, he ran into one of those wire tethers, flipped over, threw his shoulder out—which he did quite frequently—and landed on his face, giving him a couple of black eyes and scrapes and bruises.

Meanwhile, his car plowed into one of the planes, snapping the rudder.

After hearing the story, Bobby Nystrom said that guys started to greet him in the morning with, "Hey Al, hit any planes today?"

The fact that he was intimidating and yet you could still tease him was one of the things that made you love and respect Al so much. At our pre-game meals, he would tell stories that would motivate us. He knew how to push buttons. He had this uncanny ability to use the phrase "some of you." Like, "Some of you aren't going hard enough." It would make you want to go through the wall for him. When he said that, everyone in that room would look at himself and think, "Geez, I'm not getting the job done. He's talking about *me*. I'm not giving my all." On other teams, you might have guys thinking, "Oh I'm going. I'm going fine." But not on our team. Al inspired each of us to look at ourselves and go, "Aw man, I gotta pick it up. I gotta do better."

Don't get me wrong. Al knew when to tear us down too. He had a few choice words for us on occasion. One time after a game in Pittsburgh, he didn't like the way I played. It was right after Christmas, and because the Penguins had won, he looked at it as my giving Pittsburgh a big gift, so he called me Santa Claus for a few days. And not in an affectionate way.

I don't think there were any three-car-garage kids on our team. So if Al saw us getting pompous or arrogant, he'd give us a couple of verbal shots to bring us back down to earth.

Al would often remind us about how privileged we were. One thing he'd say that always got to me was, "Think about your parents." I was really proud of my dad. Not that he was treated poorly, don't get me wrong. Pepsi was fantastic to him, but it was clear he wasn't management.

Say we were in a slump. Al might ask us if we noticed all the telephone lines as we drove in to practice, and then he'd talk about the guys who had to climb the poles in the freezing cold to fix the wires. He'd say, "You think *you* got it tough?"

In the early '80s we were playing the Rangers at Madison Square Garden. They were our bitter rivals. We had some other good matchups with other teams, but nothing like the Rangers. We lost that night, and on the bus ride home, it was very quiet because we knew Al was mad.

We got back to the Coliseum parking lot, and he stood up at the front of the bus and he said, "I didn't like the way you guys played tonight. I didn't like your work ethic at all. Tomorrow we're going to have a workday like your parents are used to. Be at the rink at 6 a.m. and be prepared to be there until suppertime."

On a non-game day, professional hockey players are usually at the rink at nine thirty in the morning, practice at ten thirty and home with their feet up in the living room, having a sandwich and watching *Days of Our Lives*, by 1 p.m. The next day, we got there early. He showed us what a full day at the office was like—practice, video, lots of meetings and several cups of coffee. We got the message loud and clear. He was so good at that.

For Al, it was team first in every way. He understood how to get the absolute best out of all of us. What you hear all the time from current coaches is "You've gotta be a good communicator."

I agree with that. I think in today's world, every coach should have about five personal interactions with each player each week. Today's player needs to have more conversations about what's going on in his personal life. It has to be the head coach who talks to him, because other than his immediate family, the head coach is the most important person in a player's life. When you are a player, your ultimate goal is to be a winner, and the coach is the guy leading you there. Al was unique in that he could do it with one conversation per week.

Remember, back then it wasn't a touchy-feely era. Think of coaches like Eddie Shore. There was very little of this type of interaction. Al was one of the first to do it.

That all being said, guys are supposed to get out there and play. Coaching has never been about babysitting. The coach's responsibility is to put the right people on the ice so that you have the best chance of winning. Al knew when Clark Gillies was going, and when it was time to sit him for a couple shifts and then bend down and put his mouth to Clark's ear and politely ask him if he wanted to play.

There was a brilliance in Al. That's why we loved him. He saw the world from more than the perspective of a hockey coach. He grew up in Sudbury, Ontario. He knew about hard work and everyday people. In '84–85, during a period when we were struggling—and keep in mind, when I say "struggling," we were a great team, and our struggles would have been minimal compared to most other teams—he came into the dressing room before a practice and asked, "How many of you guys go into Manhattan?"

A few of us tentatively raised our hands. I immediately regretted it. I thought, "Oh crap. He's going to think we're at the clubs, partying all the time." He looked around and said, "Well, all of you have to do it more often. You have to go into Manhattan and experience life. It's an unbelievably great city. Go out, have dinner and make sure to get to Broadway."

I thought, "Wow, I didn't expect that. I thought he was going to tell us, 'Don't you ever go there. You should be thinking about hockey twenty-four hours a day.'" And then he said something that always stuck with me, "When you go to a Broadway play, picture yourself as a Broadway performer. That's what you are. When you're on the ice, you're performing for everybody. Your stage happens to be a sheet of ice, but remember, people pay to watch you perform."

Al took every win or loss personally, which was also a great lesson. Winnipeg had a good team in '83–84. That was my first season in the NHL. Dale Hawerchuk, Paul MacLean and Morris Lukowich were exceptional together. We played the Jets the day before New Year's Eve.

Despite the fact they outshot us 39–26 and we took two more penalties, the score ended up 4–3 for them in overtime. So I thought we'd played pretty well. Al didn't see it that way. He would often address us on the bus, although sometimes if he was mad, he wouldn't say anything because he wanted a cowed environment to really send the message home. But this time he walked down the aisle and pointed at each and every guy and said, "Don't. You. Ever. Fucking embarrass me like that again."

The next night we went into Minnesota and slaughtered a good team 7–3. We broke a 2–2 tie in the second period with four goals in a row. Al was half coach and half psychologist. He was in command.

I was having a tough time my second year, '84–85. I had no idea how to behave after a win, or especially after a loss. I really didn't. I didn't know if I should be down in the dumps or pouting, or how the hell to react. If I was smiling, I worried it might look like I didn't care enough. The truth was I cared too much. Al picked up on that. He didn't like it if you got too down on yourself. He'd often say, "Take all that negative energy you are feeling and turn it into positive energy."

There was a sauna off the dressing room at Nassau Coliseum. A bunch of us younger guys—Gord Dineen, Greg Gilbert, Brent Sutter, Tomas Jonsson, Mark Hamway and Ken Leiter—would practise, have a sauna together and then go to TGI Fridays for lunch. This one day, I was a bit pokey getting off the ice. I undressed and headed for the sauna, expecting all my friends to be there, laughing and joking and telling stories as usual.

But when I opened the door, I saw Al. He was sitting there, sweating on the cedar bench. Alone. In all his naked glory, and trust me, gravity had not been his friend. When I saw him, I thought, "Oh crap, what do I do? Do I go in or . . . ?" But it was too late. I was already halfway through the door. I had no choice. I sat down next to him and he got right to the point, in a nice, understanding way.

"How's life?"

"Great," I said. "It's going really well."

"How's the family?"

"Everybody's good, thanks."

"It's pretty great being in the NHL, isn't it?"

"Yeah, it's better than I expected."

He smiled. "Listen, I want you to go out there and have some fun again. Relax, Kelly. Enjoy yourself."

Al was a pretty intimidating individual, there's no question about it, and as a player at any level you'd never want to be isolated with just you and the coach. But he was so great at relating to his players that every time he talked, your eyes and your ears were wide open. It turned out to be pretty special sitting in there and listening to what he had to say. It helped me to grow and move forward.

We were playing in Montreal a day later, and he started me, and I left my troubles behind. I was like, "Okay, it's all right to enjoy being around, playing even if you're not performing as well as you'd hoped. You don't have to act as though the world is crashing down around you." Al could have told me to meet him in the coach's room for that talk, but I don't think I would have really heard him. I would have been intimidated and distracted by being called in there. Instead, he was able to make it clear he was talking to me person to person. He was open and vulnerable, like I was, with everything hanging out there.

Sometimes coaches don't like the way you do things off the ice. My first season with the Islanders, I set up an NFL pool for the team. Well, Al put an end to that pretty quick. He was very blunt. He said, "This is a distraction, and I don't want you doing it anymore." We weren't playing for much money, but it didn't matter. He wanted me focused on hockey before a game, not thinking about football.

But I couldn't stop. I loved football. Still do. We had this little lounge near the locker room with a TV and a beer fridge where we could gather before and after games. The rule was that you had to be out of there half an hour before you started getting dressed for warm-ups. I knew Al didn't like me watching NFL games before our games—so I'd pretend to go in there to get another cup of coffee, but I'd linger.

This one time I went in there and the Dallas Cowboys were playing. I loved the Cowboys. I grabbed a coffee and started watching. I heard a noise and turned my head and there was Al, watching me. He didn't say anything. He just gave me this look of great disapproval. That weighed on me the entire game, and we lost. Afterward, I was the only guy he came up to in the dressing room. In front of everybody, he said, "You weren't prepared to play tonight. You had other things on your mind and you let us down today." Wow. He was right, and it changed the way I prepared for a game for the rest of my career.

As I got older, I tried to follow Al's example of getting right to the point and to say something in the dressing room if it was warranted. I tried to do that in my personal life too. Obviously, I had to alter my approach a little because I have three girls. You can't just say what I would have said to one of my teammates—"Why the hell would you do that?"

Chapter 7

Character

I TOLD YOU ABOUT AL'S RELATIONSHIP with Denis Potvin. In the early days, Al worked on moulding Denis into that special player. Denis was the ultimate captain for me. There are guys who are leaders based on what they say, and there are guys who are leaders because of what they do on the ice. Denis was both. He commanded so much respect that when he said something in the locker room, it meant something. Obviously, he's one of the all-time great defencemen, and that carried a lot of weight with our team. Denis passed on a lot of the lessons Al taught him.

Early on in my career, we flew to Los Angeles for a game. One of the cookies that the Islanders management always dangled in front of us was that if we played well, we'd get a few extra days in L.A. "You'd better win the game, because if you don't then next time, we're getting right back on the plane." Sure enough, we won on a Saturday night and were scheduled to take the next twenty-four hours off in the City of Angels. We were staying at the Marriott in Marina del Rey, and Denis arranged for us all to get together for beers on Sunday at 3 p.m. in one of the conference rooms. And then the plan was to head out and have some fun.

Well, I'd partied pretty hard after the game Saturday night, so I took a Sunday afternoon nap and made it to the get-together about five minutes late. When I got there, the guys were all chatting around this big, long table. Denis stopped the conversation and looked at his watch. He said, "Where the hell have you been? You're four minutes late. We've been here waiting."

I looked around and saw the faces were fairly serious. Embarrassed, because he had ripped me in front of the whole team, I said, "Sorry," but I was thinking, "You asshole, we're just meeting to drink beers." But after thinking about it for a while, I came to a different realization. Denis was right. It was a team get-together, and me being late said to everyone that my time was more important than theirs. I took that lesson and incorporated it into my personal and professional life. I was never late again. That was one of the cornerstones of the Islanders' success. We weren't afraid to call each other out.

In my third year, we played in St. Louis and I had the best game of my National Hockey League career up to that point. I made forty-seven saves, including twenty-seven in the first period, and we won 5–2. Doug Wickenheiser slipped a late one in on me in the final minute. It was a wrist shot from the blue line. I knew it was a weak goal that I shouldn't have let in, but I shrugged it off, telling myself, "That's excusable, considering."

Al Arbour would shake your hand after a victory—not after a loss—in the dressing room. When he got to me, he shook my hand and he said, "You let your guard down." Now, at the time I was feeling awfully proud of my game. His words pissed me off. We had a bunch of beers that night, like we always did, flew back home the next day, and headed to the practice rink the next morning. The first drill was sort of a pick-up-your-speed drill. You skate laps, round and round, and then the coach blows the whistle and you pick it up to get your legs going and the blood flowing. I was still a little sore at Al for coming down hard on me, and I was hungover, so I wasn't skating as hard as I should have. Bobby Nystrom saw that and skated right up beside me and said, "Get. Fucking. Moving." It was always "Have fun, but this is serious business too."

Bobby Nystrom never wore a *C* or an *A*, but he was definitely a major factor in the locker room. Like a lot of championship teams, we didn't have one or two leaders on that team, we had eight or nine of them. Denis was the captain, but there was Butch Goring, Bobby Nystrom, Clark Gillies, Bryan Trottier, Mike Bossy . . . right on down the line.

Bobby was one of the strongest leaders on the team. You couldn't help but feel a sense of responsibility to play your best when Bobby Nystrom was out there, giving his all every shift. He'd always make sure we were ready. He'd talk a fair amount right before the game, reminding us to "get out there and get your legs going and remember, keep your head up." And he was always ready to stand up for anybody on the team.

Kenny Morrow tells a story about playing in Quebec when there was a fight on the ice. Quebec had a pretty tough team, and so did the Islanders. Moose Dupont had cross-checked Mike Bossy in front of the net, and Bobby Nystrom got so pissed off about it, he started to jump over the boards so he could chase Moose down.

Al had a bad shoulder that constantly popped out, but he forgot himself and grabbed Bobby by the back of his jersey to keep him on the bench. Of course, Al put his shoulder out, and when that happened, he lost his balance and dropped like a sack of potatoes. Fell onto the rubber at the front of the bench where there's water and honk and all kinds of gross things.

So Al was lying in front of the players' skates with a dislocated shoulder and he couldn't get up. He used his good arm to crawl back behind the bench and over to the trainer, who helped him up and took him to the dressing room. But now the team had no coach because assistant coaches weren't on the bench back in the day. Lorne Henning was the assistant, but he was up in the press box. The players needed him to come down and coach, so they got his attention by waving at him with their sticks. By the third period, Al came back with his shoulder in a sling and finished the game.

Bobby Nystrom retired at the end of the '85–86 season and was hired as our assistant coach. Recently, he told me he thought he was a bad assistant coach. He said he realized he was too critical when he went home one night and watched some old tapes and saw a few things about his game that he was disappointed in. I was surprised to hear that, because I couldn't disagree with him more. I thought he contributed greatly, both when he played and when he was behind the bench. Occasionally he'd blow a gasket, but only because we weren't playing the way we could. It was his way of getting us to pick it up a hair. "We gotta get our rear ends going! We gotta go. We're playing like crap!" And it worked. He'd get us all fired up.

Bobby had character, and in my opinion, you need a lot of character to win as a team. The word *character* is overused in the game of hockey. If you ask half the people in the game you'll hear several different interpretations. A lot of guys think it means "heart," or that a guy showed a lot of grit. Bryan Trottier described it this way: "Character is about celebrating certain personality traits. It's like a caricature. When an artist exaggerates a particular feature that's unique to that person, that's character and that's wonderful."

I think you need that blend of character on a team to make something fun happen. People talk about chemistry, they talk about a blend of skills and all that kind of stuff, and it's true, it's all very important, but character is a big factor for me. Gordie Lane was a great example. He was a loose cannon. Some might say borderline nuts. And he didn't hide it. Before games, he'd get this menacing look in his eyes, like he was in a different world, and he was honest when he'd tell opponents in the faceoff circle that he was going to carve their eyes out. Most guys would say it, but you wouldn't believe them. Everybody believed Gordie.

There was a dark side to Gordie Lane. He'd slash guys and punch them in the head. You know, I rarely felt bad for anyone on the other team, but sometimes when you'd see him cross the line, it was so scary I'd cringe. Oh, Gordie was mean. Gordie was mad-dog mean. But you need those big brothers on a team, and he was out for one thing—he wanted to win. When you take a guy like Gordie Lane out of the lineup, all of a sudden, you're a different team.

That was the great thing about that Islanders team. Everyone was accepted for who we were. Butch Goring was maybe more unique than most. The guys all said Butch injected life into the team right from the get-go. He stood up in the dressing room and said, "You just don't understand how good you are." There's no question that when he joined the Islanders in 1980, just before the trade deadline, it was a key move. The team was so deep that when Butch came in, he ended up being their second-line centre. The number one centre was Bryan Trottier.

In the playoffs, Butch ended up playing on a line with Duane Sutter and Clark Gillies, and they won their first Stanley Cup. In '81, Goring won the Conn Smythe Trophy as playoff MVP. In fact, the Smythe went to Trottier, Goring, Bossy and Billy Smith in the four years they won the Cup.

Butchie was not only a good hockey player, he had pizzazz and he brought an element to the dressing room that was good for that group. He kept the room loose. To this day, when I think of Butch I can still hear him laugh, and it makes me smile. The guy had a good heart. And when the puck dropped, he was a catalyst. He wasn't a big guy, but he was extremely smart and a tireless skater. He was one of the best penalty killers I've ever seen, thanks to his hockey IQ. What a gutsy little playmaker. Very underrated.

He'd been in the NHL for a long time by the time he joined our team, which made him slick and sly and full of deception, which I loved. He didn't play a tough, slashing, beat-you-up kind of game, but man, he was gritty. He went into what Trots called the "dirty, slimy areas." And that fit like a glove because he had this gnarly look. Both Gordie Lane and Butch were Manitoba boys. We loved them because they were Western Canadian to the bone.

Butchie liked to gamble. He was always at the racetrack. I went with him one time. I'm not a gambler, but it was a lot of fun. He knew every horse. He must have done well because he had a yellow Lamborghini, one of those cars with the gull-wing doors that open up vertically. This was in an era when very few players could afford a car like that.

It's interesting that he bought a Lamborghini, because he was tight with a buck. Butchie could squeeze a nickel until the beaver cried. It was comic relief sometimes. He took a lot of razzing about his wardrobe. He always wore this old, raggedy lime-green Gatorade sweat suit. After practice one day, the guys took those green sweat pants and nailed them to the end of a hockey stick and set them on fire. He wouldn't take any extra clothes on a road trip. Just a shaving kit, a tan-coloured turtle-neck and a corduroy sports jacket. Halfway through the trip, he'd turn the turtleneck around to hide the stains.

Billy Smith is another example of a guy with character. When Billy was getting ready for a game, he was all business. He is the most serious guy I've ever been around in my life, bar none.

Billy was a guy who didn't address the team a lot, but when he did, he was passionate. He spoke straight from the heart. And because we recognized his sincerity, we listened.

During the '81 Stanley Cup Final, I was called up as a spare. I wasn't dressed, but I was standing in the tunnel, watching as the Islanders walked out onto the ice for the warm-up. Back then, they didn't have the tarps that protected the players from fans. Some lady reached out to touch Billy, to pat him, and he hit her with his stick. Just whacked her. I was like, "Holy geezus, this guy is intense."

We all know about how Billy liked to protect his crease, but the most vicious thing he did was during Game Six of the 1980 semifinals. You can still watch it on YouTube. Sabres versus the Islanders. The play was around his net, and it ended up going back towards the Buffalo zone. Lindy Ruff, who had been skating in and out of Billy's crease, overstayed his welcome, and Billy flicked out his elbow, quick as lightning, and with the knob of his stick he got Lindy hard in the temple, next to his right eye. It sent Lindy sprawling, and he jumped up in a fury and tackled Billy in his crease. The knob on Billy Smith's stick was a couple of inches lower than the end of his stick. It was built like a weapon. Later on, they changed the rule on where the knob on your stick could be.

As a player, Billy was combative in every way, and that meant for ice time too. In '85–86, I improved more and more and I got more starts. Billy was one of the earlier guys who made the partial transition into a butterfly style of goaltending. Guys like Ken Dryden and Bernie Parent were stand-up goalies. They very rarely went down. As my style evolved, I incorporated the butterfly, but back then, I still made the old-school skate saves with the kick, and I stacked the pads too.

I think what set me apart from the other goalies was that I could handle the puck. I'd go out and skate with the guys without my gear, and I got fairly decent at puck possession and stickhandling. Gerry Diduck was just an outstanding young defenceman from Sherwood Park, Alberta. Gerry's defence partner was Denis Potvin, so every time Gerry would get up above the red line, all he'd hear was Al yelling, "Get back! Get back! Get back!" Basically, Al didn't want him crossing the red line. Gerry started passing back, using me as a third defenceman. I loved that and got better and better at handling the puck thanks to the great defencemen on that team. I mean, it was always better if I left the puck for a guy like Denis Potvin, who could make a better tape-to-tape pass than I ever could. But there were certain circumstances when it worked, like if I'd push the puck up ice when taking advantage of a bad line change by the other team.

Denis was invaluable in teaching me to move the puck effectively. He taught me to pay attention to who was coming back for the puck, because where I positioned the puck depended on whether it was him or Ken Morrow or whoever. Each guy liked to pick up the puck a certain way. Years later, when I played with Paul Coffey, he liked to pick up the puck on his backhand behind the net, so I would put the puck much closer to the boards behind the net so he wouldn't have to break stride. That would allow him to accelerate and power through up ice.

In November of '84, Rollie Melanson was traded to Minnesota. Now it was just Billy and me.

Al believed in rotating. I'd play a game, Billy would play a game. But as I said, I was getting better and better, so Al started giving me more rope, maybe two or three games in a row. Billy did not like that. He'd go into Al's office and say, "I'm going to play the next game. Kelly's playing great, but I'm your guy and don't you forget it."

Watching Billy do that instilled in me the idea that once you believe you're the guy, you should take ownership of your position. I fought back hard for those next few years so that I would get more playing time than Billy, and eventually I did. Especially in '86–87, when we made the coaching change to Terry Simpson.

Terry was more open to me because Billy's game was in decline, but as was his right, Billy continued to fight for minutes. I do recall one time where we went toe to toe. Billy told me, "I'm going to go in and ask the coach for more ice time." I followed him into Terry's office, and after Billy said what he had to say, I said, "Terry, screw that. I'm playing better. Don't listen to this guy." Billy was fine with that. We were great friends. We golfed together, played tennis together, went to dinner all the time. It was a great lesson in defending what you own.

I was combative in the game too. People might suggest to you that I learned that from Billy Smith, but that's not true. I was that way naturally, and maybe that's one of the reasons they drafted me. As with Billy, it wasn't a good idea to talk to me before a game. Other times, I showed my competitiveness in a different way. I liked a lot of shots in practice, whereas Billy didn't appear to give a crap if he got scored on in practice. He stood at one post and the guys would shoot at the other side. Once in a while, a rookie or a new player on the team would take a high slapshot at him. That'd really piss him off. He'd come out of his net and whack the guy with his stick, or if he couldn't catch him he'd swear and point at the guy and draw a death line across his throat. Al would shake his head and pull the shooter aside and advise, "Best to just aim for the pillows."

When it came to games, both Billy and I were pretty fierce. We had to be—we were up against guys like the Oilers' Glenn Anderson. He would fly in at you at a hundred miles an hour. We'd punch him, we'd slash him, we'd jab him in the nuts from behind. We'd do anything and everything to him. But he was fearless in taking the puck to the net.

THERE ARE TWO THINGS MOST PEOPLE don't think of when they look at a goaltender getting hit. First, goalies are static, not moving, so we feel the G-force. On top of that, we're usually bent over in some kind of awkward stance. Think about sitting behind the wheel of a car and being hit from behind. Are you going to be more injured if you are sitting upright with your hands at ten and two, or if you are shoulder-checking with your head turned?

What I would try to do so that I could be strong and sturdy, and not go flying, was to anchor myself to the ice. You can do that in many different ways, but I'd get low and hug part of the post. It can be dangerous because it can lead to an injury, but I found that the lower I got, the stronger my foundation.

I don't have a reputation for being dirty, but I remember getting into a lot of fights in junior. Not too long ago, I met up with Barry Trotz, who's now the head coach of the Washington Capitals. He played for the Regina Pats when I was with the Tigers, and so we were sharing stories about our intense battles back in the late '70s, early '80s. We were laughing about the regular things that happened, like all the brawls we had, you know? And then, much to my surprise, he reminded me that I used to be "a frickin' dirty player." He told me that he'd be down in the crease in a scrum or something, and I'd go around, kicking out with my skate. While Barry was telling me this, I started feeling sick to my stomach. It threw me back into the net in one of those scrums, and I started to remember my skate connecting to the back of guys' legs, and I was horrified.

I also remember being pretty combative. I'd punch a guy if he came too close. I had no problem with that. But until that conversation with Barry, I didn't realize how dirty I was. There was another guy, a big left winger named Troy Loney, who I played against in junior when he was with Lethbridge, and then again through the '80s and early '90s when he was with Pittsburgh. He won two Cups with the Penguins in '91 and '92. He told me the same thing. Troy played twelve years in the NHL and had more than a thousand penalty minutes. Unfortunately, I was the one who gave him the only concussion he ever had.

In 2009, I was in the parking lot near our television production truck in Pittsburgh when they were up against Detroit in the finals. Troy was walking into the arena with his sons, Reed, Clint and his youngest, Ty, who went on to play for the University of Denver and was the leading scorer for the ECHL's Adirondack Thunder in the Pittsburgh organization in 2016–17 before moving to the American Hockey League with the Albany Devils and the Chicago Wolves.

Troy spotted me and came over. He introduced me to his boys and then pulled back his hair, showing us all a two-inch piece of rope behind his right ear. He said to his boys, "See this scar?" He pointed at me. "This guy did that to me. We were on the Island in 1989 and he was in goal. Four of my teammates were on one side of the net and I was on the other. And for once the puck came to me. I bent over to pick it up, and this guy flew at me and got me behind the ear with the butt end of his stick. I skated over to the bench on a wobble board. All I could see was that little black circle at the end of the Looney Tunes cartoons, and it was getting smaller and smaller."

On one hand, I was very disappointed in myself for injuring a player like that. On the other, I knew it was that kind of fierce competitiveness that not only took me to the NHL but kept me there.

Chapter 8

The Islanders Love Wayne's Story

OUR RIVALRY WITH THE NEW YORK RANGERS got going right from the time the Islanders joined the NHL in 1972. I remember Denis Potvin talking about how it pissed him off that Ranger fans used to buy the more affordable tickets to our rink, the Nassau Veterans Memorial Coliseum, to cheer for the Rangers.

Al put me in a game at Madison Square Garden on February 17, 1985. Back then, goalie equipment was stiff and inflexible—you had to break it in over a long time. You didn't just get it from the manufacturer and wear it in games. You had to practise in it to make everything mushy enough to move in. Some guys would run their pads over with their car.

Stupidly, I strapped on a new set of pads. Why I chose that game, when I knew it was against the Rangers, I'll never know.

We skated out, and Al could see I was wearing the new pads. I knew he would be pissed at me if the game went sideways, and it didn't take long to see that that's what happened. The Rangers wound up winning 9–3, but in the second period, when they were up 7–3, there was a skirmish at the other end. A lot of the guys joined in, starting with Trottier and Clark Gillies. I skated up to centre ice and then stopped, because if the goaltender crosses the red line, it's a penalty. But I was ready to get involved and slug it out if need be. In my opinion, the Rangers' goalie, John Vanbiesbrouck, was getting too involved. He was chirping at our guys and getting a little handsy.

This attracted some attention, and so Duane Sutter came in and grabbed the bars of Vanbiesbrouck's mask and started using it as a steering wheel. Vanbiesbrouck took a swing, and that was it. I raced down, wheeled him around and did my best to beat him up. That was the way it worked back then. If one goalie got into the fray, the other goalie stepped up. In the dressing room afterward, there was jubilation. Al was smiling. The new pads were forgotten. We were all in it together.

The awkward part about this story is that my lawyer, Lloyd Friedland, represented Vanbiesbrouck too. My wife, Donna, had hired a sitter and come into Manhattan to stay over so that we could go to dinner with Lloyd and his wife, Carol, and John and his wife, Rosalyn. Needless to say, that didn't happen.

Al had a real hardhat mentality, and that was the culture he instilled in the team. One of the reasons Bill Torrey hired Al in 1973 was because he hated Al as a player. Al would clutch and grab, but he was really smart defensively. He knew how to stop turnovers. I cannot tell you how many goals get scored because somebody turns the puck over close to the goal crease.

It was generally perceived—and pretty much true—that teams had to learn how to win a Stanley Cup. First, they had to get over a hump to do it. The Islanders were favourites in '78. They'd had a really good season and then got knocked out early in the playoffs by Toronto because they were too beaten up. The following year, they lost to the Rangers, which was a devastating defeat. In 1980, there was talk about the team being broken up at the end of the season. Not unlike you hear nowadays when teams have great regular-season records but fail to close the deal in the playoffs, when they don't achieve what people think they should. Much like the conversation most people are having about the current-day Washington Capitals. Tons of regular-season success, but just not a successful playoff team. Is it time for big changes?

In 1980, the "hump" came in the form of the Boston Bruins in the quarter-finals. Boston was a big, tough, mean team. The Islanders would have to fight them—the expression everybody used was "beat them in the alley"—if they were going to move on. There were a ton of bench-clearing brawls as the Bruins tried to intimidate the Islanders. The Islanders were pushed to the extreme and prevailed. They emerged as a team. Clark Gillies and Bobby Nystrom and Garry Howatt stood up and led the way.

After the Rangers, the second-biggest rivalry we had was with the '82–83 Oilers. I played the entire 1982–83 season with the Indianapolis Checkers in the CHL and was called up to the Islanders after we won the Adams Cup on May 4, 1983. I was a Black Ace, which means I wasn't in the lineup, but I accepted that because Billy Smith and Rollie Melanson were ahead of me in the pecking order. Rightfully so. Don't get me wrong, I didn't want to be a Black Ace for long.

We went on to play the Oilers, and I could see that under the leadership of Al Arbour and due to their previous Cups, the Islanders were patient. They waited for opportunities and could handle more pressure. We won the first game of the series in Edmonton, and Billy Smith had a shutout. It was a great game.

On the way back to the hotel, Al had the bus pull over, and he nicely asked the driver to step outside for a moment. He stood up, and in a measured tone he said, "That was a great victory. But remember, don't say anything stupid to the press. Be respectful tomorrow at practice. We haven't completed the job."

The Islanders did take home their fourth Stanley Cup in a row in 1983, but a lot of people thought Wayne and the boys were going to win. If I were to analyze it, I would say the Islanders won because they willed it to happen. We ended up breaking the spirit of the Oilers, similar to what the Oilers would do to us a year later.

Wayne Gretzky always tells the story about losing the '83 Cup. He and Kevin Lowe were relatively fresh after the last game, and as they walked past the Islanders' dressing room they saw the vets loaded down with ice packs, sitting back, quietly sipping beers. It looked to Wayne and Kevin like the Islanders had given everything they had on the ice and were too beat to celebrate.

That taught the Oilers a big lesson in what it took to win the Cup. Wayne's right, in that there is a price you pay to win. Pull up the Bob Gainey interview from 1979. He won the Conn Smythe that year. He's got two big cuts on his forehead and a bloody nose, and there he is, taking the trophy for the most valuable player in the playoffs.

But the Islanders love Wayne's story. They still chuckle about it as a group whenever they hear it, because they partied harder than they'd ever partied when they beat the Oilers that year. The Oilers were a scoring machine, so beating them was a tremendous accomplishment for the Islanders. When they heard Wayne's story, they viewed it as a compliment. I asked Trots about it and he said, "The only thing I can think of is that they walked by during a lull."

It was different in 1984. To the Oilers' credit, they used Wayne's dressing-room story as fuel. That year, Bossy and Trottier had ice bags hanging from their shoulders long before the playoffs. They were physically beaten up but still running on mental toughness. In the Wales Conference final against Montreal in the Forum, we lost the first two games. I was quite worried, but I could see it was like water off a duck's back for the veterans. It wasn't like they were laughing and joking. It was more like, "Don't worry, we'll come back and win four straight," and they did. I remember Bryan Trottier walking out of the Montreal Forum after losing the second game. And I gained great confidence and strength from his swagger. It didn't look to me like he was concerned at all. That kind of attitude is a hallmark of a true championship team.

I also remember Ken Morrow sitting in the dressing room with huge bags of ice on his knees after every practice, every game. He could barely walk, and he still has a ton of knee problems.

Ken Morrow was a winner. He was part of the USA's 1980 Miracle on Ice team that upset the Russians and won an Olympic gold medal under coach Herb Brooks. Ken went on to win four Cups with the Islanders. Our trainer started calling him Wolfman when he joined the team, because he kept his Olympic beard. Later, his name got shortened to Wolfie.

We had a hard time getting through the Rangers, our first-round opponents. Back then, the first-round series was a best-of-five. In the Game Five decider, Kenny Morrow scored one of the biggest goals of his career when what he always calls his "patented fifty-mile-an-hour slapshot" found its way through. It was one heck of a game. At the time, probably the best play-off game ever. Dick Irvin called the overtime "the greatest overtime that was ever played," thanks to all the up-and-down action. Billy Smith made a game-saving stop on Bob Brooke, and it was nonstop madness for the next nine minutes. One of the defencemen changed, and Morrow jumped on the ice and skated across the blue line. The puck came off the boards, and he stepped into a slapshot on Glen Hanlon and it went in. It wasn't a hard shot. Billy Smith used to tell Kenny he could read "Made in Canada" on the puck when Morrow took shots on him.

To this day, Rangers fans hate Kenny because they thought they were going to win the Cup that year for sure. Rangers winger Rod Gilbert, who is a terrific guy, told Kenny Morrow a great story. He was at the game in one of the boxes with the Rangers management team, and when Kenny scored, Rod turned to the guy next to him in disbelief and went, "They got Mike Bossy, Bryan Trottier, Brent Sutter, John Tonelli and Denis Potvin . . . and who scores? Kenny-fucking-Morrow."

Next, we played Washington. They were tough opponents too. And in the third round we were up against Montreal, and believe me, that series took its toll.

And then we came up against the Oilers. Our guys were businesslike, as usual, but I could see that we weren't as sharp, weren't as quick. There were a lot of injuries. Billy Smith injured his wrist. He didn't even finish the third or the fifth and final game of the series. Rollie filled in. I'm pretty sure Denis Potvin had some ailments. Typically, you'd never know it because those guys, they could play through anything.

The Islanders were a special team—they had skill, chemistry, determination and maybe most important, they were as tough as they come. For nineteen series, no one could beat the Islanders. But then that final series, our twentieth, after the game on the bus heading to the airport, I walked by Clark Gillies, who was slumped forward in his seat, elbows resting on his knees. I said, "Great season, Clarkie." He turned his eyes up towards me and said, "I'm exhausted. I have nothing left."

We lost to Edmonton in five games. It was the end of the run. Four Stanley Cups. Montreal won the Cup five times in a row from 1956 to 1960 and also won four in a row from 1976 to 1979. The Islanders are the only other team to do that. And it's unlikely any team will do it again. There's much more parity now in a salary cap era. But to win nineteen playoff series in a row . . . it happened only that once, and I don't see it ever happening again.

Chapter 9

It Made My Toes Curl

ONE OF THE HIGHLIGHTS OF MY CAREER, and the game I'm probably asked about the most, is the Easter Epic. That and the 1993 stick incident in the finals between the Los Angeles Kings (I was L.A.'s goalie by then) and the Montreal Canadiens. Another question I get a lot involves the headband I used to wear. I'll get to the stick incident and my headband in a bit. First, the Epic.

In 1987, we faced the Washington Capitals in the Patrick Division playoffs for the fifth season in a row. We won the first three series against them in '83, '84 and '85, and then in 1986 we had a good season, with a record of 39–29–12, but they were coming off a tremendous season—they were 50–23–7—and they beat us in a three-game sweep. I was in net for two of those games. It still burns to think about it.

April 1987 was an even tighter race. The Caps were second in the division, with a 38–32–10 record and 86 points, while we were just four points behind at 35–33–12. They had an incredible roster. Two of their top scorers, Larry Murphy and Mike Gartner, were very dangerous. Mike Gartner scored 708 regular-season goals in the NHL and 43 more in the playoffs. He's near the top of the list. But he's not a natural goal scorer. I'm serious, he's not. I even said that to him one time after we were both retired, and he agreed with me. My reasoning is, he had three weapons: he improved his odds, he had an incredibly hard shot and he was a great skater. You don't see goals like his anymore. Back in the day, he had blinding speed for a right winger. He'd come down the wing and pick up a pass, and because of his speed and the fact that defencemen didn't turn nearly as well back then, he had great opportunities coming off the wing. He wasn't like a Bossy or Gretzky or some of the other great goal scorers, but he was smart. He knew he needed about seven or eight shots a game to score, so he took lots and lots and lots of them. I was always afraid of him because I knew he wasn't going to give the puck away if he had a chance.

Larry Murphy, a defenceman, had a unique ability to know when to sneak in from the point in the offensive zone and make himself available. He always had a number of really good chances. He also had a deceptive shot—very accurate, but the way he released made it hard for my eyes to pick up the puck.

Oftentimes I'm asked if it matters whether a guy uses black or white tape on the blade of the stick. It doesn't. A professional goalie sees the puck in a three-dimensional way. We are able to discern the puck from the tape no matter what colour it is. So guys who use black tape to fool an NHL goalie are wasting their time.

Goaltenders focus on the blade of the shooter's stick. Some guys cup the puck with the blade, some guys have a curve that kind of opens up, but it all comes down to how the puck comes across and the way the blade is going to swipe at it. NHL goalies have been watching the puck on the blade for so many years that when the rubber meets the road, we have a good idea where the puck is going. You learn this day in and day out on the ice, from your teens to the pros. In other words, if I could see the puck leave the blade, I had a pretty good chance of stopping it. But Larry Murphy had such soft hands, he could suddenly change the angle, and when he did that, it fooled my eyes for a split second.

The series between us and the Caps got underway at the Capital Centre in Landover, Maryland, the rink where I played my very first NHL game. For whatever reason, I played quite well in that building.

I think everybody thought Washington was going to take the series without too much trouble. And at first, it looked like everybody was right. We got off to a bad start. They won the first game. We won the second and then we lost Games Three and Four at home. Trouble was, we were missing some of our top players.

Mike Bossy was playing hurt all season. He had a disc problem at the base of his spine, and it constantly radiated pain. The doctors tried everything to help him, but nobody seemed to know exactly what was wrong. I recently read an article he wrote for *The Players' Tribune* where he says he wrecked his kneecap doing the long jump in high school and it never healed properly. The injury caused an imbalance, and that's what triggered his back problems. His injury limited him to only sixty-three regular-season games in 1986–87, but he still managed to score thirty-eight goals. It was the only time in his ten-season career that he didn't top fifty. But what sidelined him in that series was a knee injury resulting from a hit by Lou Franceschetti in Game Two. He wouldn't return to the lineup until Games Four to Seven of our next series, against Philadelphia. And unfortunately, those last four games were the final games of his NHL career.

We had other injuries too. Denis Potvin hurt his back in Game Four of the Washington series. He didn't return to the lineup until Game Two against Philly. And Brent Sutter, our fourth-leading scorer that year, injured his groin in a 7–6 win over the visiting New Jersey Devils a month before playoffs and was still out of action.

That series was a changing of the guard for our team. It was the point where we transitioned from the players who'd been there through the Stanley Cup years to new skill guys like Pat LaFontaine, Patrick Flatley, Mikko Makela and Gordie Dineen. There were still some of the older guys, like Bryan Trottier, Duane Sutter and Ken Morrow, but they weren't as pivotal as they once had been.

We flew into Washington down three games to one. One of my friends, Barry Meisel, was a reporter for the *New York Daily*

News. He came up to me after the morning skate. "So, what are your plans after the season's done?" And although I've never told him this, I took exception to that. I thought, "What the hell? It's not over. We still have a chance."

And sure enough, that night Greg Gilbert scored a tiebreaker. That goal lit a fire that carried us over to a win in Game Six. Still, the odds were stacked against us. At that point, only two teams in NHL history had overcome a series deficit of 3–1 to win a best-of-seven series. In the 1942 finals, down three games to none, the Toronto Maple Leafs battled back and won the Stanley Cup in seven games over the Detroit Red Wings. In 1975, the Islanders came back in the quarter-finals from three games to none to beat the Penguins.

Which brings us to Game Seven against Washington, the game they now call the Easter Epic. They call it "the Epic" because it was long. Very long.

The Caps' goalie, Bob Mason, was remarkable. I mean, watching him from the other end of the ice, I remember thinking, "This guy is out of his mind." Pete Peeters was their other goalie. He was a very established guy. To a certain degree, I was surprised that Bob played. I thought they might go with the more experienced goalie.

This game would end up giving Mason a window of opportunity—the Chicago Blackhawks signed him immediately after the playoffs. But he never rose to the same level again. The Easter Epic was the game of his life. Like I said, some of the overtime saves he made were truly remarkable. And as for me, you know how a guy who loves golf can tell you about every hole on a course he played? It's funny, but like a golfer, I remember most of the seventy-five shots that came at me in that game.

First period, they came out blazing and just bombarded us. With forty-eight seconds left in the period, I left a really juicy rebound in front and Mike Gartner scored. I was really, really pissed at myself, because it was a bad goal. Of all the shots in that first period, I shouldn't have let that one in. When the red light lit up, I said to myself, "Oh my God, how could I be so stupid, leaving that rebound out there? C'mon Kelly, get it together. You're better than that." And then I turned and tapped the crossbar with my stick a few times. That always calmed me down. I didn't know it then, but it was going to be a long night.

Michal Pivonka, one of their top checking centremen, had some really good chances. I always thought he was a skilled, determined hockey player who didn't get the respect he deserved. He was difficult to play against because he was so clever. You had to be aware of where he was. He was one of the Washington guys I keyed on. Whenever one of the best scorers on the other team had a chance, it got me going because I wanted to be the top dog. I got this great feeling whenever I managed to stop Pivonka on his chances. Those saves gave me the confidence that carried me through the rest of the game.

They outshot us 15–5 in the first period and we were down 1–0. Halfway through the second, Pat Flatley tied it up for

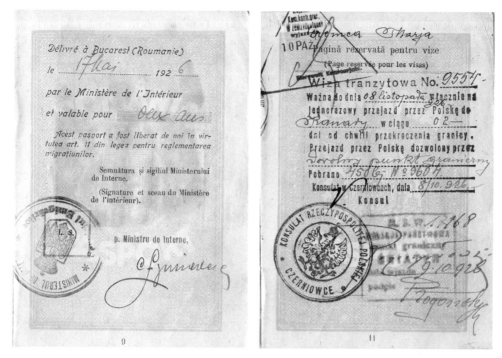

My grandmother Mary Yaremco's passport, issued in 1926. We called her Boona. My grandfather Dmytro Karpo sent for her once he settled a piece of land near Smoky Lake, Alberta.

My *dida* (grandfather) Dmytro Karpo (left) and his brother Wasyl (William), who was later wrongfully arrested for being an enemy alien. *Circa* 1925.

John Hrudey and his bride, my grandmother Maria Cheborak, *circa* 1926. He settled near a town called Zawale in central Alberta. All that's left there now is a post office.

My dad, Steve, my brother, Ken, my *baba*, me and my mom, Pauline, at Baba's house in the community of Beverly, Alberta. I'll never forget the great food from her incredible garden.

Here I am at the age of eighteen months, tricycling in our backyard in the summer of 1962. Look at the stumps on that baby!

Me (left), Dad and Ken at our favourite viewpoint overlooking the Athabasca Valley in Jasper, Alberta, in the summer of 1967. We stopped there every summer on our way to Maligne Canyon.

My brother, Ken, and me. I'm the smart aleck giving the peace sign. Christmas 1969.

Wearing my Elmwood Community League baseball uniform with my athlete-of-the-year trophy, 1972.

Grade 7. I started life as a blond.

Elmwood Peewee A, 1973–74. My first year in hockey. I was a goalie right from the get-go.

Edmonton bantam football, 1976. I loved all sports as a kid.
—**Courtesy Wajo Studios, Ltd.**

With the Medicine Hat Tigers, 1979–80, looking pretty dangerous. My brother, Ken, painted my mask for me.

With the Medicine Hat Tigers, 1980–81. Check out those handsome new pads I got from the Islanders. I liked them small because they made me more agile.

Indianapolis Checkers, 1981–82. We were a powerhouse! We won the league championship two years in a row. **Front** (left to right): Rob Holland, John Marks, Kevin Devine, Fred Creighton, Lorne Stamler, me. **Middle**: George Schmitt, Neil Hawryliw, Randy Johnston, Charlie Skjodt, Steve Stoyanovich, Mats Hallin, Kelly Davis, Garth MacGuigan, Tim Lockridge, Don Niederkorn. **Back**: Glen Duncan, Frank Beaton, Darcy Regier, Bruce Andres, Mike Hordy, Monty Trottier, Red Laurence.
—Courtesy M. James McAdams

Donna and me in 1981. My brown-eyed girl.

Our wedding, June 30, 1984.

It sure was a lot more fun playing with Wayne than against him.

Oilers vs. Islanders, 1984–85. Glenn Anderson was always crashing the crease. I'm sure he went home black and blue. I know I did.
—Courtesy Oilers Entertainment Group

February 17, 1985. Donna and I were scheduled to have dinner with John Vanbiesbrouck (34) and his wife after this game. It was called off.

us. Al Arbour used to call Pat "Secretariat," like the racehorse, because Pat had these skinny little legs but he could really fly. A few minutes later, Washington was back on top. Again, they outshot us, this time 10–5.

With about six minutes left in the third, I was in my net and my team was attacking. As a goalie, you always assume that the other goalie is going to make a save on every shot. Again, it's like golf. You're always pretty sure the other guy is going to make the putt. Watch the pros in a tournament—whenever his opponent misses, the player always has this surprised look, like, "Holy geez, I sure didn't expect that." Bryan Trottier had a separated shoulder, but he still managed to come down the ice and sneak a backhand through Bob Mason's pads. I was stunned. It was a strange goal to let in when you're leading 2–1 in Game Seven. I recall thinking, "Wow, that's not the shot I thought would tie it." But that's how it goes. Fancy plays and dipsy-doodling make the highlight reels, but those aren't the shots that win games. It's usually something pretty straightforward.

Our guys had started to drive to their net hard with pucks, and the Caps were taking their feet out any way they could. The ref, Andy Van Hellemond, had basically put his whistle away. Kenny Morrow remembers tackling guys, literally. Somebody would come in front and he would wrap his arms around them. I loved it. It was a real dogfight.

We were tied 2–2 and headed for overtime. We had seven penalties and they had six. That may seem like a lot today, because now they're skating at top speed and it's all finesse. But back then it was "take the man." Wear the other guy down and intimidate him. And if you couldn't intimidate him physically, do it verbally.

Like I said earlier, put me in sneakers and when I jump, I can barely get off the ground, but in the first forty seconds of the first overtime, Lou Franceschetti sent a slapshot my way from the blue line. Somehow, I caught it with a fair bit of air under me. Every once in a while, I'd surprise myself.

By the second overtime, we were just trying to get enough water down to rehydrate as best we could. We had some oranges and things that the trainers always had on hand, and we brought in some other starchy stuff, like bread and peanut butter.

The guys changed socks going into the third overtime just to lighten the load, but their skates were so soaked that when they put them back on it was like sticking their feet in a bucket of water. Everything was soaked. Some guys even tried going without socks. It was a challenge to stay fresh. Our gloves were so wet, you could squeeze your stick and the sweat would drip onto the ice in puddles. Today, players have equipment guys who blow-dry their skates and gloves before and halfway through each period.

Franceschetti was dog tired. He fell on me while trying to score. I was face down on the ice and he used my helmet as leverage to push himself up—like my head was a handrail. I was super offended and hated that, and I hated him for doing it.

Years later, after I became a broadcaster, I had a conversation about that very thing with Lance Armstrong, the road-racing cyclist, when I interviewed him in Saskatoon, Saskatchewan. I said, "So when you're racing against these guys, do you have a hate-on for them?" He said he did, but he'd never heard the term "hate-on." And then a couple of months later, I heard him use it when he was being interviewed by someone else.

Anyway, at the end of the third overtime, there was a play where Franceschetti made a determined effort to score. He made an incredible rush up the ice and tried to overpower me, pushing me into the net. And that kind of put me in awe of him because I thought he had nothing left. I responded by doing the thing I'd always got shit for from Al. I kept my paddle down so I was able to seal off the net down low and not allow him to end the game.

When you put your paddle down like that, it anchors you to the ice, making you powerful, strong and secure down low. It's now a legit goalie move called "paddle down." Ron MacLean credits me with creating it. You fall on your knees and you lay the paddle of the goalie stick down horizontally on the ice to form a barrier. It helps protect the five-hole and defend against wraparounds. Denis Potvin sparked me to come up with it. He said, "If you can't see the puck, because there's a screen, get as low as you can and spread out."

Al Arbour hated it. Despised it. He wanted me standing on my skates, not low on the ice. The first time I tried it in a game, they scored on me and Al was really mad. I did it again in practice the next day and he yelled, "Get back up on your skates! I don't ever wanna see that again!" But I was stubborn, and despite my respect for Al, I knew it would work if I could perfect it. Dominik Hasek used it and always did an incredible job with it.

Andy Van Hellemond, the referee, kept a lid on things, but like I said, he let us play and we appreciated it. His demeanour was perfectly suited for that game. He was good-natured and there was a calmness about him. He didn't want to influence the outcome. He'd let the players decide it. Obviously, if something very serious happened, they would call it, but otherwise he let us battle it out. I think that's what made the game great back then—when it came down to crunch time, especially in overtime, referees let us sort it out. During the season, a referee might come up beside you to make a comment, but in the playoffs they stay away from the goalies because we're concentrating so hard.

In order to get a little rest, both teams were constantly flipping the puck over the glass. If you do that today, it's an automatic penalty, even in overtime, but back then it only resulted in a faceoff.

Van Hellemond, who seemed to be enjoying the game as much as we were, blew the whistle after one of the flips and skated to my net. I had stopped about seventy shots by that time. He said, "Wouldn't it be something to stop a hundred shots in a game?" And we shared a laugh.

My mom and dad were watching, and later they told me *Hockey Night in Canada*'s Harry Neale said something like, "Wouldn't you want that to be your goalie? Look how relaxed Kelly is." And in truth, by that point, I *was* relaxed because the pressure was off. Here we were, in a multiple-overtime Game Seven, and nobody was going to be pointing the finger at me to say I hadn't done my job.

The ice wasn't the greatest to start with, so by the fourth overtime the guys were pretty much skating in sand. The rink staff had done a great job of trying to keep the ice up to speed throughout the course of the game, but the Cap Centre was a tight building. It was hot in there. We had a hard time. They couldn't get the compressors cranked up high enough to freeze the entire ice surface, so there were puddles everywhere. It was tough sledding. At that time of year, it felt like eighty-five or ninety degrees Fahrenheit at ice level.

The shifts were getting shorter and shorter. We were looking at twenty-five seconds, maybe thirty. There was no energy left in the tank. We were trying to find any edge. So, our trainer, Craig Smith, asked the Caps' trainer for oxygen and got some. You know, those little tanks with the hose and mask.

I chose not to indulge because first of all, I was in net and so I wasn't free to suck back on it on the bench like the skaters, and secondly, I worried about relying on it. What if it gave me a big lift and then a letdown? I know some guys swear by it. In 1960, the game they call the Forgotten Miracle, the U.S. men's Olympic team borrowed oxygen from the Russians, and look what happened there. They won the gold medal.

Bobby Nystrom was our assistant coach at the time. Recently, he told me, "I didn't realize that we'd gotten the tanks from Washington, but that was very nice of them, wasn't it?"

One of the funniest things was just looking up at the stands and seeing half the people gone and the other half sleeping. And going into the fourth overtime, the organist was playing the theme from *The Twilight Zone*.

Pivonka was driving to the net when Gord Dineen tied him up. Pivonka slew-footed him in retaliation. That means he stuck his foot in behind Dineen's skates and then used his upper body to push him backward and down. It's considered a dirty play because it can really injure a guy. Van Hellemond was right on the goal line and saw the whole thing. So when Gordie got up, Van Hellemond held his hand up and said, "It's okay, Gord. I saw it, I got this."

But Gordie was hot. He punched Pivonka in the nose, knocking him right off his feet. Now, that action put Van Hellemond in a bind. He had to either give them both two minutes or give them both nothing. While he was thinking about it, the Caps' coach, Bryan Murray, started yelling, "Tell me that's not a penalty! Tell me that's not a penalty! Andy, you tell me that is not a penalty!" He screamed it out about ten times. You could hear him all over the rink.

Van Hellemond blew his whistle and skated over to Murray. He leaned in and said, "Okay. It's not a penalty."

Murray was friggin' purple with rage. "What? Why the hell not?"

Van Hellemond shrugged. "Because you told me to tell you it's not a penalty." Murray's brother Terry, who was also behind the bench, had to run over to calm Bryan down.

Ron MacLean and Don Cherry were the intermission ana-
lysts, and if you go to YouTube and see their comments, it's amazing how on target they were. Don was a pretty gracious guy back
then. He talks about how goaltenders get tired, which means
that when they go out and play the puck, they start to make
simple mistakes. I know that's what was happening to me. I was
starting to become loose, pushing the puck up too far instead of
making the simple play by handing if off to my defenceman.

Here's the chain of events, as I remember it, that led to the end
of the fourth overtime. Many paying fans had left, but the doors
were left open and the ticket takers were gone, so the seats had
started to fill up with people who had been watching the game
on TV and had come down to the Cap Centre out of curiosity.

The goalie has the best seat in the house, so I was able to
observe a lot of what was happening around me. Halfway through
the fourth overtime, Gord Dineen sneaked in from the point,
circled behind the net and threw it out front. But it deflected
off a stick back out to the point. As he should, Pat LaFontaine,
a forward, moved back to Gord's position to cover for him. Patty
spun around and picked it off with a desperate slapshot. And
this is how bad the ice was. He tried to get it away as fast as he
could, but the puck wouldn't lie flat. It was up on its edge when
he shot. Patty always said it was like watching a butterfly take
off toward the net. And for me, watching the puck move toward
the goal, well, it looked like it was going in slow motion.

Now, there are two schools of thought about that goal. I
always say that, even as beautiful as that play is, if it wasn't for

Dale Henry, a former Saskatoon Blade, standing right in front of Bob Mason, screening him, I doubt that shot would've gone in. But other guys, like Greg Gilbert and Gerry Diduck, saw it differently. They didn't see a deflection. They saw a knuckleball.

The Caps' goalie, Bob Mason, was screened by Rod Langway, one of his own defencemen. Bob was standing with his legs wide open, trying to find the puck, when it floated past his man, dropped about a foot and fluttered in. Mason swears that it was deflected off the stick of his other big defenceman, Kevin Hatcher. All I can tell you is that it was great to see that puck go in, giving us the game, 3–2, and the series.

Part of the beauty of that game was the execution. Nobody wanted to be the goat, so everybody stayed keen. It wasn't just one individual act or one great play, it was the effort from all of us and a number of great plays. Look at the energy Ken Leiter had to expend charging up the ice, and Gord Dineen doing the same thing. Everybody was dog tired. We put fifty-seven shots on net, while they put seventy-five on ours. For all the guys to have found the energy to make those plays, it speaks to how people can dig deep, even when they're on the brink of exhaustion.

The longest game ever played in NHL history began on March 24, 1936, when the Detroit Red Wings beat the Montreal Maroons 1–0 on a goal scored at 16:30 of the sixth overtime. The Easter Epic lasted six hours and eighteen minutes, continuing well into the early hours of March 25. Overtime alone was sixty-eight minutes and forty-seven seconds. The winning goal was scored in the seventh period of that hockey game.

Half the guys went over and celebrated with Pat LaFontaine, which was natural because he was the goal scorer. Randy Boyd led the other half of the team back to me for a group hug. I can remember shaking hands with the Capitals and coming up to Rod Langway. He'd played so hard that the top of his boot was spilling blood. Everyone looked cut up and beat.

In the dressing room, there wasn't much of a celebration. We were too exhausted. Guys sat back against the locker room wall, too tired to take off their equipment. I think most of us were breathing a big sigh of relief and reflecting on the fact we had to get out of there and get packed again and head to Philadelphia for the next series.

When the skates finally came off, you could see buckets of sweat pouring out of them onto the floor. Times were different. We didn't hydrate well enough. We were running on empty, not an electrolyte in sight. There was nothing there to get your energy back up. We got into the dressing room and I tossed back two cold beers, which is not the best thing. But they sure tasted good.

We all reached for the Pripps Plus, a Swedish energy drink made from powdered packets. It was like Gatorade, only sweeter. I thought it was delicious. I think I drank about a gallon, but it was too late. About ten, fifteen minutes after the game, when I finally took off my skates, I was so dehydrated that my toes curled under. I don't know how much weight I lost that night, but I bet it'd be between ten and fifteen pounds, for sure.

That summer, people would come up to me and tell me they'd started watching the Epic on television, gone out for dinner, come home, flipped it back on and thought they were watching a replay of the game.

It sure was a weird game. Probably the most memorable of my life. It was the game that put me on the map in the hockey world, there's no question about that.

We lost to Philadelphia in the next round. But because of that series, I was added to the '87 Canada Cup team.

I flew back to Alberta for the summer. A couple of weeks before I was scheduled to head out to Montreal for the Canada Cup training camp, Wayne called my mom and dad's place, looking for me. Now, I had never talked to him before. Despite the fact we were opponents, I was a little in awe of him. C'mon, he's Wayne Gretzky.

He told me he had ice at Argyll Arena, on the south side of Edmonton, and asked if I wanted to come out and start getting ready for camp.

I said, "Sure!"

I showed up early because it takes goalies a little longer. I was dressed and stretching when I looked at the clock. Twenty minutes to ice and nobody was there. I started to wonder if I got the date or time wrong? He did say *Argyll* Arena, right?

Five minutes later, Wayne and his wife Janet walked in. They both laced up and skated onto the ice, and for the next hour or so we did some drills and he was shooting on me. She was too, to the best of her ability.

It was incredibly strange and a lot of fun. What a great way to meet someone and get to know them a little.

Chapter 10

Brown-Eyed Girl

DONNA. THAT'S HER NAME, THE LOVE of my life. She first caught my eye in high school. I was in Grade 12 and she was a year younger. She had to pass by my locker to get to hers. Every day, I looked forward to watching her from behind as she walked away from me and made her way down the hall.

Donna had other nice qualities too—trim and blonde with big brown eyes like the Van Morrison song, and what I liked even better was that she knew absolutely nothing about hockey. It was her graduating year and my second year with the Tigers when I finally asked her out. I invited her to our first playoff game. I figured if that didn't impress her, what would, right?

Our coach, Patty Ginnell, frowned upon girlfriends, or even dates, so I'd asked Donna to wait in the car for me after the game. Unfortunately, I had a terrible game and was pulled halfway through. Of course, I was pissed off at myself and came out in a bad mood. She asked me what was wrong. I said, "Weren't you there? I only played half the game."

She shrugged and said, "I don't understand. It was the other goalie's turn, wasn't it?"

Like most guys, I don't like being on the phone for long periods of time, but I found myself calling her and talking for hours and hours. She was sweet and calm. There was no drama. We didn't fight and make up all the time, like a lot of our friends did.

My family loves the mall. The way the lights sparkle off the glass windows and how the clothes look real sharp on the mannequins, combined with that new box smell, mixed in with Mr. Clean and french fries. It all just wraps around you and makes you feel good. I have such great memories of the mall.

When I was growing up, Mom worked at the Jack and Jill kids clothing store at the Meadowlark Mall in Edmonton. I'd head over there after school and meet up with her when she took her coffee break. She'd always be waiting with a carton of milk and a cookie. When I got older and played hockey and then went home for the summer, I was in the habit of hanging out at the West Edmonton Mall. Literally four or five times a week, me and my buddy Jeff Marshall would head over, grab a bite, walk around, chill out and people-watch.

Donna was twenty and I was twenty-one. We'd been dating a couple of years, and I gotta be honest, I was wild about this girl, which made me kind of scared of losing her. During the season, I was either at the rink or on the road, and summers I was home in Edmonton while she was still in the Hat.

I started thinking about putting an offer out there, and so I kept my eyes peeled for a ring. In early July, I noticed an ad in the *Edmonton Journal.* Jason Goldsmiths was having a "Federal Budget Relief Sale"—half off their entire inventory. I headed over to West Ed for a look. I found a beauty, pure gold and a quarter carat for $1,500, reduced to $900. I was making $25,000 that year, with close to $6,000 in bonuses, but I had living expenses, rent for my apartment, taxes and car payments, which didn't leave all that much. The ring cost a fortune in relation to my finances, but this girl was worth it.

I drove down to the Hat every other weekend in July and August with the intent of asking Donna to marry me, but each time I chickened out. Just before September long, I told myself, "Okay Kelly, the season is about to start and you're running out the clock. It's time to clinch the deal." I made a reservation for us at this nice steak house called the Beefeater.

It was super fancy with a firepit in the middle. Delicious smells were baked into the big, heavy wooden tables and velvet chairs. It was the kind of place that made Caesar salad right at your table, and if you ordered a baked potato, the waiter would bring over sour cream, bacon bits and butter and heap it on until you told him to stop. The steaks were amazing too, big, juicy cuts of Alberta beef. I was training and so I couldn't wait, but that night, when my food came I just picked at it. I didn't like much in my stomach before a big game.

Donna was tiny, but she managed to stuff herself. She leaned back and said, "I'm full!" But when the waiter came to take our plates, I blurted out, "Let's order dessert!"

She looked at me, "Dessert? You barely ate your dinner."

"Ya, but I'm really in the mood for some . . ."—I grabbed the menu—"chocolate brownie."

We ordered, and then I jumped up and said, "I gotta go to the bathroom." I made it to the men's and stood at the mirror, leaning in close. "Focus, Kelly," I told myself. "It's the right move. She is the one. You can do this."

My fist around the ring box in my pocket, I moved quickly to our table, sat down and saw the waiter coming our way with the brownies. Suddenly, I grabbed her hand and blurted out, "I love you. Will you marry me?"

I JOINED THE ISLANDERS IN 1983–84. We got married in the summer of 1984 and spent the first while in a beautiful little community on the North Shore of Long Island called Sea Cliff, then moved to a place called Huntington. We finally bought a place of our own in East Northport in 1985. I felt secure with the team. I was a guy who hoped to be the guy who played with the same team his whole career and won Cups and retired with the organization, like Bobby Nystrom and Ken Morrow.

I'd learned to love Long Island. It wasn't my favourite place when Donna and I first moved there as newlyweds in 1984 because it was completely different from growing up in

Edmonton or playing junior in Medicine Hat. It was big and it was fast. There were so many people around. The population of Edmonton was a little more than half a million. In Nassau and Suffolk counties on Long Island, where we lived and practised, there were more than two and a half million people. Nearly twenty million in the greater New York area. Traffic was horrendous. But the location was amazing. The North Shore beaches are beautiful and the parks there are incredible.

Donna was due to have our first baby in the middle of March of '86. On March 8, she went to see Dr. Levy, the gynecologist all the wives on the team went to, and while she was there her water broke. She wasn't in any pain or anything, so Dr. Levy called our dressing room and left a message with the trainer. He said, "Let Kelly and the coach know that Donna's going to be having this baby within twenty-four hours."

I came off the ice and got the message and went directly to Al. "I gotta be there for Donna. Let me sit out the game tonight. Billy's playing anyway. And if it's okay, I'd like to stay home from the road trip to Washington tomorrow."

Al gave me this stern look and said, "You're backup on the bench tonight, and you're playing tomorrow afternoon in Washington. Listen, Kelly, I wasn't there for any of mine and they all turned out okay. Yours will be fine too."

I came home just sick about it. Here's my twenty-two-year-old wife, in a strange city, all alone. (Her parents had plane tickets to come up the week after.) As soon as I saw her, I got emotional. "They won't let me be with you. They won't let me stay. I have to go to the game tonight to sit on the bench because they don't have anybody else."

Donna smiled. "It's okay, I'll be fine. Don't worry about it." Inside, I'm sure she was going, "Oh my God, what am I going to do?" But she wasn't giving me any guff about it. She knew my hands were tied.

In those days, the team's insurance covered four days in the hospital for a baby. Dr. Levy told her, "Stay at home tonight as long as you can and try not to get to the hospital until after midnight, because if you come in before midnight, it counts as a whole day." I headed for the game, and Brent Sutter's wife, Connie, came over to stay with Donna and to drive her to the hospital when it was time. You know what's funny? Life gets busy, but you make friends in the game who will always be your best friends, even if you don't see them much anymore. Connie and Brent are two people we became close with back then, and they are always going to be a part of us.

Donna and Connie turned the game on, and Donna told me that every ten minutes or so, they watched me signalling one of the trainers to come over to the bench. I'd whisper something and the trainer would walk off, and then our house phone would ring. The trainer would ask, "Hey Donna, how you doing? Are you in labour?"

She'd say, "Nope, all's good. Tell him I'm fine." And then they'd see the trainer walk back over to the bench, lean down and say something to me. I'd nod and turn back to the game.

Ten minutes later, I'd call the guy back over and Donna's phone would ring, and that's how it went all night.

I had to fly out to Washington right after the game, and I have never been more upset in my life. Donna called me and tried to calm me down. She told me she was going to check into the hospital after midnight, but not to worry because Dr. Levy was meeting her there.

As it turned out, she did check in and even managed to go to sleep. She woke up at about two-thirty in the morning and went "Oooo."

The nurse came in and she said, "Your husband is hilarious. He's been calling every fifteen minutes." Jessica was born at 6:58 a.m. Donna called me from the delivery room so I could hear the baby crying and stuff. I was a bloody mess. We lost 3–1 that afternoon, and for the first and only time in net, I didn't care. I just wanted to get home to my girls.

Now I'm going forward three years. Donna was pregnant again. It was a Tuesday afternoon, February 21, 1989, and we were playing Detroit at home. I was the starting goalie that day and looking forward to it, and so I was having my pre-game nap. Donna came in about half an hour into it, which she never did, and said, "Kelly, I just got off the phone with Lloyd [our lawyer]. We're getting traded."

I said, "No, no, you've got it wrong. We're not getting traded. I haven't heard any rumours."

She shook her head. "Lloyd says you're getting traded, and it's going to be today or tomorrow."

I said, "Well, how does Lloyd know?"

She said he'd had a really good discussion with John Davidson. John was the analyst on the Rangers telecasts on the MSG network, but he was an insider and we all knew it. He was the hardest-working broadcaster in hockey at the time, and as a former player, he had his ear to the ground.

"Somebody told him."

"Do you know who?"

I never did find out, but I knew that John and Gretzky had a great relationship. Of course, I couldn't get back to sleep. Greg Gilbert and I carpooled together to the games. When he picked me up, I told him, "I'm getting traded today or tomorrow. But I don't understand—why would they be playing me tonight?"

Greg said, "No chance, they're not trading you. No way."

We got to the rink, and I was expecting someone to pull me aside and say one of two things—"Go see Mr. Torrey" or "You're not playing tonight." But that didn't happen. I prepared like always and changed into the underwear that I wore under my gear. I was sitting around, waiting, drinking my coffee as usual, and nobody was coming up to me. I went into the equipment trainer's room, where we kept all of our sticks and looked around. I bet I stood there for fifteen minutes, going, "What the hell is going on here?"

Finally, I got dressed and I played. I was terrible. We lost 6–5, but we were a much better team. It was my worst game ever as a New York Islander. Right after the game, we were chartering to Buffalo. I was sitting in my stall, and I remember Al coming up to me and saying, "Kelly, you're staying behind tonight. We're going to rest you."

I looked down and swallowed. "Clearly, they must see my loyalty to the team and how much I want to be here. How could they do this to me?" I looked up at Al, searching for a glimmer, some sort of indication of what was going on. Nothing. It broke my heart.

I said, "Okay." And I knew it was a done deal.

The drive home was awfully quiet. When you get traded, it's the biggest kick in the teeth. You think that you're not good enough.

Chapter 11

I'm Not Doing This by Myself Again

ABOUT SIX THIRTY THE NEXT MORNING, Bill Torrey called the house and said he'd like to see me. So my brother, Ken, who happened to be visiting, and I drove down there. Mr. Torrey came straight to the point.

"We've traded you to the Kings. This is going to be a great opportunity for you. You can come out from under Billy Smith's shadow and show everyone that you're a number one. The other thing is you will get to play with Wayne Gretzky, the best player in the game. Watching his work ethic is going to be a life-changing experience for you."

I heard him, but I was too crushed to digest what he was saying . . . until much later, when his words turned out to be true.

Al called me up and said, "You were like one of the family." I could tell that he was really sad. He was a good man, but I wasn't kidding myself. I knew that Al and Mr. Torrey lived around the corner from each other. They drove to the rinks together, played golf together, so there was no way Mr. Torrey had just picked up the phone and said, "Hey Al, I just traded your goalie."

That being said, I think I really did have a special bond with Al. After I retired in 1998, we were at a banquet together, the night before an All-Star Game. He turned to me and said, "So, do you still hate me?" I couldn't believe he thought that.

I said, "God, no. I never hated you. You were like a dad to me." What a burden he must have carried. As tough as Al had to be at times, at the end of the day, whenever I put my head on the pillow I always felt like he cared about me, and here he thought I hated him for it.

The Islanders were looking for defence. Our season had not been going well. Potvin had just retired. Our team had Tomas Jonsson, one of the best guys I've ever played with (I've never met a bad Swede—they're all fantastic human beings—and Jonsson was one of my great buddies on the road), but he had some recurring injuries.

Los Angeles, meanwhile, had two guys the coach, Robbie Ftorek, wasn't playing for whatever reason: defenceman Wayne McBean and goalie Mark Fitzpatrick. They were both former Medicine Hat Tigers, just like me, and had played on Memorial Cup winners in '87 and '88. They were high draft picks, fourth and twenty-seventh overall respectively. The Kings offered up the two of them, plus future considerations (which turned out to be established defenceman Doug Crossman) for me. In other words, Bill Torrey got a very solid return in the trade.

I was to find out afterward, because Wayne Gretzky and I became friends, that at the all-star weekend just before I was traded, he went to Bill Torrey and asked, "What have we got to do to get Kelly in L.A.?" And Mr. Torrey said something like, "Not possible." Apparently, Wayne didn't accept that, and so he went to the team owner, Bruce McNall, who figured out a way.

Less than twenty-four hours later, I landed in L.A. and was taken straight to the rink. The Kings were playing the Caps. They were in the third period, and the Kings were getting friggin' smoked.

In the dressing room after the game, I met all the guys and Wayne said, "Wait for me and we'll grab a couple of beers." I thought that was awfully nice. I went upstairs with him and it was good to see Janet there too. A few minutes later, Pat Sajak, the host of *Wheel of Fortune*, came in and sat with us. He was with a girl who had been in *Playboy* that he was dating and later married, named Lesly Brown.

Their goalie, Rollie Melanson, wanted to see me at the hotel when I got back. We went for more beers and he vented. He told me all the things that were wrong with the organization. Since we'd played together on the Island, he'd been traded to Minnesota and then to the Kings, and soon after I arrived in L.A., he would be sent to the minors and then he'd sign with New Jersey as a free agent, only to be traded again to Montreal, where he played a handful of games before injuries took their toll. So, Rollie had a run of bad trades due to timing, and I seriously felt awful for him, because Rollie was a great talent.

Glenn Healy was L.A.'s other goalie. Glenn and I have become really good friends over the years. He's a great analyst on TV because he's so hockey-smart, and he's really funny. He'd been with the Kings pre-Gretzky when they still wore yellow (the Kings called it gold) pants and yellow sweaters and yellow helmets and didn't have much success. Glenn told me at Wayne's very first training camp in Victoria, there were so many reporters around, Glenn spent most of his time telling them to stop stepping on his socks and get the hell off of his equipment.

Glenn and I clicked right away. He was one of the best partners I ever had. He was playing most of the games until I got there, and then that was it—I was in net for the rest of the season. Glenn was a real class act about it. He told me, "Kelly, you are just what we need. Someone with lots of experience, who is really good, ready to take this team to the next level. The way I look at it is, playing you as number one is okay by me. We win as a group, and they don't put your full name on the Stanley Cup unless you're Robert Orr."

He and I had a lot of fun together. He has such a great sense of humour. Because there were so many guys from the Oilers, with their proud history of all those Cups and a roster stacked with Hall of Famers, they told a lot of stories, including tons about Grant Fuhr. He was a legend, and Glenn and I heard all about him—a lot. We started to make up our own stories about Grant. We'd be getting ready to skate before a game and Glenn would say, "Hey Kelly, did I tell you about the time the Oilers were on the road and the trainer forgot Grant's skates, so he played the game in Kodiak work boots and made seventy-nine saves?" Of course, we'd both be in stitches, and the rest of the team would be looking at us like, "Are Moe and Curly ready to play or what?"

I do remember that the Edmonton guys accepted me right away, though. We headed out on a five-game road trip to Edmonton, New Jersey, New York, Buffalo and St. Louis. I was getting my legs under me, but I felt I played okay at times. Just before the last game in St. Louis, Marty McSorley stood up in the dressing room and said something like, "We've got to start to play a lot better. Our goaltender's giving us a chance every single game."

When I wasn't playing, I tried to be supportive and keep things positive. You know what I really disliked? When coaches made the backup goalie take notes, like charting plays and shots and stuff like that. Oh, I hated that. My feeling is, when you're the backup, you're watching the game. That means you're learning, not only your own teammates' strengths, but the other team's weaknesses. And I always studied the other goalie. I would take things that I liked and try them out the next day in practice. Sometimes it worked, and sometimes it was, "Mmm, no, I don't like this. It's good for him but doesn't work for me."

I was in a big transition from a stand-up goalie—the style I'd grown up playing—to recognizing that, the way the game was moving, I had to learn to go down a lot. The way I played was often compared to the way Dominik Hasek played. He was in transition too. To the uneducated eye, we looked like sprawlers. But if you watch me, I had my go-to points, and I was consistent in my play. There were certain times I left my feet and went down on my knees, and I attacked a shooter in a calculated way. If you look carefully at Hasek, you'll see that the way he played was intentional too. By the way, I think he's the best goalie that ever played. Anyone who says, "All he did was fling himself this way and that," is wrong. It was much, much more than that.

He couldn't possibly have been that lucky. I watched Dominik very closely and took a lot from him, including his post work and how he positioned himself. I took things from Mike Vernon too, like the way he'd hold his glove up a little bit higher because he's not the tallest guy. I added that to my game. I'd watched a lot of guys moving the puck and picked that up. In fact, I heard one of the reasons why Wayne wanted to trade for me was because I was good at pushing the puck up the ice.

The really lousy part of a trade that most people not in the business don't understand is that for the player, it's pretty straightforward. You pack up your gear, some sticks, a couple of suitcases and you hit the airport. You show up at the new rink and say hi to the guys. Next thing you know, you're in the lineup. But you leave your family back home to pick up the pieces. I was five thousand miles away and Donna was young, in her mid-twenties, eight months pregnant, and we had a three-year-old, and she had no family around to help out. She had to slug it out on her own.

She did draw the line on having the baby. While she drove me to the airport, she pointed to her belly and said, "I'm not doing this by myself again. You make sure to tell them that."

The Kings' GM, Rogie Vachon, was a wonderful guy. He was a former goalie, so we connected right away. He got on the phone with Donna and guaranteed that I would be there for the birth of our second baby.

Dr. Levy was her doctor again, and so we looked at the schedule. I was playing in Montreal on March 15, a week before her due date. It was an easy flight from there to the Island, so we scheduled the next day, March 16, to induce Donna into labour.

The Kings were amazing. They agreed I could miss the game against Calgary on March 18 and return for the game against the Oilers on March 21 in Edmonton. Turns out we didn't need to induce Donna. She went into labour naturally the morning of the 16th, and Megan was born four hours later.

I loved being with my girls back home on the Island, but by the third day, when L.A. lost to the Flames 9–3, I started getting antsy. Donna looked at me and said, "Just go. As soon as I get the all-clear from my doctor and the pediatrician, we'll join you." I hugged her and headed for the airport. I was already packed.

Donna really understood about being a player's partner. Al Arbour's wife, Claire, a phenomenal lady, summed it up best. She said, "The guys play hockey. That's what they do. They never accomplish much else. You can talk about getting new furniture, getting stuff painted, working in the garden, and they'll say, 'Yes, I'll do it next week.' But they won't. They're focused on the games, playing and winning. So whatever needs doing, do it yourself. Just get it done." Glenn Healy said Claire's advice cost him about $300,000 because, instead of consulting with him on every purchase, it became, "Hey Honey, I just bought new furniture. By the way, we got a new car. Oh, and we painted the house!" But Claire was right, the wives had to do it all.

Two weeks later, I was missing them a lot. Donna was ready to fly out, but our pediatrician said, "No, the baby has to be eight weeks old. Her immune system isn't built up to be on a plane with all those people and all those germs. It would be dangerous." Donna was really upset. She called me and told me the bad news.

I said, "What? Oh, my God, I can't go that long without you guys here." Our owner, Bruce McNall, came up to me later that day and said, "Hey, how you doing? How's the family?"

I said, "They're doing okay, but I really miss them. Donna just told me the doctor won't sign the form to allow our new baby to fly for another month!"

Bruce said, "Well, when would she like to come out?"

I laughed and said, "As soon as she can get packed." And the next thing I knew, Bruce sent his private jet out to Long Island to pick them up.

What Donna didn't know was that I'd caught the nastiest flu I'd ever had in my life—thanks to Glenn Healy, who had it the week before—and was staying at the hospital, hooked up to intravenous antibiotics, between games. I didn't tell her about it because I was worried she wouldn't come.

She got off the plane and there was a big limo waiting. The driver loaded them up and took them back to the Marriott Residence Inn on Manhattan Beach, where I was set up because it was close to the practice rink. The front desk gave her keys and she hauled everything up to the room. I'd left a note on the table with a set of car keys. It said, "I'm in the hospital," and I had drawn out a map of how to drive there. I think she thought it was a joke.

She drove to the hospital and made it up to my floor. I remember Jessica flying into my arms and Donna standing in the doorway holding Megan, not daring to come near me because of the germs. It didn't matter. At least we were all together again.

That was the beginning of the playoffs. I didn't come home through the first round. I continued to stay at the hospital. Donna would come to the games and drive me back to my room after each one. We ended up losing in the second round to Calgary. I thought I played really well for the most part, but in the second round I wasn't as sharp as I needed to be. It happens.

When the season was over, instead of heading straight back to Edmonton, we stayed to find a house. We bought a brand-new place in Redondo Beach, a seven-minute drive from the ocean. I was with a great group of guys, in a fantastic organization, living in an amazing place. I remember asking myself, "How could life get any better?"

Chapter 12

Grace Under Fire

THE ISLANDERS WERE A REALLY GOOD team when it came to responsibilities. Every player had a job and they took care of business. When I played there, I hardly ever faced a break-away. Then I went to L.A., and there were a ton of them. I'm not complaining. I embraced the fact that L.A. was a wide-open team. It made things more challenging and kept me on my toes, and I got a lot better thanks to all the scoring chances that came my way. By 1995, I had faced thirteen penalty shots, at that time the most in NHL history. Statistically, I went from letting in seven of the first eight to stopping all of the last five.

My first year with L.A., I remember a conversation I had with a guy I think was the greatest goaltender ever to play in Boston, Gerry Cheevers. I always thought super highly of him, and I loved the way he played. He was with the Bruins on

Bobby Orr's team and won the Stanley Cup in 1969–70 and '71–72. I would've been nine and then eleven. Those are ages when you start to notice the world around you. Gerry was fantastic at his job, and he did it with humour and a bit of a showman's flair. Look at his mask, with all the stitch marks on it.

Gerry was the colour analyst for the Bruins, and I saw him standing at the Zamboni entrance when I came into the L.A. Forum for a morning skate. He had a big personality, full of confidence, but not in an arrogant way—he was just comfortable with who he was. That day, he told me something that freed me up for the rest of my career. He said, "Kelly, enjoy. This is a fun way to play. Who cares if you win 7–6? As long as you win the game." I went away thinking about how kind he was. He didn't have to try to help me whatsoever, but he did, and that was very gracious of him. That's one thing you learn when you play hockey—goalies stick together.

Robbie Ftorek was my first coach in L.A. I didn't play for Robbie all that long, so I didn't get to know him very well. In the playoffs, we beat Edmonton in the first round, but then we were swept by Calgary.

Just before our fourth game of the Calgary series in Los Angeles, Sylvester Stallone came into the dressing room to give us a little speech. He told us, "Look, we're down three, just like Rocky. And it's a good thing, right? You don't wanna be up three games to one, you wanna be down, on the ropes. It's better when their fighter's givin' it to ya, so you can fight your way back on top." When he left the room, Glenn Healy leaned into me and said, "I don't know about you, but I kinda think it's better to be up three to one."

After we lost that series, Robbie Ftorek was gone. I liked him. I thought he was a good guy. He was the first guy on the ice and the last guy off. I think he tried to be a good communicator, but it didn't seem to come naturally. There seemed to be some conflict going on in the dressing room between Robbie and some of the guys.

In his playing days, which weren't too far behind him, Robbie had gone from a high school star and silver medallist with the 1972 U.S. Olympic team to a sort of middle-of-the-pack forward, but he was well regarded. He was the first English-speaking captain of the Quebec Nordiques, and then the Rangers traded for him because of his reputation in the dressing room. He spent three years as the head coach of the Kings' farm team, the New Haven Nighthawks. They loved him there and considered him a players' coach. But they were kids, and that's the difference. Remember when I said that Al Arbour connected with all of us by treating us all differently? Well, Robbie had this philosophy that you should treat us all the same, and you can't. You just cannot do that.

In the NHL or NFL or NBA, there are stars and they get special treatment. Like when my dad worked at Pepsi, there are the workers and then there's management. There are double standards, and that's just a fact, Jack. Put in simple terms, when Al was dealing with Mike Bossy, Bryan Trottier and that core group of superstars, they enjoyed benefits—like optional practices—and more leeway. I didn't have optional practices under Al Arbour, not until I earned them.

I had no problem with Wayne being treated better than me, and me being treated better than another guy. Now, I have to say, comparing any other coach to Al Arbour isn't fair, but Robbie didn't get it.

I think the guys were frustrated. It seemed Robbie truly believed the coach had to have total control, so the team felt they were being treated like kids. Before they are pros, players spend years in hockey being treated like kids. So when they get to the National Hockey League, they want to be treated like men. And a coach had better understand that, or he won't last.

So, you go to that incident in Detroit on November 23, 1988, where Robbie benched Wayne. I wasn't there. I was still with the Islanders. I hadn't been traded yet. But I heard all about it. Wayne was having a great night. First period, he had a goal and two assists. Second period, he had two assists. But when the puck got by him and Stevie Yzerman scored, he got pissed at himself and whammed his stick on the crossbar.

The Kings went into the dressing room at the end of the second period, and Robbie told Wayne he was going to be benched in the third so Robbie could make an example of him. I don't think Wayne had been benched since he was seventeen years old and Glen Sather sat him through the first period of a game against Cincinnati. And it made Wayne so furious he came out in the third period and scored three goals.

The story about Robbie benching Wayne spread around the

league like shampoo in the shower. Everybody heard about it. When someone told me at the time, my immediate thought was, "Geezus, he's mishandling Wayne." It's so silly to imagine that Robbie would take the best player in the world and bench him for showing the kind of passion you want a player to show.

Later, Bruce McNall told me he was clueless about what was going on that night and hadn't even noticed Wayne sitting out the third. He went into the locker room afterward and Wayne stormed past him, which was very unusual for Wayne. When Bruce found out, he went to Wayne and said, "Wayne, what happened?" But Wayne was so mad, he wouldn't even talk about it.

And then, after Wayne cooled down a little, Bruce said, "Okay, Wayne, what should we do?" And Wayne said, "Nothing. Leave it alone." But obviously, from that point on, tensions increased in the locker room. As I said, treating everybody equally, that's just not the real world.

I know it was difficult for Robbie too, because here you've got a guy and it's his first year coaching in the National Hockey League, so of course there's an adjustment period. And then you've got a superstar, not that Wayne was hard to handle. Coaching in the NHL is difficult, understanding the players is difficult, and a guy with zero experience was supposed to know how to coach Wayne Gretzky, the best player to ever play the game? There was no operating manual for this.

I played with Wayne in Los Angeles for eight seasons, from '88–89 to '95–96. People, and not just hockey fans, know his name because of all the points he scored, but I am not sure they really understand that he was one of the greatest hockey minds of all time. His general knowledge about the game really surprised me. No, not general knowledge. That's not giving him enough credit. I couldn't believe his in-depth knowledge of everything going on in the game, not just in our organization, but everybody else's organization. I recall when the Winnipeg Jets brought in Luciano Borsato in 1990–91. They had drafted him in 1984. I had never heard of this guy. But Wayne knew all about his college career at Clarkson. He was aware of everybody.

One time, we were getting ready for a home game. We were in the dressing room, getting our equipment on, and he came in. Like all of us, he had his own routine. I was sitting there, tying up my left skate. That was the one I always tied up first.

I tried not to be too superstitious, but it crept in. My second year with the Islanders, we were in Washington, and I had my sticks lined up perfectly on the wall. One of the young stick boys, a local boy, real nice kid, moved my sticks and I snapped at him. Denis Potvin looked at me and said, "Kelly, where your sticks are positioned has nothing to do with the outcome of the game." He knew what I was doing. I thought that was great. It helped me move forward. After that, if my sticks were moved, I'd give myself a little reminder. "It's not a big deal. Don't worry about it." The only real non-negotiable I kept up my entire career was on game days at home. I had to eat a piece of boneless, breaded chicken at 12:15 p.m. sharp.

Anyway, as we were getting ready for the game, Wayne

sat down in his stall and told us all about how important
it was to win that night. He said, "This is a really important game. We have to beat this team because Edmonton's in
Philadelphia tonight, tomorrow they're in Long Island and in
three days they're in New York City . . ." He had every Campbell
Conference team's schedule mapped out in his head. And he
did the math for us—why that game was important because it
meant we'd move up into second place and they'd fall back into
third. It was fascinating to see how his brain works.

The way he looks at the game hit home for me when he
was chasing Gordie Howe's record for most points. In the fall of
1989, about five games before he broke Gordie's record, we were
having lunch together and I asked him, "So, when do you think
it might happen?" And he knew. He went through the upcoming games and how many points he thought he would get in
each game. It was nuts how he nailed it.

I sat closer to the front of the bus than Wayne. But sometimes I'd lollygag because I wanted to follow him into an arena.
It was so cool to see. He knew everybody. He'd walk by the
Zamboni driver, and he'd say, "Hey Bill, how's your wife, Anne?"
It seemed easy for him. I don't know if it was, but I was blown
away by how he cared about people. Look, most of us don't
think of that as being important, but maybe because of his stat-
ure, Wayne knew. "It'd be nice if I took the time to remember
the guy's name." I put Wayne and Ron MacLean in the same
category. Generous with people that way, and both have what I
would call photographic memories. That's unique.

Wayne taught me one of the most important things I ever learned in the game of hockey, and it was something I carried into the rest of my life. Instead of lecturing people or telling them what to do, let everyone find their own truth. We had this young left-shooting defenceman, Petr Prajsler. Petr was highly skilled. I remember he used a wooden Christian stick that had this super-straight blade. Petr was from Czechoslovakia, and like a lot of guys who came over from Europe at that time, he didn't like to get hit. Whenever anyone came after him, he'd throw the puck away. He didn't care where it went. He'd just get rid of it to avoid a tough check. That made for a lot of turnovers.

On January 27, 1990, we were playing at home against the Rangers, ten minutes left in the third period, and he threw a puck away from behind our net. It was intercepted and they scored the game-winning goal. I was furious. Typically, when we lost, I'd be pissed at myself—just berate myself, really nasty. It would push me to become better, and I do think that's one of the reasons why I made the NHL. I had this goal in mind and I was going to will it to happen, no matter what obstacle was in my way. I refused to be denied. Having said that, I could have relaxed a little bit. I think life would have been a little more enjoyable at times.

But I was really effin' mad at Petr. Super pissed. Now, Wayne was always the guy quickest to get undressed, into the shower and out the door. He learned that from Guy Lafleur at the end of a Canada Cup game in 1981. Flower came up to him and said, "Wayne, the game's over. Let's go. Get undressed. There's no reason to sit around in your gear all night." And I learned that habit from Wayne. So now I was in the shower with Wayne, and I was having a major tantrum. One of the things that made Wayne so great was he knew that no one could ever play at his level, and he had a great understanding of everybody's abilities.

I was saying a bunch of terrible things about Petr Prajsler. I was ranting and raging and chucking bars of soap and shampoo bottles, which were exploding against the tiles. Of course, all our teammates were hearing this, so no one was coming in.

Finally, after about five minutes, the tantrum was over. And then I felt bad because I knew Petr was out there and he'd probably heard everything. But Wayne gave me the kindest look. He went, "Kelly, let everybody earn a living. If he's not good enough, they'll find somebody else." That humbled me. I thought, "What a great lesson." Here's a guy with all this pressure on him to win. If there's anybody who should have been upset, it was him. But instead, he sees it differently. After that, I never had a tantrum over a teammate again. Man, Wayne was grace under fire.

Chapter 13

Tunes

IT WASN'T JUST CONFLICT IN THE DRESSING ROOM that cost Robbie Ftorek his job at the end of that year. Yes, he was a worker, a guy who came in every day and gave everything he could, but what happened in Los Angeles was that Robbie wouldn't change, even though Bruce McNall and management were asking him to. He seemed proud of his inflexibility. For instance, some felt he should have worn a suit instead of one of his fancy cable-knit sweaters on the bench. They thought he was being disrespectful. Their opinion was that when you're playing in the greatest league in the world, you've got to show respect, not only for the people you're playing for and against, but for tradition and the people who came before you. So a Sunday sweater didn't cut it for management. For me, when I first saw Robbie in a sweater on the bench, I thought, "Oh. That's kinda cool." I knew from the way he interacted with the team that he respected the game.

So Robbie was out and Tom Webster was in for three seasons, '89–90 to '91–92. Webby said it was a dream job for him. Rogie Vachon was one of his good friends, and so when Robbie Ftorek was let go, Rogie called Tom. I knew who Tom was because he coached in the Central Hockey League with the Tulsa Oilers when I played for the Indianapolis Checkers.

After the announcement that Webby had taken the job, Bruce McNall came up to him and said, "Tom, I'd like to see you in my office tomorrow. I just want to sit down and talk to you."

Webby said, "Sounds great, Bruce. No problem."

The next day, Webby walked into Bruce's Hollywood office, and on Bruce's desk were three big stacks of papers. One on each side and one in the middle. Bruce said, "Tom, you're probably wondering why I called you in here."

Webby said, "Yeah, I am, Bruce. But I want you to know, I'm pretty excited. I'm looking forward to getting it all going."

Bruce said, "Well, that's what I wanted to talk to you about. Tom, I'm going to fire you."

Webby said, "What?! I just got here!"

Bruce said, "I know, but I'm going to fire you—eventually." He pointed to all the papers on his desk and said, "On the left hand of my desk is the history of coaching in the NBA. On the right is a history of coaching in baseball. In the middle is the history of coaching in hockey. You know what all this stuff tells me? That coaches get fired."

Webby said, "I can't argue with that."

Bruce stood up and shook his hand and said, "What I'm trying to tell you is you are eventually going to be fired anyway, so you might as well do it your way."

Webby laughed. "Thank you, Bruce. I appreciate that information."

And Webby did come in with new ideas. He tried Luc Robitaille on Wayne's left wing, which made sense because Luc was a goal scorer and Wayne was a playmaker. Wayne had that combination in mind from the time he came to L.A., probably due to the success he had with Mario Lemieux at the 1987 Canada Cup. Of course, when we're talking about Lemieux and Gretzky, we're talking about a Ferrari and a Maserati. They'd both get to the same place at the same time.

But Wayne and Luc couldn't find that same chemistry. The one thing about Wayne that not many people talk about is that he processed so fast. He was the iMac before there was an abacus. You can make the same argument today for Sidney Crosby and Connor McDavid. People think they are easy players to play with, but it's the opposite. They make plays that no other players make. If you are on the ice with them, you have to anticipate more than you normally would. You have to get really creative and go to an area of the ice that the other team doesn't expect. That's why it is so tough to play with them. Most players see the ice the way they were coached. Plays are drilled into guys from the time they are very young. And unless your brain works the way that Wayne's, Sid's and Connor's do—where they see things shaping up far ahead of the play—how can you figure out where to be? Look at Crosby's goal on March 21, 2017. He opened the scoring by splitting four guys and shooting it top shelf with one hand. Who does that? Nobody. Well, Wayne could, and maybe McDavid or Ovechkin, but that's about it. It takes a unique player who thinks differently to play with guys like that.

And so, a change was made. In January 1990, the Kings traded Bernie Nicholls to the Rangers. It was a loss in the dressing room. Nothing seemed to bug Bernie. He kept things loose. One time he was suspended, and Glenn Healy was backing up. So Bernie called Glenn and asked him if he wanted to go golfing that day. Glenn said, "Bernie, it's a game day."

He went, "It's okay, we'll take a cart!"

Bernie was so naturally skilled. He had this incredible shot and the ability to turn the puck on its side. He could score from anywhere and everywhere, and he made whoever he played with dangerous too. Chris Kontos scored eight goals in seven games when the Kings defeated the Oilers in our 1989 division semifinal. Granted, three of them went off Kontos's rear end and two off his shin pads, but Bernie assisted on five of the eight goals.

Bottom line, we let go of a seventy-goal scorer for Tony Granato and Tomas Sandstrom. It was a move questioned by a lot of people at the time, but Tony and Tomas filled out a number one line to play with Wayne. Luc went back and played with Dave Taylor and Todd Elik, who we brought up from our farm team. Webby called them his two perfect lines.

Webby was a good guy. He was stern when he needed to be, and I like that in a coach. I remember we were in Buffalo and I let in a horseshit goal in the second period. I was trying to play the puck and I screwed up. They scored and I lost focus. They scored a couple more times, and when Webby came into the dressing room after the game, he gave it to me for getting rattled. And he was right. I thought, "Geezus, Kelly, it's your eighth year in the league. You can't crumble like that. You have to be strong. Stop being weak." I couldn't believe that first goal threw me like that.

Tom Laidlaw was a hard-nosed stay-at-home defenceman who had a tremendous sense of team. He was perfect in the three, four or five role. He was also one of the best practical jokers in the game.

The one that cracked me up the most was his "three-shower prank." After practice, we'd be coming out of the shower. As we exited, we'd grab one of the white gym towels that were folded on the bench outside the room. Tom would fill the towels ahead of time with shaving cream—and so, when you threw the towel around your waist, you'd be covered. Of course, you'd have to head back to the shower.

Back then, most of us would use a blow-dryer to shape our hair. I had flowing locks, and I liked the VO5 too. What Tom would do was fill the dryers with baby powder. When you turned it on, it was like a pie in the face. So . . . back to the showers.

The first prank would be the shave cream, and then he'd hit you with the baby powder. He was pretty crafty about it. He'd wait a couple of months before trying it again. He got a few of us more than once.

Anyway, on the plane after the game where Webby gave it to me for getting rattled, I think Tom could see I was a little off, so he sat down beside me and loosened me up with a few jokes. I really appreciated that.

Barry Beck was this monster of a man. He was a former number two draft choice by Colorado in 1977, and he found success and fame with the Rangers. He left the game in 1985–86 and then attempted a comeback with us, playing fifty-two games in 1989–90. He was the funniest guy I'd played with since Clark Gillies. I was lucky because he sat beside me in the locker room at the Forum. He loved the song "Love Shack" by the B-52s. I can see him sitting there, swaying his big body back and forth, singing, "Love shack, baby, love shack . . ."

Remember, we flew commercial back then, and so that meant we waited for flights at the airport. Barry's best gag was to take a dollar bill and thread a piece of fishing line through a little hole in the top. While we sat in the waiting area, he'd throw it out onto the concourse. Trust me, there is nothing funnier than grown men in expensive business suits chasing a dollar bill and not catching it. When they realized what was going on, reactions were varied. Some guys would find it funny, but most would come up to him and call him an idiot or a child or tell him just how juvenile he was. Of course, that would make Barry laugh even harder.

Except for that bout of flu when I first joined the Kings, I was the healthiest guy you'd ever meet. I had an awesome start to my first full season with the Kings, 1989–90, under Webby, and then suddenly, about midway through November, I was dead tired. When I played, I'd run out of gas. When I wasn't training or on the ice, I was sleeping. I constantly had that lousy feeling you get when you first get the flu. At the end of November, I woke up from a nap with a headache so bad it was like a knife through my temple. I sat up and held on to my ears and squeezed my head between my palms as hard as I could. It hurt so bad it almost took my hearing away. And then the pain started moving around, like I was being shot in the head. I tried everything—heat, cold, massage, steam, sitting, standing, lying down—and I gulped down handfuls of Aspirin and Tylenol. Nothing worked. The only relief I got was when I went to sleep. The idea that it might be a brain tumour crossed my mind, but I was too tired to get worked up over it. It turned out that I had caught a virus called cytomegalovirus (CMV). The doctors told me it's like an adult version of mono. And at the same time, I had a raging sinus infection. That's what was causing those horrendous headaches.

Mario Gosselin was our backup goalie at that time. I went to Webby and said, "Listen, I'm not feeling good, but I feel I can give you two periods of play and Mario can come in for the third." I told him, "I'll battle through this, don't worry." But I found out there was no way to battle back from it. Time is the only thing that allows you to get better. It was an awful time. Your first full year with the team and you want to be good, right? Instead, I was bagged by the end of the first period. My blocker weighed a hundred pounds, and my pads were like bags of wet cement. You want to be a difference maker, and I wasn't. I was part of the problem. I really didn't start to feel like myself until March. I went through a five-month stretch of hell.

In his second year coaching us, Webby laid down the hammer. He gave us a specific set of rules about how we were going to play. More like a team. No more wide-open play, trying to win every game 8–7. We weren't the Edmonton Oilers of the '80s. We were going to play *our* way, and that meant more discipline and structure.

We accepted that. We played his way, and we were really good. His philosophy was that our defencemen had to stop joining the rush on every play. You can't be looking for cookies all the time. You've got to be responsible. Now, if there is an opportunity where you can beat the other guy up the ice and create an odd-man attack, go for it.

The following year, 1991–92, I felt great. I was in really good health, and after Webby implemented his system, look at my numbers. They improved dramatically. In the second half of the season, I went 15–2–1. I was on fire. In March, I was the NHL's player of the month. The team finished third overall, the best they'd done yet. We came in first in the Smythe Division ahead of the Flames, the Oilers, the Canucks and the Jets in that order. It was a strong division, and we were on top.

When I looked up in the stands, I saw a few kids and long-hairs wearing blue headbands. So how did the blue headband become my trademark? It started on Long Island. I had long hair most of my life, even when I was a kid. And then in junior, I got contact lenses. Think about it—the combination of sweat and contact lenses is not good. Sweat stings your eyes and makes your vision blurry.

I would buy those regular stretchy headbands, but when I got to the NHL and played games that sweated off ten pounds, the store-bought headbands weren't absorbent enough. I tried wrapping all sorts of different materials around my head under my helmet, and then one day before practice, I was pulling on the blue underwear I wore under my equipment—basically, Stanfield pyjamas—and I thought, "Hey, what about this?" I grabbed an extra undershirt and cut it up and I was like, "You know what? This is pretty good. I like it!"

I didn't intend for it to become my trademark, but it did. Especially when I got to L.A. and Don Cherry did a stand-up in the tunnel before a game in April 1991. In his book *Cornered*, Ron MacLean said that Don didn't like it when Wayne said in an interview that he wanted fighting out of hockey, so Don decided to poke fun at the Kings by pretending he was a flashy L.A. sports announcer. He put on the earrings and sunglasses and all that, and when I came through and skated onto the ice, he said, "First of all, let's talk about Kelly Hrudey. Here comes Kelly right now. Here's Kelly. I love the little blue string that hangs from the back, don't you? I love him. You can see that little string there. I think it's blue chiffon."

My mom and dad hated it. They thought that Don was a total jerk for saying that. I thought it was kind of funny, but now that I'm a parent, I get why they didn't see the humour in it.

Oh, and my nickname never was Hollywood. That's a big misconception. Hollywood was just something I had written on my mask because it was iconic and Hollywood is the first thing you think of when you think of Los Angeles. My real nickname was given to me by Wayne Gretzky and Brent Sutter at the '87 Canada Cup. Very few people know it, but it's Tunes—simply because I love listening to music. I was just getting into Springsteen, U2 was big for me, and so were the Eagles. Rock 'n' roll got me going. I gained a lot of emotional strength from it. I was always looking for inspiring songs like "Life in the Fast Lane." I like the guitar riffs in it, and Don Henley on drums and his raspy voice. I didn't live that lifestyle, but I dug the attitude. When I see Wayne today, he would probably call me Tunes. Brent for sure still does.

I MENTIONED EARLIER THAT BRENT SUTTER and I stayed close. I talked to him after he was traded to Chicago in October 1991. He'd been captain of the Islanders since 1987. Brent knew that the ownership of the Islanders was in question. John Pickett had been the majority owner since summer of 1978. He was an excellent, hands-off owner. But after moving to Florida in the late 1980s, he seemed to lose interest, and by early 1991 he had put the team up for sale for $75 million.

Now, this shows you the level of respect the Islanders had for Brent. Very few guys, and I mean you could count them on one hand, get a heads-up that they are going to be traded. But after training camp, Mr. Torrey called Brent in for a good sit-down. He wanted to talk about the direction the team was headed. Mr. Torrey told Brent he was going to step down at the end of the year and that he was looking at moving to Florida in 1993 to help the expansion Panthers get going for their first year. He told Brent that Al was to either going stay on and coach, or the Islanders were going to keep him as a consultant. He mentioned they were looking at trading Brent, and then, even though his contract didn't give him a choice, Mr. Torrey asked for a list of four teams Brent would like to play for. Brent told him, "Chicago, Calgary, Los Angeles or St. Louis." Chicago because Mike Keenan was head coach and general manager there, and he had won two Canada Cups with Mike. He had no idea at that time that his brother Darryl would become the head coach of the Blackhawks just one year later. Calgary had a good team and was close to home. He liked the way St. Louis played and thought he could do well under his brother Brian, who was coaching. And L.A. had Wayne and me. Besides, he knew our coach, Tom Webster, because Webby had been the assistant coach at the Canada Cup in '91. He thought we'd be a good fit for him.

The day of the trade, Mr. Torrey called Brent in to tell him he was going to Chicago.

Brent stood up to go, and Mr. Torrey said, "You gotta go speak with Al first. He wants to see you."

So, for the last time, Brent opened the door to Al's big office. It was configured strangely. It was rectangular, maybe twelve feet wide but thirty feet long, and Al's desk was situated at the far end in front of a large wooden bookcase. The room was dark except for the glow from a gooseneck lamp, which threw a circle of light onto Al's desk.

Like I told you before, Al was a big man, so he had this enormous high-back leather chair, but it was turned away from Brent, facing the bookshelf. All Brent could see was the top of Al's slicked-back salt-and-pepper hair.

Brent walked in and said, "Al?"

No answer.

Brent moved closer. "Al?"

Again, no reply.

All kinds of thoughts ran through Brent's head. "Did Al have a heart attack, or even worse, a stroke? Oh my God, is Al dead?"

Brent took a chair in front of the desk and cleared his throat. This time, he was firm. "Al!"

Slowly, Al's chair began to turn around until he finally came face to face with Brent. His glasses were all fogged up, and there were tears running down the deep ravines in Al's cheeks. It was heartbreaking. Brent got all teary-eyed himself. Neither of them said anything for a moment.

And then Al took a deep breath and said, "It's over. You're the last. The last link to the Stanley Cup years."

Brent was swallowing hard.

Al said, "You've been like a son to me."

That was too much. Brent started crying and they both just sat there, bawling their eyes out.

Whether you were a veteran or a rookie, Al was always there for you. He knew when to motivate and when to back off, and he had so much respect, not just for the players, but he cared very deeply about everyone's family. You'd go to the rink and Al would be the first to say hi to your wife and kids. He was a genuine, caring guy who was the right amount of firm when it came to the hockey side of it.

Chapter 14

Q-tips in His Ears

IT'S FUNNY HOW THINGS HAPPEN ON the spur of the moment. Close to the playoffs in March 1991, we were taking it to the Flames, which is incredible when you think about it. Their top scorers were Joe Nieuwendyk, Doug Gilmour, Al MacInnis, Sergei Makarov, Gary Suter, Joe Mullen and Theo Fleury. We were leading 3–0. Just having a really good game. Gilmour was taking the losing score badly, so he started poking Webby, getting under his skin with his constant stare and little comments that Webby felt went beyond what was acceptable.

The benches were right beside each other, and Webby said something back to Doug and one or the other took a swing. They both started going at it and Doug went down, but I don't think anybody landed anything. I remember Joel Otto and Tim Hunter joined in. Webby thought they were going to beat his brains out, and their coach, Doug Risebrough, was jumping up and trying to get at Webby too. And then all hell broke loose. The glass came down and Webby was suspended for four games and fined $5,000. Gilmour was fined $500 and given two games. Webby felt terrible about it afterward. Recently, I asked him what Doug said that made him so mad and he replied, "He told me he wasn't going to send me a Christmas card that year."

I FIRST MET LARRY ROBINSON WHEN I was lucky enough to be on the 1987 Canada Cup team. He'd broken his leg playing polo in August. It would cause him to miss the first twenty-seven games of the season, but he was at training camp in Montreal, getting rehab with our trainers. I really enjoyed his interaction with all of us. It was obvious he loved to be around the guys. He was a real guy's guy. He'd punch you in the arm to say hi, and he was funny. He'd walk around with Q-tips in his ears to make us laugh, silly stuff like that. I thought, "Man, I like this guy. He's so good-natured and happy-go-lucky all the time." But later, when he went from player to coach in L.A. from 1995 to '99, he was a much different guy.

When Webby came to L.A. in 1989 to coach, one of the first things he did was talk to Bruce McNall and Rogie about signing Larry, who was thirty-eight years old and a free agent. Montreal had offered him close to half a million dollars on a one-year contract. Bruce upped the ante by offering $1.5 million for three years. Larry was a great presence on our team because of all of his experience and his winning attitude. As a defenceman, he would play extremely well for us. Rock solid.

Larry wasn't the take-charge kind of guy he'd been with the Canadiens, when he was at his all-time best, but he was exceptionally crafty. He knew when to rush the puck and how to take advantage of the other team. He was great for me because he shared his understanding of goalie positioning from his playing days with guys like Ken Dryden. I absorbed everything he said and my game improved. The other thing I liked about him was the fact he was totally dedicated to playing in his own end. As a goalie, you have tremendous appreciation for someone who's going to stay back and worry about goals against. He understood that we could win in lower-scoring games.

Larry also did a lot of things with the younger guys at the end of practice. He was especially good with Rob Blake. Blakey came in rambunctious. He wanted to run around and hit people. One time, Rob raced into a corner to hit somebody and ended up out of position. Larry was his D partner and was quick, right on the ice, covering for him. The whistle blew and the three of us met in front of my net. Larry said something like "Rob, no need to run to guys. Wait, be patient, they'll come to you. Stay between the net and the puck carrier and the hits will come." In the defensive zone, Larry was the master of putting his stick in the passing lanes, and he taught Rob how to do that. Rob seemed to take these lessons to heart and became a better defenceman because of it.

Larry and I became close before his second year with the team at training camp in Lake Arrowhead, about two hours outside L.A. A beautiful little spot. Dave Taylor and Larry and I would have dinner together. I'd met Dave in Moscow in 1986 when I played for Canada in the world championships. The three of us were a little older and married with kids, unlike some of the younger guys, like Luc Robitaille or Steve Duchesne. Dave and I became good friends. He could make me laugh like nobody else. He had a dry sense of humour with perfect timing. Dr. Lombardo was our team's orthopaedic surgeon. He had a get-together one evening at his gorgeous home. It really was something, very contemporary and clean-looking and filled with expensive furniture. The whole team went, and so there weren't enough places to sit. Dave could see me looking around, and he pointed to a large urn and said, "Have a seat on that. It's only from the Ming Dynasty."

Dave, Larry and I would laugh and make jokes and down a couple beers. Donna became close with Dave's wife, Beth, and Larry's wife, Jeanette. Those three had a really nice connection.

As I got to know Larry, I saw he was very trusting, like a big kid. There were scams all over L.A., and you had to develop a kind of crusty cynicism there. But Larry never did. He stayed the guy he always was. One time, Larry was driving down the freeway and some guy in a nondescript van rolled down his window and yelled over, "Hey, I got a great deal on some speakers in the back!" They pulled over and he gave Larry this spiel that he was down at the docks when the ship was unloading and they discovered extra speakers. He said he had permission to sell them at a discounted price.

Larry thought this was just great! He laid a couple of hundred bucks on the guy. They loaded up the speakers, and Larry came into the Forum while we were all stretching before practice and told us all about it.

When I was with the Islanders and camcorders were new to the market, scammers would set up on the street and demonstrate them and then pull out a box and sell you one cheap. When you got home, you'd find an empty box. I looked at Larry and said, "Oh my God. Larry, man, you've gotta go open those boxes." He went out to his car, and sure enough, there was nothing in them but chunks of cement.

And then there were the horses. Larry loved polo, and from what I understand he was really good at it. His polo partners were all millionaires and billionaires, just rolling in it. They thought nothing of flying a horse to Belgium on a 747 for a tournament. Larry was the kind of guy who fit well into that life as well as the life of an NHLer. That sort of paints the picture of Larry and how much I liked him.

Unfortunately, by his second year with us, Larry's game was really starting to slide. I felt bad for him because he was making a whole bunch of poor decisions and causing bad plays, and there was nobody who felt worse about it than he did. I recall a number of times he'd pass the puck and it'd be intercepted, which meant the other team got a scoring chance. Larry would start banging his stick on the ice, disgusted with himself.

Still, there was no question Larry was one of Webby's favourite players. On November 16, 1991, early in Larry's final season in the NHL, we were playing the Wings at the Forum. It was a fast game with a lot of rough stuff going on. Larry went back to get a puck and was completely run from behind by Vladimir Konstantinov. Referee Kerry Fraser called both of them for cross-checking, and Webby lost it on the bench. A penalty for receiving an illegal hit? Webby grabbed a stick, which happened to be one of Luc's, and javelined it toward Fraser, hitting him in the foot. This time Webby was suspended until New Year's Eve. You know, Webby wasn't a garbage-can-kicking kind of coach, but he had some residual health problems from an ear fistula (a leakage of fluid between the inner and middle ear). I always wondered if that had something to do with it.

The 1991–92 Kings didn't have the playoff success that we wanted. We were learning to win together as a team, but in order to make it through the playoffs, we had to find a way to beat the Oilers. We couldn't get by them in the second round in '90 or '91, and then we lost to them in the first round in '92. It was frustrating because we were competitive with them. I think we sometimes even had the advantage over them, but when the pressure was on, we seemed to be the first to cave. They had our number. Looking back, I think the Oilers expected to win because they had gone through it so often. All winners will tell you to continue to bang away until you win. If there's a secret, winners seem to have it, and they make a habit of it.

I don't think Wayne liked playing against the Oilers. I think it was uncomfortable for him. He looked as though playing against them didn't bring him joy. He was usually so ready to go, and I'm not saying he didn't give his all, but playing against his old teammates Mark Messier—before he was traded to the Rangers in '91—and Kevin Lowe, who were his best friends in life, seemed to cause him some consternation. And Esa Tikkanen—my God, Esa really bugged Wayne. He was all over him, like gum on a shoe. In his book *99: Stories of the Game*, Wayne talks about how, when a guy like Esa was shadowing him, he would respond by shadowing somebody else, which would take two of their guys out of the play. Webby once said, "It's funny how, through the course of a hockey game, you're the person in charge and you're looking at ways to get Wayne on the ice. You're racking your brain to try to get him away from checkers and get him the freedom to go out and be the magic man that he is. And then, when it comes down to it, you go, 'Let him play.'"

That being said, John Muckler and Glen Sather and Kevin Lowe, all of those guys, they knew what it took to get Wayne off of his game. Normally, you shadow by taking away time and space. What they were doing to Wayne was so tight, it was arm to arm, leg to leg. The officiating at that point was different than it is now. They let that stuff go. Refs gave players a lot of leeway when it came to clutching and grabbing and hooking. There was a ton of interference. If those games were played today, the Oilers would be in the penalty box every shift for tackling and mauling!

Webby tried moving Marty McSorley up with Wayne to play forward. Theoretically, a guy like Marty up front can add muscle to free up Wayne. And Marty was effective to a degree. There were times when we would try to work pucks into Marty's corner so he could use his size to finish checks, create some space, draw some attention, and let other people know that he was on the ice and that "If something goes wrong out here, look out, I'm coming."

You could see how hard it was on Wayne. He loves to win. He wanted to beat Edmonton so bad. He would do everything and anything that he could, especially in the playoffs, because great players rise to the occasion. So, to be shut down and prevented from playing his game was tough. I think he took it personally and it frustrated him. But hey, credit to the Oilers, it was a tactic that was allowed at the time and they took it to the extreme.

The thing that stopped us in the 1990 playoffs was their young Kid Line. Adam Graves, Martin Gélinas and Joe Murphy. Those boys scored some big goals. Originally, they were a depth line. We weren't concerned about them, but they turned out to be maybe the biggest factor on that team.

We'd played good hockey all throughout the year, but that Kid Line was outrageous. Their speed and skill level pushed the pace. Full-on north-south hockey. I don't remember them having a bad period. Every single shift was an energy shift. Their main advantage was that they played free. They didn't feel the pressure yet. They were all young guys surrounded by cagey veterans who covered up their mistakes. If you can be relaxed and play with energy and a free mind, then you're going to have a lot of success. They put us back on our heels. We really had no answer for them, no way to stop them. The Kid Line was a major factor in the Oilers' making it all the way to the Cup finals, where they beat Boston.

Getting stopped by the Oilers was the reason Webby was fired. It still haunts him to this day. But I honestly have no idea what else we could have done to get by them.

From left to right: Pat Flatley, mc, Randy Boyd, Brent Sutter and Greg Gilbert at the 1985 Islanders team Christmas party. Brent Sutter and Greg Gilbert would become two of my best friends.

When Clark Gillies lost his temper on the ice, those eyebrows would come up and scare the hell out of the opposition. We joined a recreational bowling league together in 1985–86.

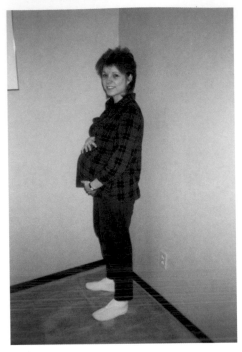

Donna pregnant with Jessica in March 1986. I was playing in Washington the day she gave birth. I couldn't get the time off.

Duane Sutter and me at an Easter Seals event on Long Island, around 1986. I loved playing with and against Sutter brothers Brent, Duane, Ronnie and Richie.

Denis Potvin tries to give me a hand against Vladimir Krutov in the Canada–USSR game at the 1986 world championship. Krutov went on to play the 1989–90 season with the Vancouver Canucks.
—Courtesy Nick Didlick

WASHINGTON CAPITALS

VS. NEW YORK ISLANDERS

DATE APRIL 18, 1987

SATURDAY -- 7:35 PM

HOME GAME NO.	W	L	T	POINTS
4	1	3	0	

NHL NO. D-7 ATTENDANCE 18,130

REFEREE Andy vanHellemond
LINESMEN John D'Amico
Ron Finn
Alts: Kerry Fraser
Gord Broseker

GOAL #	PER. 100	TIME	TEAM	SCORED BY	ASSISTS	E	P	S	PLAYERS ON ICE
1	1	1912	W	GARTNER 4 ADAMS	STEVENS				H 3-4-11-20-22 / V 4-20-12-20-28
2	2	1135	NY	FLATLEY 3 KONROYD	TROTTIER				H 3-4-17-27-32 / V 2-33-19-26-35
3	2	1845	W	MARTIN ADAMS	MURPHY				H 3-8-22-25-32 / V 4-5-10-16-20
4	3	1437	NY	TROTTIER KERR	KONROYD				H 3-4-17-22-32 / V 2-33-10-19-35
5	7	847	NY	LAFONTAINE DINEEN	LEITER				H 4-5-9-20-22 / V 4-39-12-16-28

RECAP

GOALS BY PERIOD	1	2	3	OT	T
CAPITALS	1	1	0		2
ISLANDERS	0	1	1		3

SHOTS ON GOAL	1	2	3	OT	T
CAPITALS	15	10	11		75
ISLANDERS	5	5	11		57

POWER PLAY GOALS	PPG IN	ATTEMPTS
CAPITALS	0	2
ISLANDERS	0	1

PENALTIES	NO.	PIM
CAPITALS	9	26
ISLANDERS	9	18

★★★ THREE STARS ★★★

1. LAFONTAINE
2. HRUDEY
3. MASON

#	CAPITALS	SHOTS 1	2	3	OT	T	#	ISLANDERS	SHOTS 1	2	3	OT	T
1	MASON						30	HRUDEY					
3	STEVENS	1	1			2	7	DINEEN	1				
4	HATCHER	1	2	3		8	3	JONSSON		1			3
5	LANGWAY						4	DIDUCK					1
8	MURPHY	1	1				6	MORROW			2		2
9	JENSEN			2		2	7	GILBERT					3
10	MILLER						8	BOYD	1				1
11	GARTNER	3	1			4	10	KERR		1			2
14	DUCHESNE	2		1			11	WOOD					4
25	MARTIN		2		1		12	D. SUTTER	1	1			4
17	RIDLEY			1			16	LAFONTAINE					6
19	SMITH						19	TROTTIER			3		5
16	KUOWLA	2				4	20	HENRY					
22	ADAMS		1				21	MAKELA		1			7
23	GOULD	2					26	FLATLEY		1	1		4
27	CHRISTIAN	2	1	1			25	BASSEN		1	2		
34	KASTELIC	3				3	33	LEITER			1		5
32	FRANCESCHETTI	1					23	KONROYD			2		2
33	BLUM						35	KROMM		1			
1	PEETERS						31	SMITH			1		

PENALTIES

PER.	TEAM	PLAYER	MIN.	OFFENSE	TIME
1	NY	KONROYD	2	HOOK	236
1	NY	KERR	2	ELBOW	
1	W	GOULD	2	HOLD	1951
2	NY	BOYD	2	SLASH	355
2	W	BLUM	2	CROSS CHECK	
2	NY	GILBERT	2	HIGH STICK	604
2	W	KASTELIC	2	HOLD	
2	NY	TROTTIER	2	HOLD	1458
3	W	MARTIN	2	HOLD	731
3	W	DIDUCK	2	HIGH STICK	1021
3	W	FRANCESCHETTI	2	HIGH STICK	
3	NY	SUTTER	2	HIGH STICK	1906
3	W	JENSEN	2		
2OT	NY	KERR	2	SLASH	846
2OT	W	STEVENS	2	HIGH STICK	
4OT	NY	FLATLEY	2	HIGH STICK	1049
4OT	W	DUCHESNE	2	CROSS CHECK	
4OT	W	ADAMS	10	MISCONDUCT	1647

NOTES:

THIS IS LONGEST GAME IN BOTH WASH AND NY HISTORY. (7TH LONGEST IN

OUT OF TOWN SCORES

NHL HISTORY)

BCD 14128-81A5

The game sheet from the Easter Epic, April 18–19, 1987. We won the game in the fourth overtime at nearly 2 a.m.

The 1987 Canada Cup was my first opportunity to play with future teammate Wayne Gretzky.

The 1987 Canada Cup team. *From left to right*: me, Doug Gilmour, Ray Bourque, Brian Propp, Rick Tocchet, Craig Hartsburg, Brent Sutter, Dave Poulin, Dale Hawerchuk, Wayne Gretzky and Mike Gartner. It's always a privilege to play for your country.
—**Courtesy James Lipa Photography**

Mom, Boona, my daughter Jessica and me, about 1989. Hanging out in Mom and Dad's basement rec room.

My first year with the Kings, 1988–89. Getting traded there turned out to be the best thing that ever happened for my career. **Front** (left to right): me, John Tonelli, Bernie Nicholls, Wayne Gretzky, Bruce McNall, Rogie Vachon, Dave Taylor, Tom Laidlaw, Steve Duchesne, Luc Robitaille, Glenn Healy. **Middle**: Cap Raeder, Bryan Maxwell, Jim Fox, Steve Kasper, Phil Sykes, Dean Kennedy, Ron Duguay, Mike Allison, Tim Watters, John Wolf, Ron Muniz, Robbie Ftorek. **Back**: Pete Demers, Bob Burgan, Jay Miller, Marty McSorley, Ken Baumgartner, Mike Krushelnyski, Doug Crossman, Igor Liba, Dale DeGray, Mark O'Neill, Mark DeCola. —**Courtesy the L.A. Kings**

With everybody's favourite celebrity, John Candy, around 1989.
—**Courtesy Wen Roberts**

With actor Kurt Russell. Lots of people said we looked alike. I wish. —**Courtesy Wen Roberts**

With Sly Stallone. He gave us a pep talk in the dressing room during the playoffs against Calgary in 1989.
—**Courtesy Wen Roberts**

Michael J. Fox and me, 1992. He's always been a huge hockey fan.
—**Courtesy Wen Roberts**

Here I am with actor James Woods (left) and former Kings owner Bruce McNall, around 1990. It was a ton of fun to play for Bruce, and he was very generous.
—**Courtesy Wen Roberts**

Mike Myers, me and Matthew Broderick, about 1993. We often had celebrities walking around the dressing room. —**Courtesy Wen Roberts**

With baseball and football great Bo Jackson. A lot of athletes came by the dressing room, too. —**Courtesy Wen Roberts**

Being interviewed by KABC-TV (channel 7 in Los Angeles), 1991. As a goaltender, I always felt it was my responsibility to talk to the media after a game. Win or lose.

Once the whistle blew, I hated the other team.
—**Courtesy the L.A. Kings**

From left to right: Larry Robinson, John McIntyre, Dave Taylor and me during the 1991–92 season. We shared a lot of laughs that year.

Chapter 15

The Worst Goalie in the League

WEBBY WAS OUT AND BARRY MELROSE was in. When you look at hiring Barry, the optics looked right. He was young, good-looking and charismatic. He was from the new school of coaching and used inventive and interesting techniques to send us subliminal messages. When he addressed us before a game, he would go up to the whiteboard with a marker, unbutton the cuffs of his starched white dress shirt and then roll up his sleeves like, "Time to get to work now, boys."

It helped put us in the right headspace. We thought, "I get it. You want us in the trenches, down and dirty."

Barry wore his hair all business in the front and party in the back, and he had these flashy suits. He'd stand behind the bench, kind of like, "Look at me." I recall a conversation I had with Wayne when Barry first came in. I said, "Do you like this guy?"

And Wayne replied something like "I don't know if I need to like him. I've just got to follow him."

I thought, "Yeah. Good advice."

As it turned out, Barry earned our loyalty, trust and respect. I think he was a guy who woke up in the morning and said, "You know what? I'm gonna have a great day today. Whatever it presents me, I'll figure out the solution and we'll go from there." He had a great sense of humour, and he shared it with us all the time. That's what I thought was unique about Barry. Even when things got tough, his humour carried the day. There were times we'd be laughing as we walked down the tunnel because of something he said in the locker room. He wasn't afraid to rip on you about your haircut or your clothes. That meant everybody. If Wayne walked into the room wearing a different-looking pair of shoes, Barry wasn't afraid to throw him a zinger either.

Sometimes Barry used humour as a tool to get a serious message across without ruffling any feathers. Let's say we finished a period and we got outplayed really, really badly, like, outshot twenty to one. He'd come into the dressing room, look around and say, "Okay, which one of you assholes got that shot?" It was a good way to let us know that it was time to get out and get going.

Did he treat Wayne any differently than the rest of us? Yeah, he did. Wayne was a superstar. Did he treat Paul Coffey differently? Yep, same reason. Did he treat me a little differently? Yeah, he did, because I was his number one goalie. But it wasn't like Barry was sucking up to us or that we never caught hell. He was very honest with each and every one of us without assassinating our character.

Like Al Arbour, Barry knew that it was important for a coach to know what makes a guy tick. Not everybody responds to a kick in the ass. Not everybody responds to a pat on the back. Now, what you need to understand is, when I was coming up in hockey, the coach had all the power. Most coaches didn't care about hurting your feelings. It was a "my way or the highway" system. Barry wasn't like that. He was honest. He might tell a veteran like Pat Conacher, "Hey Patty, we depend on you to get the puck out. That's your job. That's what you're here for. We've seen you do it. So do it tonight."

As soon as I mention Pat Conacher's name, a smile comes across my face. The way I would best describe Pat is he's a guy's guy. An old-school thinker, just rough enough so that he's not grumpy. Hard-nosed, but when he found something funny, he had one of the most infectious laughs. He roared right from the belly.

Another thing Barry did that reminded me of Al Arbour was that he made the superstars accountable while still giving them some perks like extra ice time. You cannot coach with Wayne Gretzky on your bench and not play him. If Wayne Gretzky is going, well, play the hell out of him. Double-shift him, keep him out there 'til he drops. If I'm your number one goaltender and I'm on a roll, play the hell out of me, play me 'til my wheels fall off. When Marty McSorley comes back from fighting Bob Probert, like, c'mon, man, reward the guy. Put him on the first power play, play the heck out of him. Barry did that, and he did it with everybody.

Okay, I have never totally shared this next part with anybody. Donna and I would summer in Alberta. I'd mountain-bike with my brother and train and get super fit, and hang out with my family and friends. It was a fun time. The summer ahead of the 1992–93 season, one day, kind of out of the blue, something weird started going on with my thinking. I started messing around, kind of teasing or torturing myself with questions that nibbled at the edges of my mind and began chipping away at my confidence. "Can I keep doing this? Can I sustain this?"

I know that sounds strange, but when it's just you and your thoughts . . . let's face it, people would think you were totally screwy if they knew exactly what you said to yourself half the time, right? I remember worrying, telling myself, "It's your tenth year in the NHL. It could be over for you any minute now. Look at the stats. Most guys only play three years." But I covered it up, shook it off, went back to L.A. and started the season.

First thing we find out at the top of the 1992–93 season is that Wayne is not coming in for the first half. He was hurt and needed to rehab to be ready for the playoffs. Wayne had a recurring back problem that started giving him trouble two years earlier, in 1990. It happened in a game against the Islanders. It took him out of several playoff games. And then, a year later, Gary Suter checked him by the boards in a Canada Cup game, and that revived the injury.

We were at training camp at Lake Arrowhead in the fall of

1992 when Barry came into the room to deliver the news. Barry was always good at showing strength, but you could tell something was bothering him. He told us all about Wayne's injury and the significance of it. Wayne was going to sit out, and not only that, there was a possibility his injury could be career-ending. We were all in shock, but Barry, as he did so well, was able to give us strength. "We'll get through this, and when Wayne does come back, we'll be better than ever. But for now, let's go out there and create a new culture. This team is not just about one guy. There is so much talent in this room. Each and every one of you can make a difference. This is your chance as an individual to make us great. This is your chance to *be* great! All you have to do is add your own piece to it."

Barry looked over at Paul Coffey. "And Paul, I don't mind if you make those one-hundred-foot passes right up the middle of the ice through the neutral zone, tape to tape. We don't need a Léo Boivin [a heavy-hitting stay-at-home defenceman who played for nineteen seasons] out there. Take chances. Make it happen like you can." I looked around at our defence, thinking, "These guys look excited. They're seeing an opportunity here. A chance to play their own game."

We rocketed out of the gate. Luc had a fantastic start. Everybody was chipping in. Our young defencemen—Robbie Blake, Alex Zhitnik and Darryl Sydor—were absolute studs back there. And Tim Watters was making huge contributions. We were so strong on defence. Coff was playing great, and so were Marty McSorley, Charlie Huddy and Mark Hardy. The thing about

Barry was, when he said it, he believed it. He came in every day, driving us to work together as a team. He talked constantly to the young guys, telling them the team that plays harder and with more courage is the team that wins. He convinced us there was no obstacle we couldn't conquer.

I knew that I was a big part of the equation. I was stealing a lot of games. But then came a game on November 28 in Toronto where we lost 3–2. Not really a problem, but I was like, "What's going on, Kelly? What's wrong with you? Have you lost it? How did you fuck this up? You gotta be sharper." Yeah, I was always hard on myself, but I'd never questioned my ability before. I tried to shake it off and move on, but the doubts lingered.

At that time, the NHL had neutral-site games, in part to test possible expansion markets. We were in Milwaukee for a game three days later, on December 1, 1992. In my hotel room, I ordered up a clubhouse sandwich, soup and fries with a Pepsi with lots of ice. When the food was delivered, I sat on the bed and turned on the TV and started to eat. That's when that doubt I'd felt in late August started burbling up.

I took another bite and looked at my sandwich. I couldn't really taste it. I stood up and started pacing the room. My anxiety grew with each step. I talk out loud when I'm alone, and I remember blurting out, "I wonder if I can keep this up? I wonder if I'm really this good?" And then, "Holy shit. I still have four months left where I have to be this good or better."

On the road, I'd have a bath every night before a game. It was part of my stretching routine and it helped me relax. I'd look forward to soaking in some good-smelling stuff from one of those little bottles and listening to some awesome tunes on my CD player, which I'd set up by the sink, the sound bouncing around the marble bathroom walls. The other thing I did while I was in the tub was read a book on the Canadian Rockies. Any chance I got, I'd pick up a book about climbing or mountain trails. It took me back to some of the happiest days of my life, those summers driving around in the old Plymouth with Mom and Dad and Ken.

I went into the bathroom and turned on the taps. While the tub filled, I walked back into the bedroom and continued pacing. My mind started up again, only this time I wasn't asking myself questions, I was telling myself, "It's all over. You can't do it anymore. You've lost it. It's gone. Everything. They're going to find out and you'll be outta there."

I was collapsing mentally. The running water got louder and louder and I started moving faster and faster as I made my way towards the edge of my sanity. I looked around in despair. I'm not a religious man. Never have been. My parents were Greek Orthodox, but we weren't churchgoers. But when I opened the drawer of the nightstand and spotted the Gideon Bible, I grabbed it and hung on to it like a life raft.

I opened it, paging through, looking for something, anything. I got into the tub and opened it up again, but nothing touched me. All I read was a bunch of *beholds* and *begets*. I looked around and hung my head, feeling pathetic. Here I was, in a bathtub in Milwaukee, searching through a Bible for an answer to save me.

I got out of the tub, fell into bed and crashed. It was such a heavy night. I didn't open my eyes 'til morning.

Like I said, I was playing great, and I don't know why I started to question myself.

Again, I powered through it mentally and played fantastic the next night against the Chicago Blackhawks. Lights out, forty-four saves. We put twenty-three shots on Jimmy Waite, and we won 6–3. Darryl Sutter was the coach in Chicago, and in the paper the next day he said something like, "The Hawks didn't lose, they just got beat by a goalie who played unbelievable." Next, we played at home and beat Pittsburgh 5–3 with Mario Lemieux in the lineup. I made a sprawling save in the third period that might have been the best save of my career. I remember getting up and looking around and thinking, "I wonder if the people in the stands get how great that save was?"

Our backup, Robb Stauber, played the next game against Hartford, and that's when it all started disappearing again. On December 8, 1992, we went up against Montreal. I was determined to play my best because we were playing against Patrick Roy. Every goalie in the league loved winning against Roy. Not because we didn't respect him, but because we did. First of all, he'd already won the Stanley Cup. Second, he was revolutionizing the way we played the game. We tied 5–5. Barry came in after the game. It was our first blip as a team, and I know he was trying to stop us from sliding, but he said, "We haven't done our best here yet." He added, "Even Kelly can play better." I looked at him and thought, "No, I fucking can't." I was already having these issues with "Can I keep it up?" and now my coach was saying, "You know, you can be even better."

I was average against Quebec and we lost 5–4. Next game I played was in Edmonton, and we tied 5–5. Now I was starting to give up some goals. We went on a losing streak, and I was not always getting the start because Barry had lost a bit of faith in me. From twenty wins, eight losses and three ties—which is pretty good, right?—we were suddenly down to twenty wins, *sixteen* losses and five ties.

We had a practice at home, and I looked up in the stands. There was our manager, Nick Beverley, and a whole bunch of staff watching me. I was nervous as hell. Overwhelmingly scared and wondering about my future. I had worked my way to the top, and now everybody was gunning for me. During the time I played in Los Angeles—eight seasons—they brought in more than twenty goalies. That's an unbelievable number of guys trying to take your job. A revolving door. I spent a lot of time fending them off. I mean, you want to help your partner, but you also have to have an attitude in order to survive. "Okay, you bastards . . . you think you can take my job?" I'd beat one out and then it was, "Okay, he's gone, who's next?"

Whenever I had a guy coming up, I was always nice to him—the way Billy Smith had been nice to me, helping around the net and stuff—but never did I let a guy take my job. Never, ever, ever did I say, "It's great he plays instead of me." I was a nice, respectful teammate, but I wanted to play. I was not giving anybody my spot.

My relationship with Barry was so strong that, up to that point in the season where I started losing confidence, if I hadn't had an especially good first period and I thought Barry was looking at taking me out, I'd take my helmet off, go right over to the coach's room and say, "Don't you even consider pulling me." That put the onus on me, right? I'd just promised my coach I was going to be good.

It shows you how down I was that by January of 1993, Barry was playing Robb Stauber ahead of me and even called up an older guy from the minors named Rick Knickle. We played in Vancouver on New Year's Eve, where we lost 4–0, but I played pretty well. Barry came in after the game and he was really positive. One of the things he said was, "Guys, we're okay. Kelly's back. He played like he can." We had a team dinner after the game, and I was starting to feel a bit better about myself, thinking, "Okay, I wonder if I've got this going again?"

Wayne came back into the lineup two games later against Tampa, the one-thousandth game of his career, and I was thinking, "Okay, yeah!" I felt great in the warm-up, great at the start of the game, but I couldn't stop a beach ball. We lost to Tampa—an expansion team, a team that came into the game at 14–25–2—for the second time in three weeks.

Wayne says he wears that loss, but that's not what I recall. You know why? Because somebody in the room was worse! I let in six goals on twenty shots and felt really bad about it. Their centre, Brian Bradley, scored on me from the blue line. It's not like I was screened or anything—he beat me clean.

It was one of the worst goals I ever let in. It was all coming crashing down.

Donna was my biggest supporter, as always. But I remember how we'd be sitting on the couch at night and I'd lay my head in her lap, too depressed to even sit up. None of her old tricks and conversations were working. "Keep pushing and fighting through, Kelly. You can do it! I know it. You are the absolute best." She was a rock. But I didn't believe her. I was 100 per cent convinced, without a doubt, that I was done. I started to hear trade rumours, but I didn't believe them. Who would want me? Like, honestly, I went from being one of the best goalies in the game to, bar none, the worst. Right in the toilet, and who would want to trade for the worst goalie in the league?

There was a stretch after Tampa where the game had me right down on my knees. And then we played the Rangers on January 23, and that's when it all turned around, because that's when I met Tony Robbins.

We had a night game at home versus the Rangers. Robb Stauber was playing, and I was backing up. Later, I had a conversation with a good friend on the team who told me, "Look, a lot of us felt that Robb, good guy that he is, was getting a little too much respect considering he hadn't earned his spurs yet. You were our number one, and when you have a proven guy, you've got to keep going with that guy until he absolutely can't do it anymore. You don't take his job away."

It was the first time in my career, since becoming an elite goaltender, that I didn't have the net. Everybody always thinks of goalies as being somewhat different and alienated from the rest of the team. On game days, they can't talk to people and they have their own rituals and you don't bother them and all that. No disrespect to any other goalies—some need to be a bit different in order to get in the right frame of mind for their game—but it was important to me to be one of the team. I think one of my biggest concerns was that this was my problem, and I didn't want to drag anybody else down.

Being out of the lineup was tough, but at the end of the day, it was up to me to fix it. Barry had tried all the usual stuff—benching me, patting me on the back, kicking me in the butt—and nothing was happening. Obviously, he knew it wasn't because I didn't care. In fact, I cared too much.

Barry was a big supporter of mine. He even told the press that, had it not been crazy and actually against the rules to name a goalie as captain, he would've given me a *C* or an *A*. So, despite the fact I was struggling, I think the conclusion Barry eventually came to was, "We're gonna have success around here, and it's going to be with Kelly in net."

Back to the Ranger game. I was sitting in my stall like always, taping my goalie sticks, drinking my coffee, and Barry walked in. Right behind him was Tony Robbins. I recognized Tony from the infomercials, but I didn't think much of it for two reasons: first, there were always famous people around who wanted to meet Wayne, and second, Barry was a Tony Robbins fan. Barry was always carrying around some sort of self-help book. One of the books he would often quote from was *Unlimited Power*. In it, Robbins talks about setting goals—one-year goals, five-year goals, ten-year goals and twenty-year goals.

Barry had read it three years earlier, and one of the goals he wrote down was "I'm going to meet Tony Robbins within three years." When he got the coaching job in L.A., Barry called up Tony's publisher. The guy he spoke to was a hockey fan who put Barry in touch with Tony. Barry laid out his whole story about writing down his goals and all that, and Tony was so impressed, he flew out to Santa Monica on his private helicopter for lunch. From that moment on, Barry and Tony communicated on a regular basis.

Barry and Tony walked into Barry's office, and less than a minute later Barry opened the door and called me over. And here again is an example of how down on myself I was. I thought, "Why the heck would Tony want to meet the worst goalie in the league?" Looking back, it's shocking to see how negative I was. I headed in there and Barry introduced me to Tony and said, "I've been working with Tony for a while, and I want to see if he can help you too."

My first reaction was "Wow! Barry's still in my corner!" I was thrilled. I thought, "Oh my God, he cares enough about me to go way out on a limb to introduce me to a guy who might help me?" Cool, right? Remember, this was 1993. Sports psychologists weren't around much, or if they were, they were still trying to figure out how to deal with professional athletes.

Barry said, "Would you mind working with Tony?"

I said, "Of course, I'd love to. I want to get out of this worse than anybody."

"Do you mind if I sit in and listen?"

"Sure. If you've gone to these lengths to try and help me, I have no problem with you listening to everything I'm going through."

Barry sat in the corner and I took a seat across from Tony, who stood over me. The image seared into my brain to this day is how enormous he was. He's six foot nine. Standing instead of sitting immediately put him in a power position. It was very clear to me that he was in charge. I remember looking at his perfectly groomed hair. He looked carefully put together, almost slick. That scared me a little, because I thought, "Hmm, I wonder if he's a fake."

He touches people a lot. I guess the idea is to make a physical connection, and it does feel reassuring. He touched my shoulder a couple times when he asked about what I was going through, and then again when he told me we were going to work our way out of it. There is a documentary out on Netflix about Tony called *I Am Not Your Guru*. I watched it recently with Donna. After the first scene, I turned to her and said, "I'm going to love this show." In the movie, he was exactly the way he had been with me.

I found being with Tony was like being with another athlete. He spoke our language. He'd swear, he'd curse, and so I didn't have to watch what I said or how I said it. I don't think Wayne Gretzky would mind me saying this, because I have heard him talk about it publicly, but even Wayne would swear when it was warranted. It does seem to get your point across.

I was honest with Tony right away. I told him I was really questioning myself. There was no hidden issue eroding my confidence, no scarring incident from my youth or anything. I was in a bad place mentally about where my career was going, and I couldn't get out of it.

Tony was also good at making intense eye contact. Interesting how some guys cannot look you in the eye when you are talking about something uncomfortable.

As an aside, when Wayne retired from the Kings, they raised his number to the rafters and all that. Only three people spoke that night other than him: Gary Bettman, Bruce McNall and me. I was honoured. I looked over at Wayne when I was onstage, but his eyes were aimed down at the floor the whole time. He's a funny guy that way. Greatest hockey player of all time, but super humble. He truly seems uncomfortable when people pay homage to him.

Going back to Tony, with the shoulder-touching and the eye contact, I felt a connection and I trusted him. That initial thought I had, that he's a little too smooth? It went away.

Tony said he wanted to figure me out, so we went to the negative first and then built to the positive. He said, "So, who do you feel like when things aren't going very well? Give me someone well known, maybe a Hollywood movie star, somebody in a book, another sports figure, anybody."

I looked and him and I said, "I feel like Fred Flintstone."

He laughed. I laughed. Barry laughed. And then I said, "I do. I feel like Fred Flintstone when he's called into Mr. Slate's office. He comes in and sits on a chair across from his boss, who berates him. And while that's going on, Fred starts to shrink. He gets smaller and smaller, until he's this tiny guy whose legs don't even dangle over the seat. Well, as soon as I let in a goal, I feel like I'm shrinking in the net, and that's not a good thing when you're the number one goalie on a team in the National Hockey League."

Okay, at this point you might be thinking that saying this in front of Barry was nuts. And it's true, it was very revealing and very dangerous for my career, but I was willing to lay it all out there so I could get better.

Tony said something like, "Conversely, when you're feeling great about yourself, who do you feel like?" The Gulf War had just ended two years earlier. I had followed it closely and was impressed by the strength of General Norman Schwarzkopf Jr. I told Tony that when I was playing really well, I felt like Schwarzkopf back there. "I don't care who's shooting on me—Mario Lemieux, Pavel Bure, Teemu Selanne, Stevie Yzerman—I'm in command. I single-handedly control the outcome of a game. Sometimes negatively, sometimes positively, but I feel that powerful."

Next, we talked about changing my mindset. In those days, picture-in-picture television had just been introduced. Tony explained that my big picture was a negative thought and my little picture was a positive one. He said I'd had a positive big picture for the duration of my career. For the next hour, we worked on restoring the order.

Finally, he had me fill out a little index card and put four points on it. The first one was Schwarzkopf, and then "picture-in-picture." The last two items were technical—"toes out," because I had a tendency to be pigeon-toed, and sometimes I'd get caught, and finally, "Don't get too deep in your net." Most people don't know this, but you can tell when a goaltender's struggling because he gets a little too deep in his net. It feels safer, but the truth is that coming out is a safer play. You get bigger in the eyes of the shooter, because there's nothing for him to shoot at. I laminated that cue card, and I'd look at it before every game and at the start of every new period. It was the last thing I'd see before I went out onto the ice. I did that for the remainder of my career—another five years.

When our meeting was over, Barry was energized. He told me he could see how my body language had changed. He said, "I think I might play you instead of Robb."

That he might be serious scared me, because I hadn't done any preparation. I pretended I thought he was joking—"Heh heh heh, good one"—to let him know I needed a day.

The meeting with Tony gave me such great strength that I changed back into a powerful guy, a take-charge kind of guy. My next game, on January 26 at the Forum against San Jose, I found my swagger. I was a defiant competitor like Corey Crawford or Chris Osgood. At the morning skate, I went up to Cap Raeder, our assistant coach, and I said, "You know, Cap, I don't care if I let in fifteen goals tonight. I'm going to play my position the way it's supposed to be fucking played, and if these guys screw up, it's not my fault anymore. To hell with it. I'm playing my game."

I thought he might try to talk me down. But instead, he said, "Good, I fucking love to hear that." And we won, 7–1. I played great. San Jose was terrible that year, but it was an important win. Then we played Calgary, and I played really well again. You know what I thought after that? "I'm back."

THEN SOMETHING HAPPENED THAT PUT IT all in perspective. Kaitlin, our youngest, was born January 27, the day before the Calgary game. And after she was born, Donna hemorrhaged. She lost a lot of blood and was in serious danger. We'd just come out the other end from that when the hospital pediatrician looked the baby over and told us she had a heart murmur and might need surgery. Kaitlin was only three days old when we took her to a specialist.

I remember sitting in the waiting room and seeing all these sick kids who needed new hearts, and suddenly I was wrapped up in cotton batting. My sight was still sharp, but my hearing became dull and my other senses started to shut down too. I looked down and could see the pocket in my shirt jumping up and down, but I couldn't feel my heart pounding. It was an out-of-body experience. I followed Donna into the examination room, where the doctor told us that Kaitlin had a hole in her heart, but they were going to monitor her for two years to see if it would close. I had been so broken that I think it would have pushed me over the edge if I'd heard that news before meeting

Tony. At eighteen months Kaitlin was fine, thank God, but it hung on me like a two-hundred-pound barbell the entire time.

There were still some stretches where I wasn't as good as I wanted to be. It's a long road, right? You don't go from being the lousiest goalie and turning it around overnight after just one meeting with a guy. I had to fight like hell. I knew I was back, but I needed one more big game to prove it. On April 1, we played in Philadelphia against Eric Lindros and beat them 3–1. It was a tough game, and I was rock solid. I didn't have to be spectacular because our team game was getting better and better.

I stood up in the dressing room afterward and thanked the guys. I got pretty emotional. "Thanks for sticking with me. That meant more to me than you could ever know." I think it caught a couple of guys by surprise. Tony Granato, he didn't say anything, but his eyes told me everything. The team never doubted me. It still humbles me whenever I think about it.

I met with Tony Robbins a couple more times over the course of that season. During the conference final in Toronto, we didn't have an actual session, but I talked with him just to affirm everything we'd discussed. That summer, he invited me to his resort in Fiji for more sessions, but the cost was around $10,000. I was like, "Well, I can't afford that." Maybe I could have, but I was too cheap. Didn't matter. Slump was over.

Chapter 16

Right to the Point

SO NOW I WAS PLAYING BETTER, feeling good, and we were starting to win a lot. When I was going through all that tough stuff in December and January, I continued to answer the media's questions. I was good about that my entire career. Win or lose, I'd talk to the press. Of course, they didn't always like my tone. Believe me, it taught me a lot about how to behave now that I am on the other side of the microphone.

When I think about memorable media interviews, I think about a game at the Calgary Saddledome in October 1992, before all my trouble started.

First, let me say that I really respected guys around the league who gave everything on every shift. To me, nothing was more wasteful than watching a guy's career go down the toilet because he didn't work hard enough. Calgary's Gary Roberts was legendary for his work ethic, and I found him terrible for kneeing me in the head. And it was starting to piss me off. Whenever I covered up the puck, he'd come in knee first, and *bam!*—straight to the noggin. I talked earlier about how vulnerable a goaltender is because of all the weird positions you need to be in to stop the puck. Considering that, I was pretty lucky when I played because I wasn't injury prone, but I did have a bad neck from training that past summer, and it was nagging me.

Gary came in again and got me hard this time. I was airborne, and when I landed I remember thinking, "Geezus, this hurts." A few minutes later, there was a whistle in our zone and then a TV timeout.

I saw Gary standing near the faceoff circle and I said, "Hey Gary, you got a sec?" He skated over.

I said, "Gary, I understand what you are up to, but c'mon, man. Quit kneeing me in the head every time you come by the crease. You've got a family, right? I've got a family. And I'm just trying to put my kids through university some day. So knock it off, will ya?"

He gave me an incredulous look, shook his head and skated back to the circle, but he became less of that guy, which was good. After the game, my neck was killing me. I could hardly wait to ice it down, but I took the time to talk to the media, like I always did.

The dressing room in Calgary is not very big. When you walk in, there's an open area to the left, a smaller area to the right and bench seating all the way around. Directly in front of the doorway are the two larger goaltender stalls. It was a little chaotic in there, as it always is after a game. There was a lot of buzz in the room. Players were talking back and forth and grabbing Gatorade and snacks when the reporters showed up and gathered in front of my stall. I was halfway out of my gear, and the trainers were quickly packing up our bags.

Eric Duhatschek was the main sports reporter at the *Calgary Herald*, along with Mike Board. I liked and respected both of them, and for the most part I thought they were fair. Eric and I are still friends today. But there was another guy, Monte Stewart, who wrote sidebars for the paper. Stewart was one of those guys who was big and soft with a belly. He moved kind of slowly and methodically, and he could be a major smart-ass.

We were all talking about the game when someone said something about me going down after the Gary Roberts hit. Monte looked at me with this little smirk and said, "Soooo, Kelly, was that just a case of a little play-acting there?"

I've always admitted that I did embellish at times, but that night wasn't one of them. I was still ramped up from the game, and I was insulted and pissed off by the question. There was a long pause while I tried to pull it together. I cleared my throat and said something like "Well, by the looks of it, you've never played a sport in your life, and you accuse me of embellishing? How dare you imply I'm not hurt? You know eff-all about playing goal, because you spend every day on your fat ass, and yet you're my judge and jury?"

Everybody looked over to see what was going on, and I did notice the group of reporters around me was backing up. I continued my tirade for about a minute, and when I was done, the room was dead quiet.

Again, there was a pause, and then Monte nodded and said, "Soooo, I take it that's a no?"

A few months later, in March and April of 1993 as the play-offs approached, there was a time when I stopped talking to the press altogether. It wasn't that I was mad at anybody. I just needed to focus on my game and the preparation I had worked out, and not be distracted.

On March 29, 1993, we went into Detroit. And I was hot—really hot—because I read an article in the newspaper the day before where our backup goaltender, Rick Knickle, was answering questions for me. He was giving his opinion on questions like "Well, why is Kelly not talking to us? Do you think it has to do with what Kelly went through during the slump?" Rick was an inexperienced guy, I got that, but I thought he had no business talking for me. I gave it to him as I got on the ice at the morning skate. I wasn't an a-hole. I didn't do it in the dressing room in front of everybody. Instead, I skated up beside him and got right to the point.

"Hey Rick. Mind your own frickin' business. What I went through is for me to answer, and nobody should interpret it. Don't ever speak for me. I'm a big man, I can handle it. I'll tell everybody when I'm ready to talk." To his credit, he just looked at me. He didn't try to apologize or defend himself. Instead, he said, "Okay."

We got smoked in the last two games of the regular season in 1993. I played the second-to-last game, and Robb played the last game and got pulled. I thought that was the wrong thing to do. As much as I knew Barry was rooting for me, I think he still was toying with the idea of going with Robb in the playoffs, and that pissed me off royally. You don't throw your number one into that shit so close to the playoffs for the last eight minutes of another goalie's messed-up game.

Once again, I found myself next to Wayne in the shower, pissed off and ranting. When I lost it like that, my lawyer, Lloyd Friedland, used to call it "the Hrudey volcano," but this time I was going off on Barry. I looked at Wayne and was surprised he didn't seem bothered at all. In fact, there was a look of serene confidence in his eyes, like he was saying, "Not to worry, Kelly. We'll be okay."

Wayne always put the team before himself. In January, when he had come back into the lineup after being out the first half of the season, we were playing a fast, in-your-face, heavy-forecheck game. A lot of times, that means chipping the puck in, following it and getting hit, so that's what Wayne did. I doubt he'd ever chipped a puck in in his life, but you know what? He was the captain and he knew that in order for us to go forward, he had to do what Barry was asking. He adapted to our style, and then, of course, he got his legs under him and paired with Tomas Sandstrom and Jari Kurri, and they became the best line in the National Hockey League. Beyond fantastic.

Chapter 17

The Gretzky High Stick on Gilmour

WE PLAYED CALGARY THAT FIRST SERIES. I was in goal for Game One, which we won 6–3, and Game Two, where we got our asses handed to us, 9–4. We lost Game Three at home in a close one, and then Barry made the right decision—and a brave one. He put Robb in for Game Four. Robb played fantastic, and we won. We went to Calgary for Game Five, and Barry stuck with Robb, who ended up winning the series in a high-scoring Game Six—the final score was 9–6. Robb was just a young guy, and he kept his head under a lot of pressure.

Next, we headed to Vancouver for an afternoon game to start the Smythe Division final. Robb played, but not especially well, and afterward Barry called in Wayne, Marty McSorley,

Jari Kurri, Luc Robitaille and me for a meeting. The first thing he said was, "Kelly, you're playing Game Two." We won, and I was in net for the rest of the playoffs.

When we beat Vancouver in Game Six, it was a monumental step for the Kings organization and a real high for us as individuals. The franchise had never reached the next-to-last series of the playoffs.

Wayne and I don't agree on that second series against Vancouver. It's not a big deal, but I thought it was the best hockey the L.A. Kings ever played. He thinks we played even better in the conference final, against Toronto. My argument is that the Vancouver series was fast-paced and hard-hitting. Both Kirk McLean and I played very well in goal. Game Five went to double overtime. It was everything I think you would want in the playoffs. The games in Toronto were just as action-packed, but the teams played more of a defensive style, not quite at the pace we'd played at against Vancouver. In any case, we took Vancouver in six and then went on to Toronto and the game that Maple Leafs fans can't seem to get past.

We started Game One in Toronto on May 17, 1993, but we weren't there mentally yet. We were not executing as well as we could. The Leafs were totally dominating us, especially in the third period. We showed no fight. They started to take away our will, and that's a bad way to start a series. And then Marty McSorley laid an open-ice hit on Doug Gilmour that changed everything. It led to a fight between Marty and Wendel Clark, and the entire series changed course.

I remember watching Marty and Wendel go at it from my crease and thinking, "I'm pretty sure this is going to be a game changer." Wendel was so tough to stop. He made a difference every time he was on the ice, and now Marty was going toe to toe with him. I could feel the energy from our team—"Hell yeah!" We were enthusiastic again. We got our emotions back and our heads into the game. I truly believe Marty's Gilmour check and the ensuing fight affected the rest of the series.

What most people don't know is that in Game Two, with about ten minutes left in the third period, we were nursing a 3–2 lead and I ran out of gas. I had the cold sweats and the shakes. I'm not sure why, maybe dehydration. It only happened a handful of times in my entire career. I hung on, and then with seven minutes left, Wendel Clark was coming down his off-wing, maybe his most dangerous spot, and he rifled his patented snap shot by the post, missing it by a hair. I'd come out to cut off the angle but didn't have the energy to move beyond that. His miss made me look like a genius. People said, "Wow! How did Hrudey know it was going to go wide?"

The series stayed very competitive. The Maple Leafs, led by Doug Gilmour, who was at the peak of his career, were having their best playoff run in a long, long time. Which brings us to the overtime in Game Six when Wayne swung around and clipped Gilmour on the chin with the blade of his stick. There was blood but no call from Kerry Fraser. Toronto fans went nuts. They wanted a five-minute major, which would've meant we'd play four on four for 1:09, because Glenn Anderson was in the box, and then Toronto would have close to four minutes on the power play, giving them a great chance to put us away.

To this day, when I am in Toronto, I cannot tell you how often some guy brings up Gretzky's high stick on Gilmour. Every guy on our team gets the same thing—"It shoulda been a five-minute power play. It shoulda been us against Montreal."

We are all so sick of the whining. It's gotten to the point where I just tell them the truth. I say, "Yeah, but you know what? Doug Gilmour wasn't exactly a Lady Byng nominee." I have so much respect for Gilmour as a player, but there were times he would cross the line. Besides, they had a chance to finish us off in Game Seven on home ice. C'mon.

So we won Game Six in overtime, and that took us back to Maple Leaf Gardens for the seventh game, which Wayne considers his best game ever. I remember Pat Conacher telling me later that he was sitting beside Charlie Huddy on the bench. Charlie had played with Wayne for years and years in Edmonton. Charlie turned to Pat—"Patty, look at Wayne. Look at his eyes." Pat looked over at Wayne and saw that his eyes were as big as silver dollars. He wasn't even blinking. Charlie said, "I've seen this so many times before, Patty. You're gonna witness something like you've never seen before in your life. You watch." Sure enough, Wayne went out and played the best game of his life.

Wayne had a hat trick and an assist, and oh my God, two of those goals in particular . . . wow. From my crease, I had a great view. I watched his first goal shape up. Almost ten minutes in, Gilmour brought it across on a power play but turned it over, and Jari Kurri jumped in and sent it up ice. Wayne picked it up and headed down the side for the net. Marty, who'd been trailing, broke to the opposite side on a two-on-one, and Wayne passed it to him. Marty was all the way to the paint, and I was thinking, "Marty, shoot the puck! You've got a great chance." But at the very last second, Marty passed it across.

I don't think there's another player in the history of the game who could recover as quickly as Wayne did. Watch the play on YouTube. Wayne corralled the puck with his skate, kicked it gently up to his stick and tapped it into the open net. It was one of the nicest goals I've ever seen. Thank God it was Wayne over there, because believe me, nobody else in the world could have handled that pass like that.

Wayne's second goal, at 10:20 of the second period, was one of the craftiest goals I'd ever witnessed. On a rush, Tomas Sandstrom sent Wayne a drop pass. Wayne got around Kent Manderville with such a clever move. It was so subtle. He positioned his body open toward our net, giving Manderville the impression of a loose puck. Manderville went for it, and Wayne suddenly closed up and moved around him, then rifled the puck over Leafs goalie Félix Potvin's glove. Manderville must have been kicking himself, but I mean, c'mon, how do you defend against that?

Wayne's dad, Walter, was still recovering from his 1991 stroke, but he was in the stands as always. Wayne scored his third goal with a shuffleboard bank off Toronto defenceman Dave Ellett's skate to make it 5–3. Then, when Wayne skated back to our bench with this big smile and looked up at Wally, giving him the thumbs-up, I felt like I'd just swallowed a jaw-breaker. I was like, "Geez, I can't watch." I had to look away and compose myself.

There were still three minutes left. They ended up scoring. Ellett, who was in pretty tight, scored a shitty goal, beating my glove with sixty-seven seconds to go to make it 5–4. But we hung on because we had Dave Taylor, Jari Kurri, Pat Conacher, Charlie Huddy and Marty McSorley out there, real quality play-ers, to protect the lead. They saved the day in the last fifty sec-onds, but it was Wayne's finest game.

I remember at the end of the game, Luc Robitaille came over to me with this dazed look in his eyes. I grabbed his shoulders and yelled in his face, "We're going to the Stanley Cup Final! Holy fuck!" His eyes opened wide and he was like, "Oh my God, you're right! We're going to the Stanley Cup Final!"

We had faced down Toronto, the doubters and maybe even the odds. We were in the final because we deserved to be in the final.

Chapter 18

Crushed

CLOSE TO A QUARTER OF A CENTURY later, the famous stick incident in Montreal is still hard for me to swallow. It's the most difficult thing for me to talk about regarding my entire career, not only because it involves a significant loss, but because it involves a friend and teammate.

We went into Montreal and totally dominated the Canadiens in the first game. In the second game, we were up 2–1 with a minute and forty-five seconds to go, and Marty McSorley got called for an illegal stick. The curve on his blade was bigger than the rules allowed. That gave the Canadiens a power play, and they scored, sending the game into overtime. Then they scored again. Instead of us heading home leading the series two games to none, we went home tied at one game apiece, and Montreal had new energy.

Curved stick blades started to enter the game in the early '60s but when guys like Bobby Hull started using a stick with a three-inch curve over the next few seasons, the NHL stepped in. In 1967–68, the league limited blade curvature to an inch and a half, then dialed that back to one inch in 1969–70. A year later it was half an inch, and the current limit is three-quarters of an inch. I always thought it was kind of an unwritten rule that teams didn't call for stick measurements. It had certainly never happened in the Stanley Cup Final. That being said, both our team and the Canadiens were looking for every advantage, and so some of the sticks made us nervous.

Between the second and third periods, Wayne told Luc, Tomas Sandstrom, Alex Zhitnik and Marty McSorley to check their sticks because we all knew how important that series was and because Montreal was desperate. Marty's stick was so obviously curved that, as one of my teammates said later, "Stevie Wonder could've spotted it."

Luc Robitaille used a big boomerang too, but Luc used to shave his heel and cut the toe so that if they measured the blade with a stick gauge, it would be considered legal. That's the reason Luc went through so many sticks—all that work he did on them made the blades fairly fragile. Smart guy.

In Game Two of the best-of-seven series, on June 3, 1993, at the Montreal Forum, we were leading 2–1 late into the third period. Our team was on a high. Winning this game meant we'd take a two-games-to-none lead back to Los Angeles. We'd be unstoppable.

With a minute and forty-five seconds left in regulation time, the whistle blew, and there was a little gathering that included referee Kerry Fraser over by the Montreal bench. First of all, I had no idea what coach Jacques Demers and his team were talking to Fraser about. When I realized that it was an illegal stick, I felt my heart jump—in a good way. I was really hopeful they were going to come down to my end and grab *my* stick. And the reason I was hopeful is that I knew my stick was perfectly legal. In fact, I often tried to bait teams—although it never worked. I tried to fool them into calling for my stick to be measured. You see, I used illegal sticks in practice, and I used illegal sticks for the first two periods of a game. Although, sometimes, if I had a funny feeling that I might be challenged, I'd switch to a legal stick earlier in a game.

The blades of my illegal sticks were too long and too wide, and the paddles were too big too. So that I didn't grab the wrong stick by accident, I'd mark the legal ones by taking a felt pen and swiping a line through my name, K. Hrudey, printed on the shaft.

So to let the other team know I was using an illegal stick, after the morning skate on game day, I'd leave one of my broken goalie sticks on the players' bench. I figured maybe one of our competitor's trainers or a coach would pick it up, look at it, measure it, and if they were desperate in the third period and wanted to change the tide of the game, they might decide to call for a measurement.

The risk you run if you call for a stick measurement is that if you're wrong, and the stick is legal, you get a two-minute penalty.

And so, when Fraser didn't come to me and went to Marty instead, I remember thinking, "Well, I'm certain *that's* a legal stick." I just couldn't fathom that Marty would be using an illegal stick that late in the game.

And then, once the call was made and Marty went to the penalty box, I didn't freak out or let it distract me like, "Why would he be using an illegal stick?" Nothing like that. Instead, my thoughts immediately turned to the fact we'd be on the penalty kill, and that meant they were going to generate some scoring opportunities. I told myself, "I need to make a couple of big saves here." Simple as that. "I've got a job to do, and I'd better do it well."

I was very calm. No anxiousness, no doubts. I was certain I was going to make the saves. So I was really pissed at myself when Eric Desjardins scored. John LeClair was in front, screening me, but I didn't think I did a good enough job of trying to look around him. I took a lot of pride in my ability to find the puck through all sorts of traffic. I thought, "Shit! I should have found a way!"

After that brief bit of self-recrimination, it was like, "Okay, we are going to be reeling over this, so make the next save." Montreal had their second wind, and they were all over us in the last few seconds of the game. Guy Carbonneau had a great chance just seconds later, and I made a glove save to preserve the 2–2 score going into overtime.

What followed was also the biggest ruckus in the dressing room I'd ever seen in my life. Wayne threw off his gloves and took off his helmet and chucked it on the floor. He focused the laser beams on Marty and yelled, "What were you thinking?" He repeated it two or three times and he was waving his hands in the air.

I mean, we were all thinking exactly the same thing, but I was shocked. Like I said, Wayne was really mad. Now, if you had told me Denis Potvin was pissed off like that, I'd say, "Uh huh, why? Is it Tuesday?" But Wayne—that was a different story.

It was chaos. Pure chaos.

You know how I said earlier that I couldn't believe Wayne's in-depth knowledge of the game? How his grasp of everything and how it all tied together was amazing? In retrospect, I think he understood hockey so well that when we were called for the stick, he could see what was going to happen. He had been in many Stanley Cup Finals before, and I wonder if he knew it was a monumental turning point. Did he recognize that Marty's stick was going to sink our ship? I know he knew that we had just opened the door for Patrick Roy, a great player, to get back into the series. Roy had been second-guessing himself, you could see it. And now that we were back on our heels, it would give Roy new life. I'm also sure Wayne could feel the panic and see that our emotions had gone from "We're going to win the Stanley Cup" to "We might have just given it back to Montreal."

There was pandemonium in that room for about five minutes, and then I stood up and said, "Hey! Hey! Let's stop! We're going out for overtime. We've gotta focus on this next period, and we've got to find a way to get through this."

Listen, I knew we were totally screwed. They scored on us in the first minute. I'm the one who let in the goal on the Montreal power play to put the game into overtime. Then I let in the winner. It was my job to stop the puck. That's on me. In any case, they dodged a really big bullet—or a bomb in this case—and it gave them a lot of life and confidence again.

Luc once told me that he was in Montreal at the new arena years later, and a policeman came up to him and said, "I'm sorry." Luc said, "Why do you apologize?" The policeman told him he had been working security the night of that game and was guarding our locker room. He said, "They [he didn't say who it was, but it was some guys who worked for the Canadiens] asked me to look the other way." They picked up three sticks—mine and Marty's, and one he couldn't see, before the warm-up—and measured them and then put them back in the rack.

If you go back and look at the video on YouTube, while Marty's stick is being measured, the cameras cut from Barry Melrose to Jacques Demers. You can see Demers laughing and four guys on the Canadiens bench switching sticks, handing them over to their trainer. Go watch, and you'll see. Trust me, they didn't break their sticks on the bench while there was a timeout.

The bad feelings in the dressing room totally dissipated by the start of Game Three. We were solid again. A lot of the thanks for that go to Barry. He had a really loose attitude. Guys' kids were welcome at the morning skate, and he cracked a few jokes. It was a nice relaxed feeling.

The overtime losses in Games Three and Four were a huge disappointment, but we didn't give up. We put in a pretty good effort in Game Five. Unfortunately, they had momentum on their side, and they took it to us pretty good from the middle of the second period on. Beating Vancouver, Calgary and Toronto, three of the best teams in the NHL, and then to lose in three overtime games was tough. If you are outplayed and you're not as good as the opposition, that's one thing, but to go into overtime three times and lose all three games sucks more than you can imagine.

Wayne was so discouraged, he told the press that he didn't know if he was going to play the next year. I remember that long plane ride home to L.A. after the final loss to Montreal. We were dead tired and miserable, but I felt there was also a sense of accomplishment and hope to a certain degree. We'd made it to the Stanley Cup Final. I felt good about where we were in terms of players. We had three of the best young defencemen in the NHL coming up—Darryl Sydor, Rob Blake and Alex Zhitnik—so we really thought we'd be right back at it. I knew about the Islanders' journey, how sometimes you have to lose to win. It was a dichotomy. We had been crushed, but I was optimistic about the coming season.

Years later, I found out that Barry had a much different take. He felt that the history of sports dictates that when you go that late, you're going to have a different team the next year, because there will be changes. He knew a lot of the guys were due for raises, and he was seeing the clouds on the financial horizon as far as Bruce was concerned. He looked around at our group of guys who meant so much to each other and played so hard together and thought, "This team is not going to be together next year."

Personally, my disappointment and hurt, and how crushed I am today over that loss, grew more and more as the years went by. At the time, we had to accept it. Today, not so much.

Fast-forward to 1993–94. Our team was struggling mightily. We got off to a great start, and then we went on an extended road trip where we didn't play especially well. We were hovering around .500, and then we dipped below that. Not good. And you know what? I had no idea why until I had a conversation with Kings GM Dean Lombardi after L.A. won their second Cup in 2014—they beat the New York Rangers in double overtime of Game Five, winning the game 3–2 and the series 4–1.

I had played for Dean in San Jose, and I'll get to that in a bit. He's a friend of mine, and we get along really well to this day. We've had some wonderful long talks. I listen as he tries to figure out the world. He has a theory about why the Kings struggled after their first Cup. He says they were trying to recapture what they'd had the previous year, but they forgot that each season is different. You have to start new and build again.

After our close call against Montreal in '93, there were changes. McSorley was traded to Pittsburgh. Marty's work ethic was impressive. He was always committed to getting better. He worked on every aspect of his game. He studied other players to find out what they did to have success, and he played and practised at full speed. When there was a drill and he had to get up in the play, he skated as hard as he could. Just about every guy works on his shot, but Marty wanted to be a better skater too. That, to me, is the biggest single area where every player can improve his skill set. Okay, maybe not as necessary for guys like Bobby Orr and Paul Coffey, but for most.

Marty's departure was partly about cash. He was now a very good player as well as a guy who could intimidate the other team. A year earlier, he posted 41 points and 399 penalty minutes. Like a lot of tough guys, he got really popular. I saw a guy who still worked just as hard and was still committed to being a great player, but he had a bigger ego. That happens to most of us—coming up I'm going to tell you a story about how I acted like a jerk until Donna straightened me out.

Marty started to show up late—getting on the ice for practice, for the bus, even the plane. We had our own plane back then, so we'd fly at, say, one thirty in the afternoon. Well, Marty might show up at 1:35. That bugged me.

I was never shy about telling anybody what I thought of him, and Marty knew that. I had absolutely no problem with calling Marty or anyone else on their bullshit. Marty was the same. He'd call me out too. Marty's pretty sharp, so it was a lot of fun actually. He might say something like, "Hey Kelly, you mind stopping one tonight?" And I'd be like, "Hey Marty, let's see what happens if you put on a left skate instead of two rights?"

But when I needed to be serious, I was careful with my timing. It's like with your kids. You can't be on them every day, because then they'll shut you out. Marty was one of the biggest competitors in the entire world. He battled hard. That's how he made it to the National Hockey League, and then he made himself into an excellent player through sheer hard work and determination. He had worked awfully hard to become a valuable player on our team. It didn't matter who you were or what you did, but if you came and competed and worked hard every day, Marty respected you, and I think he respected me for that reason. I was direct with Marty. I could care less if I was Marty's buddy, but I knew what it meant to be his teammate.

When Marty left, it changed the dynamic of the room, for sure. Marty had been a big part of it, and he was a big part of a lot of people's lives. He and Wayne had been together a long time. He was a unique player. He could play defence, he could play forward, he could make plays, and without question he was one of the toughest guys ever to play in the NHL.

Chapter 19

Delivering Newspapers

WHEN MARTY LEFT, WARREN RYCHEL STEPPED UP, and he was fantastic. Marty was the heavyweight and Warren was the middleweight. Together they made a good one-two punch. Even though he didn't have the size, Warren had to step into the heavyweight role. One of his first fights in 1993–94 was against Sandy McCarthy, a giant of a man. I mean, geezus, I don't think even Marty looked forward to fights with Sandy.

Warren was one of the most endearing guys I ever met. Barry brought him up in 1992. By that time, Warren had fought his way through some tough teams in junior and the minors— Sudbury, Guelph, Saginaw, Peoria and Kalamazoo. He came into what I would consider a pretty intimidating dressing room with Wayne, Jari, Paul Coffey, Tony Granato, Tomas Sandstrom and Marty. Some pretty heavy names, and he had no problem taking shots at us. He was funny as hell.

Paul Coffey has one of the best stories I've ever heard about Warren. They were living together that first year, and so they were carpooling to the rink the day Warren received his first-ever full-time National Hockey League paycheque. It was awfully exciting. In those days, you got a record of your money on paper, not electronically. Warren opened up his envelope and said, "Geezus, Coff, this is big money!" Paul was driving and he said, "Really? Do you mind showing me, kid?" Warren proudly handed over the pay stub. Paul took a quick look, and without missing a beat he said, "What? Are you delivering newspapers?"

So, we'd lost in the final, Marty was gone and we just couldn't seem to get back on track. We'd play well for a while and then we'd throw a stinker in there. We couldn't find our roll like we had the year before.

Now, here is an interesting story about the relationship that Barry and I had in relation to team dynamics and moving forward. We were on a road trip in December of 1993, and we were not playing very well at all. We were well below .500. Barry, in my opinion, was pouting. He was not the same forceful, positive individual, coaching the way he could. I think he was trying to prove to management how badly we needed Marty. And that was pissing me off.

On December 18, we lost 4–1 to Toronto at Maple Leaf Gardens. I was furious with the loss, just furious with Barry. He wasn't nearly as involved as usual. For instance, in the dressing room between periods, he was subdued. Typically, when he spoke to us between periods, he was so passionate that we drew energy from him. He got us going. But not this time.

Right after the game, I undressed as quickly as humanly possible and I went storming into the coach's room. I said, "This is bullshit, Barry. You quit on us because you want Marty back. Well, we all want Marty back. But he isn't here, so quit kicking the dog. Let's go. Let's start coaching again, let's start playing again! Let's get our asses in gear." And Barry took it. He took it on the chin.

That night, a bunch of us went out, and I remember getting pretty drunk. We flew to Calgary the next day. There was no practice scheduled. We had the day off, but Barry called a meeting in his coach's suite that night at nine o'clock.

Nobody was happy about it because in our minds, we should be out having a couple beers—it was a different world than it is today. Barry came in and he had a really stern expression on his face. He started talking about how we had to be better. He looked at me, and you know what he said? "It starts with you, Kelly. You've gotta get back to being an exceptional goalie. We're not gonna do eff-all unless you get back to being who you can be." And then he went around the room and talked to other guys the same way.

I didn't take offence at all. One time Al Arbour told me that, even with those dynasty teams, whether it was after the first second, third or fourth championship, he took the first three months of every season to see where the guys were mentally, and then he would challenge them on an individual basis if he didn't think they were the player that they needed to be. Keep them on their toes.

I was really happy to see Barry back up on the horse. The next night, we beat the Flames 5–4 in a very tough building. Now, we did go home and lose 2–1 to Dallas, but then we started to come back again, gaining momentum on the road, beating the Ducks, tying Detroit and beating Toronto. We got fairly close to .500 again, which was amazing considering how bad we were for a while, but we couldn't get it back all the way.

Then in February, Marty was traded back to us for the final third of the season. Unfortunately, things didn't improve. Our failure or success wasn't about one guy. I firmly believe it had to do with the same reason Dean told me his team, the 2012–13 Kings, had problems. We tried to recapture, as opposed to rebuilding, and as he said, that is an impossible task.

The second problem was that Bruce McNall was starting to encounter the financial problems that would eventually cost him the team. We had some great older players like Patty Conacher and Dave Taylor (who was near the end of his career), and some talented young kids in Alex Zhitnik, Darryl Sydor and Rob Blake, but we could see that there were players available that we didn't pick up. Look at the list of the guys who got traded in between 1993–94 and 1994–95: Kris Draper, Esa Tikkanen, Mike Gartner, Phil Housley, Gary Suter, Glenn Anderson, Al MacInnis, Petr Nedved, and we trade away Luc Robitaille, Paul Coffey and John McIntyre? We were making deals because of money and not because of hockey. You see that today with the salary cap. We were to find out later that the whole money issue was pretty serious. Bruce ended up being charged with bank fraud. Just three years later, he would wind up in jail.

Chapter 20

The Adventures of Bruce McNall

LOOK, BRUCE WAS A GREAT OWNER. He was fantastic. I loved playing for Bruce. He was really good to us and helped make us famous and raise our level of sophistication. We were all a bunch of country bumpkins. Most of us, including Wayne, were from small towns in Canada, but maybe because Janet was a movie star, Wayne got with the program a little faster. Off the ice, the rest of us were pretty wide-eyed in L.A.

Bruce would take us on these shopping trips. Incredible. First of all, to have a one-on-one relationship with your owner, and second for him to care so much.

In April 1992, we were on the road in Vancouver after a two-week layoff due to the players' strike. On Saturday morning, the day before the game, I had a horrendous practice. And we were 0–5–1 in our last six road games. I needed a boost.

Bruce came up to me after practice and said, "I'd like you to join Wayne and me. We're going out for lunch." So we had this great lunch, and we were walking it off down a street that had some very cool stores. Bruce looked in a window and saw that they sold Versace. Wayne used to go to the Versace store in Beverly Hills. He wore a lot of Versace. I always thought he looked so sharp in his blue, black and gold shirts and jackets with all the swirls and patterns and stuff. I couldn't afford it, but I loved it on him. We followed Bruce into this store and started looking around. I passed a rack that had a black leather jacket that maybe only Mick Jagger would wear. I went over to take a better look. It was full-on rock star, with the NFL-sized shoulder pads, gold studs, each one engraved with the Versace Medusa-face logo, and near the top, a few rows of rhinestones. I touched the sleeve. The leather was so soft it was almost silky. Bruce walked over and said, "Try it on."

"No way," I said.

But he pulled it off the hanger and handed it to me. I threw it on and stood in front of a big mirror. I turned to the left and then to the right, gave the hair a shake and then hooked my thumbs into the top of my jeans. Geezus, I looked good.

Bruce tapped me on the shoulder. "It's yours," he said. "Just make sure you get a shutout tomorrow night." He took the jacket to the till and paid for it, so I never knew how much it cost.

Sunday night, they outshot us 40–24, but we won 6–1.

I don't think I have ever played so guilty. But Bruce loved it when I wore that jacket. He would laugh and giggle, and then when we went shopping again the next year and he saw these black Versace ankle boots—high-fashion, pointy-toed, with gold rhinestones—he bought them for me. Unbelievable.

I saw Bruce at the All-Star Game in L.A. in 2017. He asked me if I still had the jacket and I told him, "Hell yes, I still have it."

He said, "You know, I always thought it was $25,000 that was well spent."

It was a fun ride with Bruce. He'd come down before the games, go over to the whiteboard and clip up five $100 bills for the first goal, and another five for the first knockout in a fight. And if a guy had a great shift, he might find a couple hundred in his stall. It wasn't the money as much as it was how happy we were to be acknowledged and appreciated like that.

Bruce did something unique for a sports owner. He tried to make us even more popular than we were. Most NHL owners, especially today, seem to want the opposite. Earlier, I told you how Al Arbour encouraged us to think of ourselves as performers and that the ice was our stage. Well, I was talking to Bruce recently and he told me the same thing. He said that we sometimes forget that professional hockey is entertainment. And the minute you forget that, you're looking at poor ratings and poor attendance.

Obviously, back in those days, hockey was a smaller business. The game is very corporate now. It cost Bruce $16 million to buy the Kings. Nowadays, the owners of the expansion

Vegas Golden Knights paid $500 million for a team that didn't even exist yet. It's a different world, and ownership is usually far removed from the players.

Bruce thinks the league and the NHL Players' Association have done a lousy job of marketing the players. I see his point. You don't know who they are. I mean, I could walk one of the league's leading scorers, Jamie Benn, through the concourse at the Staples Center during the playoffs and he might not get recognized. When we played, Wayne would be on Johnny Carson, who was the absolute king of late night at the time, and Wayne hosted *Saturday Night Live* too. There's no NHLer with that kind of profile today—not Crosby, not Ovechkin. Nobody's close. Beyond Canada, nobody has a clue. But a basketball player, a football player? They're mobbed wherever they go. Those sports embrace the idea of selling the game on star power.

Bruce did his best to promote the players. He saw us like the movie studios see their actors, as stars, as the reason people came to our games. He might not have been much of an accountant, but he was a brilliant marketer. He had us at the forefront, in the news every day.

As I said, it was a unique dynamic because Bruce was different. He wanted us to go around North America being the most famous hockey team in the world. Around the same time, the trading card industry was rapidly changing, becoming a huge industry. We saw autograph seekers like we had never seen before. For instance, we'd go into Toronto at three in the morning, get to the hotel, and there would be boatloads of people waiting for Wayne to sign their cards. I had never seen anything like it in my entire life. All of us were in demand with these autograph seekers. At home in L.A., we started to spot some of the professional card traders. These pros would pay kids to get autographs. I became a little jaded about the whole thing. No excuses, but when you are young, it's a challenge to deal with fame.

When someone asked for an autograph, I'd say, "Don't you have anything better to do? Can't you go read a book or something?" As you can see, I was truly becoming a bit of an ass.

Donna and I were leaving the Forum after a game one night, and some kids came up to me, asking me to sign a few things. I blew them off, and when we got to the car, before I could even put the key in the ignition, Donna said, "Okay, that'll be enough of that. You're going to go back to being the good guy you used to be. Even if those kids were asking on behalf of someone else, who cares? They are just trying to feed their families."

That remark hit me like a ton of bricks. I thought, "She's right. What difference does it make to me if someone is making money off my signature?"

I would suspect that, from that day forward, nobody accused me of being a jerk about an autograph.

For players like Wayne, who'd signed a professional contract prior to June 1, 1979, helmets were optional back then. We had a meeting where some of the guys seriously considered not wearing them so that fans would be more familiar with their faces. I remember talking about it in the dressing room. Bruce wanted people to have a direct relationship with us, to be able to look us in the eye. To see us as human beings, not robots. Root for us as individuals. And it worked. Going to a Kings game in the '90s was one of the coolest things you could do in L.A. We were more popular than the NBA. The NFL came first, we were second, and the NBA ranked third. Can you imagine that?

The movie stars came out to our games. Goldie Hawn, Kurt Russell, Tom Hanks, Sylvester Stallone.

There was no other rink in the league that brought in the kind of money per seat that we did—Bruce says we got up to $1,500 at rinkside, which is about $60,000 for a season ticket. Huge money back then. Still is.

Bruce had us playing all over North America, promoting us as the world's most famous hockey team—mostly thanks to Wayne, but he made all of us stars. A lot of guys still come to Bruce and say, "Oh my God, playing here for you gave me the greatest memories of my life."

It was always in the back of Bruce's mind that we should play a game in Vegas, and Bruce being Bruce, well, he made it a reality. One day, he was with Henry Gluck, who at the time was chairman of Caesars Palace, Caesars World, the whole Caesars everything. Bruce said, "Henry, what about doing an exhibition game here?" And Henry liked the idea.

Most of us embraced Bruce's ideas about hockey and how to promote it. We were all extremely excited about helping promote the game, so when we found out we were going to play in Vegas, I was super excited. Two days before the game, Bruce flew Wayne, Larry Robinson, Dave Taylor, Luc Robitaille and me to Vegas ahead of the team, and we made a whole bunch of promotional appearances, just to build the excitement.

It was a challenge putting together an outdoor hockey game in the Caesars parking lot. Daytime temperatures were close to a hundred degrees Fahrenheit—in September. They brought in an ice crew, built a rink and put in 13,000 seats. The crew decided to throw a tarp up to shield the ice surface from the sun, but before practice they dropped the tarp on the ice, and it was so hot from absorbing the heat all day, it started to melt the ice. It was uncertain whether we could even play. Another problem involved one of the blue lines. Instead of paint, the lines were made out of a thick fabric and frozen under the ice, but due to the melting one of the blue lines was coming through towards the surface. I remember Wayne being concerned. That kind of thing can wrench a player's back, twist a knee, break an ankle. In the end, they solved the problem, but it was soupy out there.

I'd been approached by Prime Ticket, the L.A. cable channel airing the game, to see if I would consider wearing a camera on my helmet to provide the goalie's point of view. It was the first time anything like that had been proposed. They called it the Hrudeycam. I said sure. I knew the importance of doing something unique. I had to go over early to make sure that the camera was working properly. There was this big, big, heavy and very warm battery pack they attached to the inside of my goalie pants that took forever to mount properly. It felt like I had hot dumbbells hanging off my ass. Not the perfect scenario for stopping Gartner.

But when I skated out, it really was something. It was totally surreal to see all the people working there, wearing their glitzy Roman costumes. Even the Zamboni driver was dressed like a gladiator. When Bruce put on a show, he was all in.

The Rangers jumped out to a 2–0 lead. I gave myself my usual pep talk—"It's cool that this game is going on and all that, but you have to pull your head out of your ass, get your shit together and focus."

In the second period, it was getting dark and the rink lights came on. Suddenly a swarm of locusts, each one about the size of a baby crow, came flying at us. Apparently, they were attracted to the ice because they thought it was water. Now, I don't want to sound like a baby here, but I hate those damn things. The way they jump around, with their buggy eyes and see-through wings and twitchy antennae. It makes the hair on the back of my neck stand up just thinking about them. I was so completely freaked out.

There were hundreds of the effin' things all over the ice, land-ing and sticking. One of my serious concerns was that a puck might pick up one of those suckers on the way to the net. What if it were to shred apart and hit me in the face? Oh my God. Remember, this was back in 1991, so Tom Webster was still our coach. Webby told me that at one point Tie Domi had a break-away but had to stop because a locust flew in his mouth and he started choking. I'm not sure I could have shaken that off. Ever.

We won 5–2 and I was never happier to hear the final horn. Bruce says that game generated the largest gate in the history of the sport to that point, over a million dollars. He had to handle the cost of putting up the rink. He paid the Rangers about $25,000, a relatively small amount, and he backed up tabs in the casino for a few of our guys to the tune of $50,000.

I'm not a gambler, but after the game I hung out with Bruce for a while. He liked to gamble. He showed me how to play craps, so I watched him throw the dice for about half an hour, and then he turned around and said, "Follow me." He led me into this private room. There was just one man gambling in there. He was sitting at a table, playing baccarat. He was dealt a new hand every thirty seconds, and he was betting half a million per hand. That's right, five hundred thousand dollars every hand. We were there about forty-five minutes, and in that time, he lost ten million dollars.

Bruce's star system worked. We were up there with the parade of celebrities who pulled up in limos and came into our dressing room to meet us. John Candy, John McEnroe, and Goldie Hawn and Kurt Russell were around a lot.

My first year with the Kings, we had a golf event that summer in Palm Springs. I got to the clubhouse early, and John Candy was already there. I'd never met him before, but much to my surprise he knew who I was. Nobody else from the team had arrived yet so we sat down for lunch.

When I was a kid we used to watch *SCTV*, a TV show made right in Edmonton about a fictitious TV station in a small Canadian town. John Candy was one of the stars, along with a whole bunch of comedians who would become really famous, including Dave Thomas, Andrea Martin, Martin Short and Rick Moranis. I also knew who John was from movies such as *Splash* and *Spaceballs*. *Uncle Buck* was another big film that had just come out in 1989. When I sat down with John and ordered my burger, I thought, "Oh wow, this is going to be hilarious." But John was just a regular guy. And you know what? I liked him even more for it. He didn't crack jokes or make funny observations or anything like that. Mostly we talked about hockey and golf. Of course, I was still star-struck on occasion, but that meal taught me that the roles that actors play are their work, what they do. It isn't who they are.

John was around all the time. He really cared about the team and the game. He was always respectful. We had a really busy dressing room, with lots of celebrities and family members visiting. But John knew it was our dressing room. He never sat down uninvited. He'd just mingle with the other guests and wait until we were dressed, and then one of us would go up to him and say, "Hey John, how are you?" He'd always come back with something positive like, "Great, Kelly. I love the way you came out on the angle and made the player hit the crossbar late in the second period."

I saw him about a week before he died. He was in the dressing room after a game, and I remember talking to him. I was concerned because he was sweating profusely. A couple of us talked about that later. I said, "Geez, I hope he's okay." And then a few days after that, we heard he had had a heart attack and died in his sleep while on set in Mexico. We were all shocked and saddened. We would miss him. He was a fairly young guy, only forty-three years old.

Goldie Hawn and Kurt Russell were regulars in the dressing room too, and they really knew hockey. Goldie and Kurt's son, Wyatt, was a goalie, and there was no sending a nanny to drive him. They'd go to his games themselves. Bruce McNall used to tell me their little girl, Kate, had a big crush on me. Today, Kate Hudson is one of the biggest movie stars in the world. Ha! I wonder if what Bruce said was true.

John McEnroe was a huge hockey fan. When I knew him, he was maybe the most famous tennis player in the world. He'd won the US Open and Wimbledon multiple times. He and I struck up a friendship. Why me? Well, I think maybe because he was a guy who played an individual sport, and although goaltenders are definitely part of a team, we play the game away from the other players. I mean, they're all on the bench with the coach, while we're out on the ice the whole game. Whatever the reason, John and I usually caught up in the dressing room after games and enjoyed each other's company.

One time, after a game in February 1991, he said, "We're having a get-together for my birthday next week. It's between games, so why don't you bring Donna and join us?" It was for John's thirty-second birthday.

Donna and I showed up at his address, which was in Malibu Colony, one of the most exclusive places in all of Los Angeles, right on the Pacific Ocean. From the outside, it looked like a regular beach house. The lots were tight together, each about thirty by one hundred feet, but when we walked in we were really impressed. He and his wife, actress Tatum O'Neal, had renovated it and they did a great job. It was modern and clean, but really warm and inviting.

Their little guys, Kevin and Sean, ran past us wearing Batman suits. We smiled and made our way over to the couch. There were only about eight to ten people there, but a lot of them were celebrities, so we were a little intimidated. We were trying to look around without being obvious about it. I caught a glimpse of some people sitting out on the deck, and I gave Donna a nudge. Out of the corner of my mouth, I whispered, "Springsteen."

She did a quick head turn, then held up her wine glass and tried not to move her lips as she whispered back, "With Bruce Willis."

John was gracious and came over and spent some time with us, but we were so out of our comfort zone, we barely said two words to anyone.

After a while, I turned to Donna and in a low voice I said, "Okay, let's go out there and try to say hi to those guys." She nodded and went to stand up, but I pulled her back down. "Wait, wait."

For the next half hour, we went back and forth trying to work up the nerve. Finally, we got up together and headed outside. We hesitated a little by the seating area, but there were no empty chairs, so we hustled down to the water's edge and tried to come up with a plan. But we couldn't do it. We could not barge into a conversation between Bruce Springsteen and

Bruce Willis. What were we supposed to do? Tell them to move over and just plunk ourselves down?

I had a game the next night so we left early, and while we waited for our car to be brought around, Donna started up a conversation with a very pregnant Valerie Bertinelli and her husband, Eddie Van Halen. They were nice, and looking forward to having their first child.

BRUCE MCNALL'S DESIRE TO MAKE EVERYBODY happy, no matter the cost, eventually landed him in prison in March of '97 for bank fraud. Basically, he got the banks to lend him money using the fortune he'd amassed selling antique coins, and he was charged with borrowing more than once on inflated collateral. I think he figured he would use the cash to build now and then somehow fix it down the road.

There were fourteen people indicted along with Bruce, but he made a deal with the prosecutor that if he pled guilty, nobody else on his team, the people who worked for him, would go to prison. And that's what happened. He served five years, less fifteen per cent for good behaviour.

People loved Bruce so much that they visited him there. Goldie and Kurt came. Luc Robitaille and his wife, Stacia, visited Bruce quite a bit. At first, Luc brought along a couple of his hockey cards to help Bruce with his popularity. But the cards caught on, and so, from about the eighth visit onward, Luc was bringing at least seventy-five cards with him each time. Inmates were lined up on the way out, asking for his autograph. When

Luc told me about it, he chuckled and said, "I think it helped Bruce get some good treatment."

Wayne would bring along signed sticks to make Bruce's life easier. In fact, Wayne wouldn't allow the Kings to retire his number until Bruce got out. In retrospect, I wish I had gone to see him. I know my teammate Pat Conacher feels that way too.

I asked Bruce what it was like going to jail and he said, "I loved it. Lord, how wonderful it was. No responsibilities . . . oh my God, talk about heaven! I used to have hundreds of employees, all these people I'm taking care of, and suddenly, no worries. I couldn't do a goddamn thing in there." Talk about a positive guy. But that's Bruce for you.

The first I heard of Bruce having some major financial issues was in 1993, the year we went to the final. In April of the next year, I bought a *Vanity Fair* magazine that had a big exposé on him. In the interview, he admitted that some of the valuables, the coins and relics that he had built his fortune on, were robbed from graves in Greece and Turkey and places like that. Legend has it that the article spurred law enforcement to focus their laser beams on him, which led to his downfall. I sometimes wonder if he gave that interview because he was so tired of chasing that he actually wanted to be caught.

Chapter 21

I Was Petrified

I KNEW ABOUT THE COURAGE OF PLAYERS who first tried to get the union going in 1957. I knew about the great Detroit left winger Ted Lindsay, from Kirkland Lake, Ontario, and how he was stripped of his captaincy and traded to Chicago the next year, and that the owners were so mad that even Montreal's greatest defenceman ever, Doug Harvey, was not allowed to play out his career there. He was traded to the Rangers in 1961. But the guys in my day were brave too, and I count myself among them.

Back in December 1991, we players pressured Alan Eagleson to resign as executive director of the NHL Players' Association. He was subsequently indicted for fraud, and there was a changing of the guard. Bob Goodenow, his deputy executive director, took his place. His appointment changed the course of the game forever because Goodenow saw his mission as speaking up for the players. There was a lot of bad blood between the players and the owners, who were a really tight-knit group. We felt they had all the power and they used it against us.

Wayne's move to L.A. helped a lot of us players to understand our value in the game. He's the guy that all hockey players should honour, respect and thank because he in large part understood that when he moved to L.A., he would be raising the bar on salaries, driving them up. Wayne shared a story with me. When he was in Edmonton, his last year, he knew that what he was making wasn't appropriate considering all that he had accomplished. Because he'd heard that Mike Bossy and Bryan Trottier were among the highest-paid players in the league at the time, and because there was no salary disclosure in those days, he told me he sent both of them a letter asking if he could see their contracts and offering to pay them $25,000 each for doing so. Mike and Bryan understood and sent him their contracts—no charge. They said, "We don't want any money. You deserve whatever you get."

The bottom line was, secrecy was holding down the salaries, and it continued to be that way until Bob Goodenow brought in salary disclosure in the early 1990s. Now, as you know, Wayne is non-confrontational. He doesn't like conflict. But he is very effective in his own way. He was always supportive of me when I was negotiating my own contracts. He told me things to do based on his experience. When I was going for my first contract with the Kings, he told me, "Make sure you get all your equipment, all your sticks, included in your contract so that you can

Come to Papa. The Kings vs. Montreal in the 1993 Stanley Cup Final. —**Courtesy Gary Hershorn**

Kings training camp in Big Bear Lake, California, 1994. With the blue bandana.

On the Ninety-Nine All-Stars tour. We're smiling, but inside I was terrified. I knew I might come home without a job. **Back** (left to right): Marty McSorley, Wayne Gretzky, Tony Granato, Rick Tocchet, Rob Blake. **Front**: Pat Conacher, Charlie Huddy, me.

Donna and me with Charlie Huddy during the Ninety-Nine All-Stars tour, 1994. I loved playing with Charlie. He made such a difference in our run for the Cup in 1993.

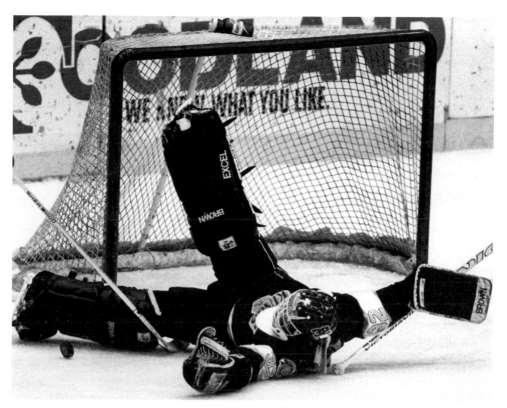

I can't believe anyone would ever accuse me of embellishing!
—© *Pittsburgh Post-Gazette*, 2017. All rights reserved. Printed with permission.

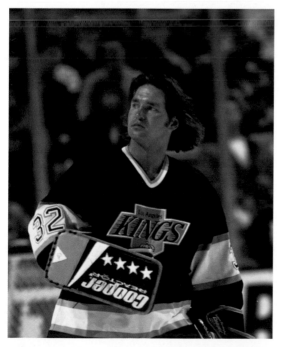

The excitement from the fans at the Forum made the atmosphere electric.
—Courtesy Steve Babineau / NHLI

The girls and me in San Jose, 1996. They loved it there. But who wouldn't?

My dad, Steve, and me in August 1998. He was the kindest, smartest father a guy could ever ask for.

Fall 1998. The first photo taken at my new *Hockey Night in Canada* job after I retired from the NHL.

Whenever I'm with Mike Vernon I'm having fun. That's Glenn Hall in the middle, one of the best to ever play the game. Around 2003. —**Courtesy Larry MacDougal**

Me, Sidney Crosby, CBC's Eric Woolliscroft, Bruce Rainnie and Scott Russell in Halifax, 2002. Crosby was a fifteen-year-old kid. Who knew?

Bob Bourne's fantasy camp at the Cove Lakeside Resort in Kelowna, British Columbia, September 2011, with my former playing buddies. *From left to right*: Greg Adams, Ron Flockhart, Bryan Trottier, Larry Melnyk, me and Doug Bodger.

More fun at the fantasy draft party in 2011 with Bob Bourne and Theo Fleury.

I'll always be grateful to Billy Smith. I was just a rookie, but he treated me with respect and taught me a whole lot.

With my good buddy Luc Robitaille in 2013. Fantastic teammate, always positive. As the president of business operations for the Kings, he finally brought the Cup to L.A. in 2012 and 2014.

With Don Cherry at the Grande Prairie Edge School sports dinner in July 2013. *Hockey Night in Canada*'s grand old lion.

Two Alberta boys at the Calgary Stampede, 2013. Nobody could ask for a better team leader than Ron MacLean.

With my lawyer and long-time friend Lloyd Friedland. Lloyd's been with me through thick and thin, so he's witnessed "the Hrudey Volcano."

Donna and me at the 26th annual David Foster Foundation miracle gala and concert, September 2014. I'm throwing this one in to show off my gorgeous wife of thirty years.

—© *Calgary Sun*, a division of Postmedia Network Inc. All rights reserved. Printed with permission.

Kaitlin (left), Megan, Matt Ling, Jessica, Donna, me and my mom, at my daughter Jessica's wedding, October 8, 2016. I can't believe my luck every time I look at my beautiful girls.

—Courtesy Jamie Hyatt Photography

sell your memorabilia down the road." And you know what? I still have two storage rooms full. That stuff is put away for the future, and I can sell it at some point to make a little bit of money if I want. That's Wayne—he kind of floats in the background for a lot of us. He always had our backs.

So, as I said, thanks to Wayne, we started to ask for proper compensation and salary arbitration, while the owners pulled in the opposite direction. They didn't want to pay us more, they didn't want arbitration, and on top of that, they wanted to sew up licensing rights and take away free agency. By 1994, we the players had absolutely no trust in the owners.

We'd played one season, 1993–94, without a new collective-bargaining agreement and we were willing to do it again, but the owners said we had to come to an agreement—on their terms—or they were going to lock us out. I mentioned earlier that in Los Angeles, we liked and respected our owner, Bruce McNall. The league's owners had elected him unanimously as chairman of the NHL's board of governors in hopes that he and commissioner Gary Bettman could work out a contract with Goodenow, but there was so much animosity, it was too hard to overcome.

Bruce kept telling us, "Look, believe it or not, guys, a lockout is not going to help you because most owners are rich. They don't really give a shit. In fact, they'll save money, and you guys will never get that season or make back the money you lost."

But the NHLPA banded together to stand up for our rights, even though, other than a handful of true superstars, we felt the owners could simply get rid of us. That's how athletes think, though. "You want a fight? You want a war? It's you against us? Okay. Bring it on." So we battled, but now the teams weren't the L.A. Kings versus the Vancouver Canucks or New York Rangers, it was us against the owners. We were bloody strong. There were guys like Ken Baumgartner and Marty McSorley, who were rock solid. Marty was a great influence. Just the conviction that he had and his resolve to keep us united. He was very much involved in the negotiations. Right at the top of the heap in terms of having a voice for all of us. He was well informed and not afraid of the consequences. I give Marty tons of credit for that.

While it's true that Wayne wasn't a political animal, he was extremely well informed. His number one concern was the future of the game itself. He had worked so hard to help make hockey popular all over the States and to build momentum. I think it was really hard for him to see what he had built come to a screeching halt. A lockout was bound to upset the fan base, which meant the game's popularity would take a step backward.

Wayne never sits around. I think he thought it would be cool to do something to help keep the game alive, and there was maybe even some thought of expanding into a European league, which someday may actually become a reality. So he formed a travelling team called the Ninety-Nine All-Stars, and we played eight exhibition games in five countries—the USA (against the Detroit Vipers of the International Hockey League), Norway, Finland, Sweden and Germany. Wayne, being the thoughtful guy he is, invited each of us to bring a guest. Some guys brought their dads or brothers. Wayne brought his whole family, including Janet. I brought Donna.

On December 9, 1994, we played a game in Stockholm against Djurgardens. Wayne got on the bus afterward and said, "Looks like the season is lost." Bob Goodenow and the ownership couldn't come together on certain issues.

I was petrified. I thought, "What am I gonna do? I'm thirty-three years old, almost thirty-four. I've got three kids to feed, and I may never play hockey again." That night, as Donna lay in my arms, she was crying. She asked, "What are we going to do?"

I said, "I don't know, but I'm going to keep my resolve, and if I have to drive a beer truck for the rest of my life, that's what I'm going to do." I had the conviction to follow through and not accept a deal that wasn't as good as we deserved. And luckily for me, there were about five hundred other guys who felt the same way. We were not going to accept a bad deal.

In the end, the owners got a rookie salary cap and some changes to salary arbitration and free agency. Look, I know there was still a long road ahead. We had two more lockouts, in 2004–05 and 2012–13. The entire 2004–05 season was cancelled, and there was dissension and dysfunction within the NHLPA between Goodenow's resignation five days after the signing of the 2005 CBA and the hiring of Don Fehr in 2010. But our action was the first step in improving trust between the owners and players. There is transparency and more control in the players' hands today, and so, both players and owners are together on many issues. So, while we all felt negative effects in the short term, over the long run I think it was positive.

It's just a shame that current players don't seem to know the reason they're making all that money now is because of the sacrifice we were willing to make, thanks to the level of commitment and passion of youth. Think about it. I was willing to let my NHL career go away for the right reasons. Would I do that again today at my age and stage, knowing all that I know? I can't say that I would.

Chapter 22

A Fun Night Turned Ugly

IN 1994, THE KINGS BROUGHT IN Sam McMaster as general manager. At the press conference where he was announced as general manager of the Kings, he said he had a three- and a five-year plan. But I wasn't convinced. There was something about the way he said it—he seemed overconfident, and my gut feeling would prove right.

From what I gathered, there was a relationship between Wayne and Sam, dating back to when Wayne played Junior B and Sam ran the team he played for. I know Sam had a reputation for having a good eye for young talent. Not knowing the man, I initially looked at the hire as a positive move, but I lost total respect for him just ahead of the 1994–95 lockout.

I talked about what happened during the lockout and the Ninety-Nine All-Stars and all that, but what you should know was that ahead of the lockout there was a dark cloud looming over training camp in September of 1994, because it looked like the lockout was going to happen. It all came to a head after our team had done quite well. We went 4–1–1 in our first six exhibition games and then lost the next two. Our last preseason game at home was against the much-improved San Jose Sharks. Before the game, we'd been told unequivocally by the NHLPA that we were being locked out the next day and that it might take the entire season to come to an agreement. We were a veteran team, so we had no interest whatsoever in playing that last game against San Jose under the circumstances. (We did end up playing the last half of the season, but at the time we had no idea what was going to happen.)

I had a wife and three kids to support. Life was on my mind, not a meaningless preseason game against the Sharks. We played a lousy and uninspired game and lost 8–4. Sam McMaster came into the dressing room and totally ripped us to shreds about our lack of character. He made some really disparaging comments. He addressed the team and said, "The effort you showed tonight will never again happen on my watch." I didn't say anything— nobody did—but he totally missed the mark.

In my opinion, Sam had no feel for people and no feel for what it takes to play professional hockey. I thought he was in over his head. He had no understanding about what we were going through. After that night, he became totally irrelevant to me.

The NHL and the NHLPA finally reached an agreement on January 11, 1995, which led to teams playing an abbreviated schedule of forty-eight games that season.

Late in the 1995 season, on May 3, we had a game in Chicago. Tony Granato is from nearby Downers Grove. One of his favourite restaurants was called the Rosebud, which was close to the old Chicago Stadium. We were all there—management, players, trainers, scouts—so they set up a long table upstairs. You might have heard of Garnet "Ace" Bailey. He was there too. An old-school third-liner. Very tough. Ace was one of Wayne Gretzky's closest friends. They played together in the WHA in Edmonton, and when Ace finished up his career in the minors in 1980–81, he scouted for Edmonton. And then, when Wayne was traded in 1988, Ace followed him to L.A. to become the director of pro scouting for the Kings. Sadly, Ace lost his life on United Airlines Flight 175, the one that crashed into the World Trade Center's South Tower when it was taken over by terrorists on 9/11.

Ace was an upbeat kind of guy. I rarely saw him grumpy or mad or in a mood. But during dinner, there was too much booze consumed while we were all trying to figure out what was wrong with our team. Now, the thing about hockey players is that we get pissed off at each other and sometimes talk to each other like brothers at a Thanksgiving dinner. Some of the guys were getting pretty opinionated, including Ace, who was way down at one end of the table. Pat Conacher was near me at the other end.

We were already being loud when somebody said something about the third line—Pat Conacher, Warren Rychel and Dave Taylor. Pat was a heart-and-soul guy, a leader in the dressing room, one of the hardest-working guys. Nothing has come easy to him. He spent a lot of time in the minors riding buses. But on our trip to the Stanley Cup Final in 1993, Pat was every bit as important as anybody on the team. He and Warren and Dave, they were fantastic. They were the line that did all the dirty work.

Ace called down to Pat, "Patty, what the hell have you [meaning his line] done this year to help us out?"

I immediately thought, "Oh, no, no." Pat might have shaken off a comment if it was just about him, but you never put down his teammates like that. He didn't even hesitate. He stepped up onto the table and walked all the way down to confront Ace. I remember watching his cowboy boots moving in between the plates and water glasses and coffee cups as he stepped on bread crusts and spilled sugar—*crunch, crunch, crunch.*

I thought, "This is not going to end well."

Ace stood up and took off his jacket, ready to go. Cooler heads intervened. All of us liked both guys, Pat and Ace, but our nerves were shot because we weren't going to make the playoffs that year. I mean, how do you go from the Stanley Cup Final one year to out of the playoffs the next two, you know? And truth be told, Ace had no business calling out one of our guys at a team dinner. If he were alive today, he'd tell you so himself. It was a fun night turned ugly.

I LOVE BARRY MELROSE AND I'M forever grateful to him, but sometimes I think he went a little too far. His intentions were good. He wanted to help so badly, and he liked to do it through frank conversation, but it's tough for men to do that. One night after a home game, we were in a bit of a slump and he called a team meeting. Not unusual, right? But this one was unique. He went around the entire dressing room and asked each of us to give our opinion on why we were playing like shit. This meant you not only had to look at yourself, but you had to call out other guys who weren't playing well. In a matter of minutes, the meeting got very heavy, and emotions started boiling over.

Guys were blaming others, while trying to defend themselves. It was awkward, uncomfortable and dangerous. When Wayne saw what was happening, he stood up and changed the entire complexion of that meeting. He said, "This is all bullshit. The problem falls on me. I've been a bad player, and we won't have any success until I start to be a good player again. And so, starting tomorrow, we're going to have a great practice. We're all going to be moving together in the right direction. We're all going to be good again, and trust me, in no time, we'll be out of this slump."

That was the end of the meeting. Wayne taking ownership like that showed tremendous leadership. Denis Potvin with the Islanders would have done the same thing. He could be a gnarly prick, and there were times I was afraid of him, but it's interesting how even though they were very different in most ways, those two guys knew how to wear the C in the NHL.

The Ottawa Senators were the worst team in the league. I remember a game in January of 1994, the year after we went to the final. We beat them 7–0 that night. After the game, we were happy, but it was tempered by the fact that it was Ottawa, right?

Roy Mlakar, our president and alternate governor, came in, opened a bottle of champagne with exaggerated flair and said, "Yay, we won a game!"

This just seemed like rubbing it in our faces. Terrible thing to do. We were all offended. We looked at each other and said, "That prick. How dare he do that? How dare he disrespect us like that?"

It was too bad, because up to that point I had an excellent relationship with Roy. But that move chipped away at my respect for him. He should have known better. Maybe he regretted it later, I don't know. We all do jerk things.

The morning of that Ottawa game, Barry had tried something else. Tony Robbins had worked so well for me that Barry brought him in to talk to all of us as a group.

I had a short private session with Tony first. It didn't take long because I was feeling like my strong self again. Other teams used "motivators." The guys from Edmonton told me that Oilers owner Peter Pocklington had them working with John Boyle, a psychologist from L.A. He'd come in and talk to them about how if you load the subconscious mind with nothing but positives, that's who you are and that's what you become.

Barry was standing with Tony and he called out, "Okay, everybody stop what you're doing and get over here." The look on Wayne's face said, "Okay, if that's what Barry wants. Just please keep him away from me."

I could see Pat Conacher. Same thing—"What New Agey bullshit is Barry laying on us now?" Normally, Barry wouldn't have asked Tony to speak to the whole team. He knew some guys were old-school, but I think he felt the best time to make a difference as a coach was when the team was struggling. If a team has won five games in a row, nobody needs any help. They're all the smartest guys in the world, right?

Tony picked Marty McSorley to come up and do a demonstration with him. He went right to the head of the snake, because Marty was a meat-and-potatoes guy. Black and white. He was skeptical about the kind of ideas Tony was offering. Marty was always the last to come off the ice, the last to shower and the last to leave, so when Tony called him over, he was still wearing a towel.

Tony started doing his *Unlimited Power* thing. He talked about how he gets people to break through solid wood blocks as a metaphor for breaking through their fears. As Tony's talking, Marty—being Marty—let the towel drop to the floor and everybody chuckled. But when Marty bent down to pick it up and tucked in his package, making a show of being modest, guys started laughing so hard they were bent over crying, holding their stomachs. Tony held up some blocks and Marty chopped through them like they were rice cakes. I mean, whether Tony pumped Marty up or not, he could have split wood all day and we all knew it. I've never met a man so strong.

But it was more than just parlour tricks, Tony talked about improving yourself. He said you only had to do it by one or two per cent to make a difference. He was all about incremental improvement—making yourself a better person today, for a week, for a month. He'd use baseball as an example—if a guy who hits the ball three times out of ten is a superstar, just think about what happens if he hits it four times out of ten. A very small percentage of improvement can add up collectively and make a huge difference. That's Tony's message.

Now, the thing about Tony's message is that you have to be receptive to it. You have to sit there and you have to think about it. Certain guys eat that stuff up and certain guys don't. I was always one of those guys that would try anything if I thought it would help me.

I was taken by surprise when Tony turned to me and asked me to tell the guys about what he and I had talked about in our sessions. I hadn't told anybody except Barry, who was there in the room with us, and I hadn't ever intended to tell anybody. But I thought, "Look, if it's going to help my teammates, okay."

I got up and started, but when I came to the Fred Flintstone part, I didn't want to climb back down that hole. I said, "I don't mind, Tony, if you share the story with the guys, but I'm not weak anymore, and I'm never going to put myself in a position to be weak again."

Chapter 23

One Point

MY CONTRACT EXPIRED AFTER 1993–94, but in that era, contracts still provided the team with a one-year option to re-sign the player on its terms. So 1994–95 was my option year, and before the start of the season I had two potential avenues: negotiate a new contract or, if I didn't like what the Kings were offering, go to arbitration. I told the *L.A. Daily News*, "If we don't get a deal I'm comfortable with, I'll go to arbitration, get my one-year deal [at a higher salary], and become a free agent in three or four months." But my number one priority was to re-sign with the Kings even though it meant dealing with Sam McMaster.

After some negotiation, L.A. signed me for two years, but the bulk of it was deferred for a few years at 10 per cent interest. This made my lawyer really nervous, considering all that was going on with the team's finances, but it was a take-it-or-leave-it situation, and it turned out to be a good deal. After I retired, I ended up being paid a good deal of money by the Kings.

I sat across from Sam to discuss bonuses. He threw out a number for a low goals-against average. I told him that was bull-shit. We both knew the Kings were a highly talented, offensive, run-and-gun team. Goals against wouldn't work. Wins made more sense to me.

He said, "Okay, what about shutouts?"

I looked at him. "Are you serious? A goalie has a better chance of starting his menstrual period than getting a shutout playing goal on this team." I said, "How about save percent-age?" This means the ratio of saves you make to the shots you face. At least I would have some control over how many saves I could make. "That would work," I said.

He agreed to a $150,000 bonus if I got a .910 save percentage. Basically, saving nine of every ten shots. Pretty effin' high in that era of the NHL. I thought there was zero probability in reaching it. I would need to make a ton of saves on a team where defence was not the priority. But there was an outside chance.

The Kings had three potential backups in Robb Stauber, Jamie Storr and a Swiss kid named Pauli (Pat) Jaks, but I was on fire. We were in Toronto on February 11, 1995, and we won 5–2. Okay, I have to say it—I was spectacular. Forty-three shots, first star of the game. As the season went on, we were in a real battle for a playoff spot, but every time I looked at Wayne on the bench, he had those silver-dollar eyes again. I could see him willing it to happen. The next night we went to Detroit and I played again, this time facing forty-nine shots. We were in over-time when Michel Petit knocked the net off its pegs and referee Don Koharski called a penalty shot for the Wings.

Sergei Fedorov got the tap. I was extremely mad at myself because he had already scored four goals on me in regulation, and now he had the chance to get a fifth in overtime. We had to come away with at least one point to stay alive, and back then there were no points for an overtime loss. It was win or nothing. He came in on me and I made the save on my right pad, right above my skate. I watched it on YouTube recently and it gave me chills to relive it. The best part was Wayne racing off the bench to hug me. I'll never forget the excited look on his face.

I was thirty-four years old and had matured into my game, both mentally and physically. I felt ready to lead the team into the playoffs, and I can't speak for Wayne, but I think he felt the same way. And that's why I was so confused a couple of days later, when I found out we had traded for Grant Fuhr.

I was surprised. I mean, look at it. Buffalo sent Grant Fuhr and defencemen Philippe Boucher and Denis Tsygurov to the Kings for defencemen Alexei Zhitnik and Charlie Huddy, goalie Robb Stauber and a fifth-rounder. Well, first of all, Charlie was a stud. Alexei went on to become one of the Sabres' best players. He was instrumental in helping them make it to the Promised Land in 1998–99, when they reached the Stanley Cup Final, losing to Dallas.

There's no question Grant was one of the league's best, but Los Angeles wasn't the right place or the right time. Boucher ended up having a strong NHL career but was injury plagued. And Tsygurov? He wasn't in shape and never really made an impact.

I'd been hearing whispers that we were looking at Grant, and I also knew that Buffalo was looking to lower its payroll after signing Dominik Hasek to a three-year, $8 million contract. But trading for Grant was just another kick in the teeth, and it told me that McMaster didn't think I was up to the job. I'm supposed to be his number one and he goes out and gets Grant Fuhr? It seemed pretty clear that he had no faith in me.

I played the next night, February 15, in Dallas, and we won 3–1. I was really sharp again. I carpooled home from our flight home with Rob Blake and Tony Granato, and I can still remember the adrenaline rushing through me. I felt like a professional wrestler standing on the side of the ring, waiting to get tagged. You know, "Argggghhhhh!"

As the season progressed, it did not go well for Grant, and I felt bad for him, because he didn't ask to be put into a difficult situation. Grant and I liked each other a ton. We were good friends before the trade. I thought too much pressure was put on him. He was always very chill, and for the first time since I knew him, he seemed nervous. He was such a competitor and had won so much. The time and place weren't right for him.

My level of play continued in an upward trajectory, but it wasn't fun for me to sit beside him in the dressing room and see him challenged. Maybe because he needed a distraction, Grant played a lot of golf.

Barry was fired near the end of the season. My feeling was that he relied too much on the mental side of the game. It worked for me, it was good for me, but not for everyone.

The game was changing. The New York Rangers won the Cup in '94 and the New Jersey Devils in '95. The combination of their success and their style of play was a strong indication the game was becoming very defensive-minded. Teams were moving to a very safe style. Using the neutral-zone trap—don't make any passes up the middle, chip pucks out, chip pucks in. These were things Barry didn't believe in. He believed in capitalizing on your natural talents. Play with pace, use your skill, don't worry about making mistakes.

The other thing was that our team was getting poorer and poorer, financially and as a team. I thought upper management wasn't doing its job, and Barry started speaking out about it in the press. He wasn't responsible for all the personnel moves, and he said so. This is the thing, and you hear it all the time: if you say the wrong things about management, you're done. Like Claude Julien, the twenty-eighth coach of the Boston Bruins. Hired in 2007. On January 22, 2017, after losing a fourth game in a row—this time 5–1 against the Penguins—Julien was interviewed after the game and he said, "There's a lot of guys now that aren't giving us enough, and this is a team that I think needs all twenty guys going in order to win. We don't have enough talent to think we can get away with a mediocre game." It was widely reported, including by *The Hockey News*, that Julien was challenging Bruins general manager Don Sweeney and president

Cam Neely with his remarks. A little over two weeks later, Julien was fired. Pretty damn good coach.

I know the Kings' ownership was in transition when Barry started speaking out, but if you look at great organizations, like the Islanders under Mr. Torrey and Al Arbour, or Edmonton under Glen Sather, you see that greatness starts at the top and filters down to the dressing room. In the end, we ran out of money and we didn't have the horses. I hate to say it, but that's what happened.

Rogie Vachon took over as interim coach for the last seven games of the season. Rogie was a wonderful guy. An ex-goaltender. He broke into the NHL with the Montreal Canadiens back in 1966–67, when there were only six teams in the league, and he partnered with Gump Worsley. He was traded to the Kings in their fifth year of operation, 1971–72. He played there until he signed as a free agent with Detroit in 1978, was traded to Boston in 1980, and retired in 1982. Then he came back to L.A. to serve as assistant coach for the 1983–84 season. He took over as GM in January 1984 and was eventually moved over to assist Bruce. I had a great connection with Rogie.

We missed the playoffs by one point that year. We had too many guys hurt—Rick Tocchet, Tony Granato and Jari Kurri. Wayne was the only goal scorer left, and even a talent like his couldn't do it all alone.

My last start of the season was in Winnipeg. I started the game with a .907 save percentage and played lights out. That night I stopped forty-two shots, only letting in one, raising my season average to .910, so I made my $150,000 bonus. Every once in a while, the hockey gods reach down and touch you on the shoulder.

Chapter 24

An A-Hole Move

AFTER LARRY ROBINSON PLAYED HIS FINAL year of hockey with us in 1991–92, he went to the New Jersey Devils as an assistant coach for two years under his long-time Montreal Canadiens teammate Jacques Lemaire. Then he put the word out he wanted to become a head coach.

Just ahead of the 1995–96 season, when Bruce McNall was trying to sell the Kings to dig himself out of the financial hole he was in, Sam McMaster suggested hiring Larry. "Look, this guy knows our team and the game so well. I think he could be a great head coach." It made sense to Bruce, and so he pushed it along.

Every time a manager or coach is hired, it puts all the players on edge. You don't know if you're going to fit into their plans. As the starting goalie on a team that had missed the playoffs the previous two seasons, I knew I was in the hot seat.

Nobody told us about Larry coming in to coach. I read about it in the papers. To be quite honest, I'd heard some rumblings about him. In New Jersey, the players thought of him as a good guy. As an assistant, he was a great buffer between players and management. He always came out with a big smile on his face.

Today, assistant coaches are very involved in designing practices, working on faceoffs, special teams, game prep and post-game analysis, but that wasn't always the case back then. Larry was more of a guy to look up to, a guy who tapped you on the pads and gave an encouraging word. The fact that he was a Hall of Famer, had won two Norris Trophies as the league's best defenceman and played on six Stanley Cup championship teams in Montreal, well, that meant something.

I was going to give Larry a chance to prove what he could do. I thought he was going to be a phenomenal coach. I had zero doubts heading into camp.

That being said, whoever was coaching didn't affect my job as a player. As I mentioned, I loved Barry Melrose, but I never had one coach in the NHL I couldn't play for. I think if you talk to any NHLer, he'll tell you the same thing. No matter who's behind the bench, your responsibilities stay the same. You owe it to yourself, your teammates, the organization and the fans to play your best.

I pulled an a-hole move that year. When I showed up to camp, I was overweight. I usually played at 188 to 190 pounds. This time, I came in at 198. Unprofessional. Inexcusable. I let my teammates down. What most people don't consider is that goalies are on the ice for all sixty minutes. Forwards are resting on the bench at least twice as much as they skate. Goalies have to be in shape. Ridiculous shape.

When you are an elite athlete and play at that level, you can't mess around with your conditioning. It throws everything off. The day before we were tested, I was skating with the guys, playing forward at the Iceoplex, our practice facility in the San Fernando Valley, and I caught an edge. I heard my ankle pop and I thought, "Uh-oh," but I had no idea how bad it really was. I missed training camp and spent almost two months of the regular season resting and rehabbing a bad, bad sprain.

When Larry started the season, he immediately reduced the veterans' ice time and started playing the young guys. To me, the way he went about it was a big mistake. Look, if I lose my job to a younger player because he is better, I can accept that. But if it seems the only reason my job's given away is because another guy is younger, I have an issue. And that's what he was doing. He was handing over jobs and not making the younger guys work to earn them. What's a job worth to you if you don't earn it? And what are you saying to your vets?

I wasn't an old, broken-down hockey player, being bitter. We'll get to this in a minute, but a few years later, I recognized when it was my time to hang 'em up. I think I was pretty honest with myself in saying, "You know, this guy is a better player. He should be playing in front of me."

Most of us in the Kings dressing room were guys who'd been around the game for a decent amount of time. We knew where we sat in the pecking order. And so, when I saw Larry—unfairly, in my opinion—take ice time away from Wayne Gretzky, Tony Granato, Rick Tocchet, Pat Conacher and Jari Kurri and give those minutes to younger, less experienced players? Well, that was the beginning of the end for us vets.

Chapter 25

It Killed Me

LARRY PLAYED WAYNE WITH A LOT of young, cheap talent. Besides being a ridiculous thing to do, using Wayne like that could get him hurt because it left him so vulnerable to physical play. When guys were closing in on him, he had no one to pass to. Some of the new guys didn't know how to break to open ice, and because Wayne was such a competitor, he hated to give the puck away when there was no outlet pass. That meant he had to hang on to the puck too long, not his style at all, and that was dangerous.

One Friday, Larry gave us a homework assignment. He said, "Go home and think about this—jot down some thoughts about our season and the job I've done so far—and bring it back tomorrow. Be honest on how I am as a coach and what I can do differently, but no need to put your name on it."

I signed my name at the bottom and told him exactly what I thought. I still have a copy. I said, "No lessons have been learned, no players sent down, no players sat out, no one yelled at, just excuses made for them. For example, 'Good game, guys, we're going in the right direction' (this said after a loss). If a young player is ever told it's okay to accept any kind of loss, he'll never become mentally tough enough to challenge himself when he's actually in a tough situation. They all think making and staying in the NHL is easy because it has been so far for them." I handed it to him first thing in the morning. He must have read it, because not long after he talked to some of the younger guys. "Maybe I've been too easy on you guys. Maybe I should have forced you to earn your jobs." And then he continued to do it anyway.

On the other side of the coin, a lot of the young guys loved Larry. They thought he was a great coach, a player-friendly coach in the way he'd talk to them. Luc Robitaille really developed under Larry. He saw him as one of those coaches you want to play for. The kind of coach who is such a good man that, when you lose, you feel bad for him. I got that. Even I felt that way.

After I retired, I remember Luc telling me about a bad road trip the team had. They were in Florida, and Larry came into the room and started getting really upset, to the point he had tears in his eyes. Luc felt terrible because he knew Larry wasn't the kind of coach who liked yelling at his players. Luc told me they won the next four games in a row. That's how much Larry meant to the team.

Coming up, I'm going to talk about Darryl Sutter, who coached me in San Jose. I was not his biggest fan, but he had a hell of a work ethic. I remember Bernie Nicholls telling me about playing for Darryl in Chicago the same season that Larry became our coach. On game day, the players would come to the rink about forty minutes before the morning skate so they could stretch. And Darryl would come into the dressing room, just screaming at them, "Look at you frickin' guys! You're not ready to go yet? This is bullshit. Go get ready!" Meanwhile, the guys were thinking, "No, we're not ready yet. It's ten to ten, we don't play hockey for another ten hours!" And by four o'clock, he'd be pacing the floor, thinking about the game—"What can I do to prepare my team?" His guys respected him for being that prepared.

I mean, no one was like Darryl, but Larry was thorough and prepared too.

It seems to me that all of us in this industry know that we have a shelf life, and in order for Larry to lengthen his coaching career, he needed to make changes to the team, and part of those changes meant moving the bigger salaries out. And who makes the most money? The vets.

My contract was due to expire at the end of the 1995–96 season, and I knew the Kings didn't want me back. In December of 1995, we had a game in Calgary, and I was in the training room, icing my ankle after the morning skate, when Larry came in and said something like, "Kelly, we'd like to have you back next year to help us develop our younger goalies, like Byron Dafoe and Jamie Storr. How much money would that take?"

I blurted out a number. But I could tell by his reaction that he wasn't liking it. We shouldn't even have been having that conversation, because he was a head coach, not a GM. After that conversation, things got frosty. So much so that Donna and I sold our South Bay house in early April and I started preparing mentally to play somewhere else. Hey, it's not that I expected anything different. That's the game. But it's funny. When I talk about that time, it brings up such raw feelings for me.

The Kings were on a long skid, and I'm not saying we were playing great, but Larry didn't help by telling the press that our team had no character.

What was too bad about playing the young guys so much was that both Wayne and I were having good seasons. Wayne was putting up a point a game. And after I returned in November from that ankle injury, I had the best save percentage in the league, .927, at the All-Star break, and the second-best goals-against average behind Chris Osgood of the Wings.

Our backup goaltender, Byron Dafoe, was struggling, and we were in a tight race with Edmonton for a playoff spot, and yet Larry insisted on rotating us. He refused to commit to me as his number one. From January 31 to February 10, we played six games. Byron was in net for four of them. On February 8, Lisa Dillman of the *Los Angeles Times* asked me about being moved back to number two. I told her I still had some good years ahead of me and that I hoped management would trade me if Larry wasn't going to play me. I think it was a fair comment. People were wondering. The stats were there. I wasn't giving away any trade secrets.

Two days later, on February 10, when I walked into the dressing room to play the Sharks, Larry had written a message on the whiteboard. I was sure it was aimed at me. "There is no 'I' in team." I didn't play that afternoon. We lost 6–1, and Larry blamed me for the loss in the press. He said I upset Byron. "It's just another distraction that we don't need."

Pat Conacher was traded to Calgary the day we lost to the Sharks. Now, remember what I told you earlier about Pat, how he stood up and walked down the table to confront Ace Bailey when Ace questioned the third line's commitment? When Pat walked into the dressing room and saw what Larry had written on the whiteboard and then heard what he told the press after the game, he found Lisa Dillman and stepped up for both Wayne and me.

One thing he told her was that Larry was running Wayne out of town. In the *Times*, she wrote that Pat was "outraged at what he perceived as attempts by management and the coaches to portray Wayne Gretzky and Kelly Hrudey as selfish players." Pat said, "I feel all the stuff said about Kelly is totally unjust and unfair." He thought it was bogus that Larry was trying to blame the loss to San Jose on me and that he accused me of being self-ish. "Kelly Hrudey is a total team guy . . . I'm not going to say anything bad about Larry Robinson. But I don't have anything good to say about Larry Robinson."

This was a brave thing for Pat to do, because he was going up against his former coach. Players just did not do that back then. On top of that, he knew that fans might think, "Eff you, Pat. Larry's a Hall of Famer and you, a third-line guy, have the nerve to criticize him? What the hell do you know? Maybe you're just mad because you got traded."

Pat called me later and said, "Look, Larry crossed the line. I had to say something. There's no two guys I'd rather go to war with than you and Wayne."

I was shocked at what Larry did. He could have told the *Times* I was horseshit, a lousy goalie, couldn't play anymore, he didn't trust me in net, but calling me out for not being a team guy? It killed me.

Larry and I had been teammates, and I felt he'd sold us down the river. I called my lawyer and I wept.

Chapter 26

Can You Read Effin' Minds?

WE WERE ALL ON THE BLOCK.

Wayne was traded to St. Louis on February 27, 1996. All my friends were traded, Marty McSorley, Pat Conacher. Everybody I played with for all those good years was gone, so I knew they weren't going to keep me.

There are certain parts of playing with the Kings I will always miss and wish never changed, and my teammates were a big part of that. When you're part of a room like we had, whether it was the '93 team or the '91 or '92 teams leading up to that trip to the final, it was the guys in the locker room who pulled us together and helped us come as close as we did to winning the Cup. That's the memory I would cherish. I had phenomenal people to play with, I had teammates who were there for me, and hopefully they think I was there for them, and that's what competition and sports is all about. So, when Wayne went to St. Louis, the team was left with the young guys feeling uncertain and veterans like me in turmoil.

The younger guys were still starry-eyed, and I don't mean this in a negative way because I was the same way at their age. But that naiveté meant they didn't understand the pending impact of all the changes. When Wayne was traded, I told all of them that not only would it have a lasting impact on the franchise, but we were going to go from big crowds of 16,000 in the stands to being lucky if half that many showed up.

Our off-ice lives would be different too. I told them not to look in the mailbox for tickets to Giorgio Armani's private fashion shows or to Grammy parties. I knew that our public profile would disappear—*phffft*! I'm not sure they believed me, but it turned out to be true. Wayne was the beacon for the Kings franchise. We all benefited from him and his celebrity. Once our star was gone, you know that sucking sound a balloon makes when you let the air out? That was happening to us.

At the time, as a player and a friend, I thought the franchise was nuts to trade Wayne Gretzky. Why the hell would they give up the seat sales and fame? Wouldn't the team make more money if they'd let him finish his career in L.A.? Consider the legacy for future teams, future sponsorships and connections.

Now I can see the other side—you've got to listen to offers. That's what managers do, and they'd be stupid not to. When you want to add depth to your organization, you look at the players that have worth. Wayne still carried plenty of weight. I'm sure they had every team in the league calling. Now, when I heard who was involved in the trade—Patrice Tardif, Roman Vopat, Craig Johnson, a 1996 St. Louis fifth-rounder, who turned out to be Peter Hogan, and a 1997 St. Louis first-rounder, who turned out to be Matt Zultek, I do remember thinking, "Seriously?" Look, I don't want to be dismissive towards those guys, because it's not their fault. But c'mon, don't tell me Sam McMaster couldn't do better in a trade for the greatest player who ever played.

I knew I had maybe a couple of good years left, but in the real world I was only thirty-five years old, so I needed a plan for what to do after I retired. The NHL is the opposite of practically every other career. Most people work their asses off, making very little money when they are young, and then the payoff comes when they are older. For us, the big-money years are in your twenties, and by the time you are in your late twenties or early thirties, it's time to retire. Then what?

I was lucky enough to make substantial money at the end of my career, but I started with guys who made very little. We used to say that the upside of playing with the Islanders in the early days was that the players got to leave with Cups, memories and injuries.

I was impressed with how well a lot of them did by creating partnerships in the community. While it's true they were being paid pretty modestly as players, just being in the NHL gave them a certain standing, and they used it to capitalize on outside business opportunities. I saw Clark Gillies and Bob Nystrom do this. I remember Bob telling me once that he didn't even have his Grade 12 diploma, but he met some community members in New York who were absolutely incredible mentors and became his closest friends. He went into the real estate business with one of them who taught him everything about business, and Bob became really successful. I think Canadian Football League players do a great job at this too.

Guys make so much money now, they think it'll last them a lifetime. When I played, there was a greater sense of responsibility. You'd ask yourself, "How do I sustain a life after hockey?"

I was never completely sure about what I would do. At first, the idea of going into broadcasting never entered my mind. I was a pretty quiet and shy guy, but because I thought it was on me, as the number one goalie, to talk to the press on behalf of the team, I did that, which helped me over the shyness hump.

Before 1994, the intermissions on *Hockey Night in Canada* during the playoffs consisted of Ron MacLean and Don Cherry wall to wall. The executive producer, John Shannon, came up with an idea designed to give both Ron and Don a bit of a break. He decided to rotate them every night during the playoffs, pairing each of them with a current hockey player. When the Kings didn't make the playoffs, Wayne was everybody's first choice. Luckily for me, he declined. I went to Toronto and got my foot in the door. The first year, I was on for two weeks, and in the 1995 playoffs they hired me for a month. I really enjoyed it and started considering it as something I might do when my playing days were done.

A TRADITION THAT DONNA, THE GIRLS and I had was that on July 1, Canada Day, we would drive to Banff, have a picnic and then go into town and watch the parade on the main street. We loved the marching Mounties, the Indigenous people dancing and drumming, and the balloons and cake, all topped off with fireworks at night.

In 1996, we were on our way to the mountains when I got a call on my flip phone. It was my lawyer, Lloyd. He had thrown out some feelers a couple of years earlier in case I didn't come to a new agreement with the Kings. He was telling me now that San Jose was interested in offering me a contract, but a couple things had to happen first. I had to go there to meet with general manager Dean Lombardi and his assistant GM, Wayne Thomas. I had to pass a physical because of the ankle injury I'd had the season before. And Donna and the kids had to check it out and approve of the city.

That last condition made sense to me. Donna was my partner in every way. Believe me, a wife who hates where she lives can tank a guy's season. But who wouldn't like San Jose? It's a beautiful place.

July 1 was a Monday, which meant July 4 was a Thursday, and in the States, that's a big holiday, so we flew in Friday night. I was nervous because I didn't know Dean. Thankfully, he and Wayne

Thomas were very welcoming. They showed up at the airport with plush Sharkies for the kids and wine for Donna and me.

The next afternoon, I met with Dean at his office. He was very direct. His first question was "Why the fuck would I want to sign a thirty-five-year-old goaltender who's more interested in being a broadcaster?"

I thought, "I like this guy. He wants a no-bullshit conversation with some meat and potatoes."

So I said, "I'm still a good goalie. I love the game and I have a ton to offer. Yeah, I want to be a broadcaster, but I'm not ready yet."

The second question was "When you were in L.A., why the hell would they trade for Grant Fuhr when they had you?"

I considered telling him I didn't understand it either, but instead, I said, "Well, I don't think the general manager there trusted me."

Dean replied, "Did he ever tell you that?"

"No."

"Well, can you read effin' minds?"

And that was the tone of the interview for two full hours. His questions weren't hurtful, just honest. We played a game of verbal tennis, and it was a hell of a lot of fun. The following day, I met for another two hours with Dean and Wayne and took my medical with Dr. Ting, their orthopedic surgeon, who gave me the thumbs-up.

You know what? I still get along extremely well with Dean. I respect him very much. We have some of the most entertaining conversations imaginable regarding the game of hockey.

The vets Dean put together in San Jose were true characters. Start with Al Iafrate. Aside from Mario Lemieux, for a man of his size to have that skating ability, and shoot like he could? Well, you don't find guys like that anymore. It's too bad he got injured so much. His back was really bad.

I remember he had these large tattoos covering his shoulders before it was the thing to do. And man, did he love motorcycles and heavy metal music and cigarettes. He'd take off out of the dressing room in San Jose and come back reeking of tobacco. We'd be waving it away—"Al, holy God, man." He'd laugh. "I feel good now. I feel real good now." Nice guy, very old-school.

I only recall facing his shot one time before we became teammates. He was with Washington and I was with L.A., and he scored on me. I hadn't really experienced a shot like that before. It was an overwhelming experience. What I mean by that is, certain guys shoot the puck so hard, it's impossible for your eyes to follow it the entire time. You lose sight of it as it's coming toward you, and you don't see it again until it's on top of you.

Most guys shoot seventy to ninety miles an hour. A good goalie can track the puck the entire way, right from the time it's released from the stick blade to when it reaches you. But with guys like Al MacInnis or Al Iafrate or Brett Hull, no way. You have to make sure you catch their release so you can observe the angle of their blade. Maybe it's tucked in or open—there are all kinds of variables. The angle will give you a clue as to where the puck is going so that you can move into that area and pick it up again. You just hope you don't have to make much of an adjustment when it arrives. That's what I remember about Al. When he hammered it, it came at you at more than a hundred miles an hour.

Luckily, he didn't hit me. We would get stung a lot back then. Our equipment wasn't very good compared to today's standards. My pads were too small—I should've gone to a larger size, but the smaller ones gave me agility.

Glenn Hall told me how important it was to be athletic and to skate a ton. Great advice. Don't get me wrong, I like the equipment and the way guys play today. It was a different time. A different game.

Chapter 27

Oh, Woe Is Me—Our Goaltender Isn't Doing His Job

WHEN I WENT TO SAN JOSE in '96–97, it was the first season where I felt my skills really start to diminish. I remember it being a mental battle to get the best out of my body. A real struggle for me to find my game. I put a lot of pressure on myself to play well. I didn't know the guys and wanted to prove myself as a free agent.

It's a different mindset when you're counted on as the number one guy and nobody questions it, but for the first time in eight years, I wasn't the top dog. I was alternating with a goalie who was four years younger, Chris Terreri. Chris was one of my favourite partners ever. In 1984–85, during an NCAA tournament, Chris was playing for Providence and Scott Gordon was in net for Boston College. Gordon would later play a few games for the Quebec Nordiques. They went to triple overtime, and so both goalies grabbed their water bottles and threw them on top of their nets, and we've been doing that ever since.

Chris had a solid NHL career. He was really smart. He was always putting money aside and investing in these fast-food restaurants. Today, he's got I don't know how many Wendy's drive-ins, and yet he continues to work for the New Jersey Devils as their goaltending consultant. I really liked him.

He got off to a really good start that year. We were eight games in, playing the first game of a road trip in St. Louis with about three or four minutes to go, when he caught a shot with his glove hand that broke a bone in his thumb. That was a turning point in my season because I knew I didn't have anybody else to rely on.

Problem was, my teammates didn't trust me. They didn't have faith in my game. We headed to Toronto, and I gave up three in the first period. I could tell my teammates were shaken. I could see it in their eyes. They knew that I was struggling, and they were playing hesitantly.

We went into the dressing room at the end of the first period and I stood up and said, "To hell with it. You guys gotta just play. I don't give a goddamn if I let in nine goals tonight. I will work my way through this. I just will. And as I battle through, you guys gotta battle with me. You can't give up out there. You can't be, 'Oh, woe is me, our goaltender isn't doing his job.' Do what you need to do."

I went back out and only gave up one more that night. I remember leaving Maple Leaf Gardens knowing that I'd earned back some of their trust. And then a couple of nights later, I stopped thirty-four of thirty-seven shots in a 3–1 loss in New Jersey. Next, we played on Long Island and tied them 2–2, and we went to Chicago and won 6–2. From that point on, I knew I had my teammates onside. Unfortunately, I tweaked my shoulder in our next game, versus Calgary, and then I did some major damage by separating my shoulder against Anaheim on a sprawling save. Didn't matter, I was in for twelve games and I played my best hockey that year in that stretch.

Before each of those games, I'd take a prescribed painkiller, and halfway through I'd take another. There were times after a game when the pain medication was wearing off and literal tears would come to my eyes because it hurt so much. But I kept playing because Chris was injured and we had nobody else who could do the job.

We had a great trainer there. He's still there to this day, Ray Tufts. He was all over the pills he gave me so I wouldn't get addicted. For instance, he wouldn't allow me to have strong painkillers for more than three or four days because they're so highly addictive.

Guys who've played a long time subject their bodies to tremendous wear and tear. No way you can play hockey, football or basketball for eight to ten years unless you have some other sort of help. In Los Angeles, I took Naprosyn, an anti-inflammatory.

It cooled off my hips and my groin, but it upset my stomach, so I had to take it in cycles.

When I hear people climb up on their high horses and talk about players taking performance-enhancing drugs, I shake my head, thinking, "Yeah, well, you have to sometimes. You just have to." And what about freezing? When a guy blocks a shot and fractures his foot, gets shot up with freezing and then goes back out, people rave about how brave he is. Isn't *that* using a performance-enhancing drug?

I'm not promoting drugs or saying I approve of steroid use, but where's the line in the sand? I group them all together. If something is helping you perform, it's in the same category. And I'll go a step further. If a guy has a really bad cold, he can't take Sudafed because he'll test positive for a banned drug, but who loses out? How about the family of four that has finally managed to scrape together enough money to watch their favourite player? But he's out because he's forbidden to take an over-the-counter drug to get him through a vicious cold. And yet, the FAA permits airline pilots to take Sudafed. The entire issue is just so political.

Anyway, I felt proud of myself for playing great. I was in really good shape and I felt that I had brought something to the organization. Near the end of the season, I played in Vancouver and we won 2–1. I was rock solid. My record was 16–20–4. A couple of days later, Dean Lombardi sat down beside me and said, "You know, that is a really respectable win/loss record considering the team that we have. I'm really happy for you and proud of you, Kelly." That really meant a lot to me. It's true that I ended up going out and losing four out of the last five, but that's how she goes.

ED BELFOUR WAS ONE OF THOSE GUYS who defied the odds. Undrafted, he played for the University of North Dakota in 1986–87 for a year, where he recorded twenty-nine wins against four losses. The Blackhawks signed him as a free agent in 1987, and he was called up for his first NHL action in 1988–89.

I had tremendous respect for Ed. He had a real feel for reading a play and figuring out what was going to happen. I recall watching him one time when I was with L.A. I wasn't the starter that game. I was on the bench. We had a good scoring opportunity on a two-on-one. Ed raced out about ten feet from his crease and took away the angle. He went down into his butterfly and the shot hit him right in the midsection. I thought, "How the hell did he do that?" I have no idea what it was he knew about the game that I didn't, but there was definitely something.

I played aggressively too, but if I came out that far, I needed to be on my feet so that I could get back to my net if I had to.

On January 25, 1997, Dean Lombardi traded Ulf Dahlen, Michal Sykora and Chris Terreri to Chicago for Ed. I'd heard all the rumours about him. He was grumpy, and if you touched his equipment he'd go ballistic on you. He was impossible to get along with because he wanted to be the guy. But it turned out that wasn't my experience with Ed. Strangely enough, and as opposite as we were, I liked him. We got along great. There was a mutual respect. He told me he liked playing with me and that he had a lot of respect because I'd made it to the Stanley Cup Final.

I didn't see him as having a big ego. One time, I told him I had no idea how he managed to figure out when a guy was committed to the shot, and he laughed and said, "Even a blind squirrel catches an acorn once in a while." I mean, that's a pretty humble thing for a guy with the talent he had to say.

He seemed to like San Jose. We were cool with each other.

Ed's first start was in Vancouver. I was backing up. We all have our little routines, but mine were pretty minimal. I knew Ed liked to come to the rink early to take care of his equipment. He'd spend hours sharpening his skates and taping his sticks, all that stuff. I got to the rink a couple of hours after he arrived. I was in my normal relaxed state of mind, drinking a coffee, reading the paper, that sort of thing. Ed was in his stall, getting ready, and lined up across the back of my stall were a whole bunch of Gatorade bottles—assorted flavours. I laughed because I thought one of my teammates was messing with me. I started moving the drinks, still kind of chuckling, when Ed snapped at me.

"Hey, you can't mess with my stuff."

I laughed again because I figured he was joking. I didn't know how important his rituals were to him. He grabbed the bottles and moved everything back into his own stall and lined them all back up in a perfect row. That's when I realized he wasn't kidding around.

He was very finicky about his equipment. His pads were set

up a certain way in his stall. Same with his gloves. Nobody was allowed to touch his equipment. You could touch my equipment all day long if you put it back where you found it. As time went on, I could see that Ed had several peculiar habits, but that was his business. That's what worked for him, and I had no objections, as long as he didn't take up my stall.

A few days later, on February 1, we beat Colorado 2–1 at home. Ed played the first two periods but took himself out of the game because his back flared up. I played the third period and didn't let anything in. A pretty good showing against the reigning Stanley Cup champions.

They had a hell of a lineup. Peter Forsberg, Joe Sakic, Valeri Kamensky, Adam Deadmarsh and Patrick Roy. Both Roy and Belfour made big improvements to their equipment that allowed them to go down all the time. Most of us didn't want to leave our feet because our equipment didn't provide the protection we needed. I ended up being a hybrid goalie—half stand-up, half butterfly. I was flopping all over the place, although there was a method to it. But I could feel the shots. Patrick and Ed realized that in order to go into that butterfly almost every shot, they needed more protection.

I admired Patrick too. He was headstrong. Look at the way he left Montreal in December 1995. His coach, Mario Tremblay, who he didn't get along with, embarrassed him by refusing to pull him during an 11–1 pounding by Detroit. Patrick came off and went over to the Canadiens' president, Ronald Corey, and whispered something like, "I'm done with this team." Whether it was the right or wrong thing to do doesn't really matter. What matters is that he believed in himself. He took a stance and he stood by it. I really admire people like that. Remember when I told Tony Robbins that when I felt good, I saw myself as a general on the ice? I looked at other goalies that way too. If they were in command and made their teammates feel like everything was under control, that would earn my respect.

I started to get on edge about getting traded. I mean, now that San Jose had brought in Ed, did they really need me? I was in the dressing room after the game against Colorado, and our owner, Mr. Gund, came in. He was a fabulous man. I just loved him. He played Santa Claus at our Christmas parties and was great with our kids. Anyway, Mr. Gund was absolutely elated because we'd beaten such a good team.

He came up to me and asked for a minute in private. We walked through the dressing-room door and took a hard right through the tunnel together, which spit us out onto the ice surface. All the fans were gone. There were no players in that hallway, no trainers, no nothing. The place was completely empty. Mr. Gund grabbed my arm—not hard, but with an air of authority—and said, "Kelly, I know you're concerned that we might move you, but you have my promise that you're staying here for the duration of your contract."

That felt really good. I remember telling Donna right away when we saw each other that night. "We can rest easy here. Mr. Gund gave me his word."

We played out the season, and because there was no way

we could make the playoffs, Ed and I were alternating. He was scheduled to play in Phoenix on April 1. I was always careful about heading out with the boys the night before a game, but we flew in a day early. What a beautiful afternoon. I looked at the big blue Phoenix sky and listened to the birds whistling and calling and chirping in the trees and thought, "What the hell. It's Ed's turn to play tomorrow. I'm going to let loose for once." At the hotel, I went up to Ed and said, "Ed, are you sure your back is okay? You're good to go tomorrow? Because if you are, I'm going to head out and light it up."

He looked me in the eye and said, "Kelly, you're good. Go have a great time." Green lights all around me. So, my buddies, Todd Gill and Doug Bodger, and I went out and tied one on at Hooters. Not my usual hangout—although I really liked their wings. After downing quite a few, I realized we hadn't had anything to eat yet, so we headed to Morton's for big, juicy steaks and some California red.

I never missed curfew. Ever. But that night, I staggered in about 2 a.m. So, what did I do? I drunk-dialed Donna. I was totally hammered, so I don't remember much about the conversation. I do know I was missing her and I was trying to tell her so, but I don't think I was getting my point across, because she interrupted me and said, "Oh my good God, Kelly. I've never heard you this drunk in my life!"

I woke up the next morning feeling like a dog that'd been hit by a car and rolled into a ditch. I crawled over to the rink for the morning skate, hoping it would blow some of the beer stink out of my pores. Now, remember how I told you Ed would get to the rink before anyone else? His stall was empty. Where the hell was he? At about 11:20, as the guys were headed onto the ice, our coach, Al Sims, came up to me and said, "Kelly, can I talk to ya?"

I went into his office and he told me, "You're starting today. Ed's having trouble with his back." I broke out into a cold sweat and thought, "Oh, my sweet geezus."

I kept the skate short because I needed to crash and sleep off some of the booze. Didn't make a difference. We got smoked 7–1. I gave up five in the first period. In fact, I scored one on myself. There was a loose puck and I moved to whack it into the corner but instead knocked it back into my own net. From that point on, it was nothing more than a game of survival.

I have to tell you that my teammates were incredible. They knew what had happened, and yet they kept coming back to the net—"You okay?" Tapping me on the pads, chuckling, having a little fun with me. It was an embarrassing loss, but those guys were great to me.

The next day, we were playing at home against Anaheim. It was another good team, with Paul Kariya, Teemu Selanne and Jari Kurri. I was playing again but feeling better—normal. There was no morning skate, so I got to the rink around 4:45 for the game. I was walking through the front doors and passed by Al Sims's office. He saw me and gave me the wave in. I was thinking, "Aw geez, he heard I went out and now he's gonna ream my ass for being unprofessional."

I sat down and Al got up and closed the door. He said, "Listen, Kelly, I've got a golf tournament in Anaheim in the summer, and you've been such a good worker for me that I'd like to invite you to my golf tournament. And as a thank you, I'll get you a free set of clubs. It'd mean a lot to me if you'd make it."

I told him, "For sure, I'd love to come."

I walked out of there thinking, "That is the strangest conversation I think I've ever had. Here I thought I was going to get ripped, but instead I feel great because the coach told me he likes me and wants me to come to his golf tournament." That night, we ended up tying a very tough team 5–5.

Chapter 28

An Absolute Stud

DARRYL SUTTER IS THE MOST INTENSE person I've ever met. He was completely dedicated to doing whatever it takes to win. It wasn't nice sometimes. Some guys can't handle getting kicked in the ass, but Darryl was going to do whatever he thought was right to get you ready to play your game. That being said, I don't think Darryl was always on the money.

I love the Sutters, especially Brent, Duane, Richie and Ron, but right from the time Darryl came in—my second year in San Jose—I felt he treated us very poorly, especially the vets.

Todd Gill, our captain, was a favourite teammate of mine. The best way I can describe him is that he played as hard as anybody I ever played with in my entire career—every shift. He played a grinding, physical game and stood up for guys when he had to. He was extremely dependable. He gave everything he could. Even if he made a bad giveaway, that never bothered me because he gave his all. We had a really cool friendship and it was hard to watch the way Darryl treated him.

Todd cared so much. The year before, on February 1, 1997, we were playing the Colorado Avalanche at home. They had Joe Sakic and Peter Forsberg—two of the top five players ever to play the game for that franchise. That morning our coach, Al Sims, told Todd he was going to match up with both of them at times throughout the game. It was kind of like saying, "Okay, your job tonight is to stop Superman and Batman."

We were getting dressed for the game and I could see Todd sitting in his stall, leg bouncing nervously, really uptight. For him, that was unusual. I'd seen him ramped up, but never anxious before. And then he got up and went into the bathroom and vomited just like Glenn Hall used to do before a game. Well, Todd Gill played the game of his life that night, and he played a lot of games in his career. He was ridiculous against those lines. An absolute stud. I'd always had a ton of respect for him, but that night . . . that night, he was something else.

When Darryl came in, Todd—as our captain—took it upon himself to try to clean up after him. If Darryl put a guy down, Todd would go up to the player after and build him back up, like every great captain does.

And then Darryl went after Todd in the papers, saying he had to pick up his game and stuff like that. Finally, Todd had had enough. He asked for a trade, and Dean sent him to St. Louis for Joe Murphy and some cash. Todd was a proud guy, and he wasn't going to go whimpering into the night. When he talked to the press afterward, he had some pretty harsh words for Darryl Sutter. He didn't back off. I was proud of him.

Darryl did seem to love Owen Nolan. After Todd Gill left, in 1997–98, Darryl gave the *C* to him. I didn't think Owen was ready for the captaincy. Not because he was younger—lots of young guys make great captains. Connor McDavid, Sidney Crosby and Jonathan Toews have all been outstanding young captains. It's just that Owen wasn't vocal enough in the locker room. He pretty much kept to himself.

I would bug him. I couldn't help myself. Owen was always one of the first guys in the dressing room before practice. I'd come in with my big coffee and go over and sit down beside him, still dressed in my street clothes. He'd be pulling on his gear—head down, not looking at anybody, as usual—and I'd go, "Hey Buster, how ya doin'? What a great day, hey? Sun is shining. I feel lucky to be alive, don't you?" Most of the time, he wouldn't say a word back. He'd just give me this puzzled stare, like, "What the hell is wrong with this guy?"

I was a clubhouse spokesperson, one of the guys who tried to create camaraderie on the team. When Darryl wasn't around, I'd tell the guys, "Don't let him get to you. We've gotta band together and play in spite of him." That kind of thing. But there were times I thought Darryl crossed the line.

Doug Bodger was one of our top four defencemen. We counted on him for special teams. He was great on the power play and at penalty killing. Doug is one of the sweetest, nicest guys I've ever met in my life. A really happy guy. Always with a big smile. It's not that he didn't take the game seriously, it's just that he loved the game, loved playing and loved being around the guys. He would come into the dressing room and spread a little sunshine—"Let's have some fun, boys! Let's go play hard!" He'd tell a few jokes, get us laughing, even when the game was still nine hours away.

Well, for Darryl, it was all about preparation. So Darryl was really hard on Doug. And I'm talking about a really good hockey player. A former first-rounder for Pittsburgh who had played a boatload in the National Hockey League. I didn't like it. Now, I will say Doug could take it. He was really strong. He'd had a coach in junior who was like that too.

Very tough.

After one particular game in Chicago, on Hallowe'en in 1997, which we lost 5–3, Darryl came into the dressing room really angry at Doug. Criticized his play, insulted his character—really put him down.

When a coach goes after a player like that, to me, well, that's going too far. Darryl left, and I went up to Doug and told him, "That's not right. He went too far. You're my friend. I'm standing up for you on this one."

Doug was blinking hard, but he just shook his head. "It's okay. Don't worry about it. Don't say anything, Hrudes. I think Darryl was just trying to fire me up."

I went in to talk to Dean Lombardi about Darryl. I said, "There's something wrong with that guy. He never, ever gives us any respect. There's no positive communication."

And Dean said, "If only you could hear the wonderful things he says about you guys behind your backs."

I said, "Well, tell him to share those thoughts with us once in a while."

The worst incident happened in March 1998 in North Carolina. We'd lost to Buffalo the night before and Darryl was really mad about it. The Hurricanes' rink in Raleigh wasn't ready yet, so we flew to Greensboro to play the Hurricanes on Saturday the 14th. We were booked to stay at the Marriott Hotel downtown. It was a beautiful hotel, maybe the nicest in the city.

Greensboro was built on the backs of the textile mill workers. And although many of the mills had shut down, it was still made up of mostly blue-collar workers like my dad. I don't know much about that area, except that's it's part of the Bible Belt, so it's full of people of strong faith.

As we pulled up in the bus on Saturday morning, I could see a whole bunch of families arriving for brunch. They were all dressed up. Every guy was wearing a suit and tie, and the ladies had on these beautiful lacy dresses with matching purses and some wore nice hats. The children were spruced up too. They looked so happy as they gathered in the lobby, chatting and laughing. There were several vehicles out front, and by the look of them, it was obvious that money was tight, and yet they'd put enough aside to enjoy this wonderful occasion. Maybe a bridal shower, or baptism, something really special at this fancy hotel.

Darryl was first off the bus and down the steps. He moved quickly into the lobby and stood next to the front desk so that we'd have to pass by him after picking up our room keys. As each of us filed past him, he dredged up something rude and dismissive for every guy on the team.

The happy chatter around us quieted. I looked around and saw everyone watching. That scene has always stayed with me, maybe because the people reminded me so much of my own family.

PATRICK MARLEAU WAS JUST SEVENTEEN years old when he came to his first training camp in 1997. He had been drafted second overall behind Joe Thornton, who was selected by the Bruins. Twenty years later, Patrick was playing on Thornton's wing for the Sharks, along with Joe Pavelski.

I had a pretty good idea that it might be my last year. I was thirty-six years old, and so Patrick and I didn't have a lot in common. Although he was a quiet and respectful kid, like I was back in the day. Just a wide-eyed youngster from small-town Saskatchewan, drinking it all in and learning from everybody. I could see him watching how guys prepared, trying to figure out the best way to approach a game. I could also see he was a little lost. He was from a farm a few hours from Regina, and when a kid is that vulnerable, he can go one of two ways. I came to find out he had a really great upbringing with grounded, loving parents. I didn't know if he was going to make the team, but I wanted to make sure that he went the right way.

Halfway through training camp, I went to Dean Lombardi and Wayne Thomas, Dean's assistant GM, and threw out a proposal. If Patrick made the team, he could live with me and my family in our little guest house if he liked. Dean and Wayne were thrilled. Patrick did make the team, and I took Donna and the three girls to meet Pat over dinner.

Afterward, he went back to the hotel where he was staying and we went home and had a family sit-down. "What do you think of him? Do you think he'd be a nice fit for our family? Do you think you'd be okay if he stayed in our guest house?" The girls were really excited. They liked him right away. Donna and I did too. Helping him enjoy his first year in the NHL and showing him what it was like to be a pro and the dedication it takes, it just seemed like the right thing to do.

We didn't want to charge him rent or anything, but I told him there was one way he could pay me back, and that was by someday returning the favour to some other kid who was coming up through the ranks. And he did. He and his wife, Christina, took in right winger Steve Bernier when it was his first year in the league.

We set Pat up in our guest house, and it was the start of a really cool friendship. He rejuvenated my love for the game because he had so much enthusiasm. After home games, we'd come back to the house and sit up until two or three in the morning, talking about hockey and life, his growing up on the farm in Aneroid and then leaving for Seattle to play junior, and my life with the Isles and then the Kings.

In front of our teammates or in a big group, Pat was very quiet, but when you got him in a smaller group with friends, like at dinner or our evenings together, he opened up a lot more. Again, he was just a wonderful kid. You look back and it's amazing that he even survived playing for our organization, let alone that he did so well in San Jose for so many years. It says a lot about what kind of a person he is, and about his easy sense of humour.

When Darryl was hard on the kids, Tony Granato or I would wink at Pat or one of our first-rounders, a left winger named Jeff Friesen, or another one of the young guys and say, "That means he loves you," or whatever. Pat would always have a good chuckle at that.

I remember Tony Granato being really good to Patrick. We both just wanted to make the kid feel welcome, and comfortable, and part of it. Selfishly, the quicker you can make a young talent feel like he's respected as a teammate, the better he's going to help you on the ice, but there were some really demoralizing conversations and meetings and things said in the locker room that I still wonder about. What were Darryl's intentions? Did he think he was being motivational? And why would he be so hard on a kid like Marleau?

I don't know the answers to those questions, but that was Darryl's style, his way of motivating or thinking he'd get the most out of a player. It's a different tactic than most coaches use, even old-school coaches. I don't think you could do that today, and I don't think Darryl used the same approach a decade and a half later in L.A., either.

There wasn't enough time for Patrick to go home for the holidays, so he spent Christmas with us. On Christmas Eve, when the girls went to bed, Patrick, Donna and I put together a Barbie motor home. There's a thousand pieces to those things, and then he helped us build a basketball hoop in the driveway. What a great night. What a great kid.

I saw the direction salaries were going, and so when Donna and I took him out for dinner at the end of the year, I told Patrick, "You know what? Based on what I see, by the end of your career you're gonna make between fifty and sixty million dollars." And the look on his face . . . it was total disbelief combined with absolute joy. It's funny, but when I saw his big smile, I realized it was the first time he understood it was a reality.

Anyway, I was completely wrong. I continued to see him when I was on the road, covering games, and in 2014, when the Sharks were playing L.A. in the playoffs, I met with him at the practice rink after Game One. I said, "I owe you a huge apology."

He looked at me, kind of shocked, and asked, "Why?"

"Do you remember that dinner we had back in 1998 at the Italian place after the season was over, and I told you that you were going to make between fifty and sixty million? Well, I apologize. I was about fifty million short."

Chapter 29

I Knew I Was Going to Be in Trouble

AS I SAID, I PLAYED WITH some terrific young guys on our team in San Jose. Late in the 1997–98 season, Jeff Friesen was playing really well on the second line. Great kid, from Meadow Lake, Saskatchewan. While we were waiting for the Zamboni to finish cleaning the ice for the morning skate, I was reading the sports section of the *San Jose Mercury News* and came across an article where Darryl was tough on Jeff. Basically, he said that if Jeff were playing on a really good team, he'd be nothing more than a third- or fourth-line player. I shook my head. Why would a head coach rip a young guy like that? It was so confidence-killing. On top of that, we needed the kid for the upcoming playoff run.

As luck would have it, the in-house TV producer came up to me and said, "Hey Kelly, can you do the first-intermission interview with us?"

I looked at him and smiled. "Sure, I'd love to."

The period ended, and the very first question the interviewer asked me was, "What'd you think of Darryl Sutter's comments this morning about Jeff Friesen?" I basically said, "I think it's wrong to go to the newspaper and rip apart my teammate like that. I don't know what Darryl was thinking. Jeff's a really valuable player for us. Really important. We are going to rely on him in the playoffs just as we have all season. He's young, but he's really come through for us."

I knew I was going to be in trouble.

Darryl always came into the dressing room with four minutes left in intermission. He showed up as usual, pushed open the double doors, stopped and looked around the room. He said, "Some of you guys give me everything you have every day." And then he walked slowly over to my stall and looked me directly in the eye. He said, "You. You make me sick. You bring us nothing! All you're good for is a TV interview." And then he turned and walked out.

The room was quiet. The guys weren't sure how I was going to handle it. I cleared my throat and looked around. "You know, sometimes I get the feeling he doesn't like me very much." Oh my God, we had a good laugh.

I had played with Bernie Nicholls in L.A. in 1988–89 and '89–90. We arrived in San Jose at the same time in 1996–97, and it was great to see him again. Bernie had a different perspective. He absolutely loved Darryl. Thanks to Bernie, I think I understand what Darryl was doing, but it doesn't mean I condone it.

Bernie said, "Look, if you're a better player than me and Darryl's chewing your ass out, then you're thinking, 'I better get my ass in gear.'"

It's true that you can't chew out a third- or fourth-line player. You're not winning and losing games with your third- and fourth-liners. It's your skill players that have to bring it every night. I've heard that Pat Quinn was the same way. A skill guy might actually be playing well, and Pat would single him out when it wasn't about what the skill player had done. It was about inspiring the other guys. Glen Sather was similar in that way. He'd sometimes yell at Gretz and Messier to get the other guys going. So, in fact, did Al Arbour. One time when Islanders defenceman Gerry Diduck wasn't playing as physical a game as Al wanted, Al came up to him and yelled, "You've got a body like a Greek god and you play like a Greek!"

Later, Al asked Gerry, "Do you know why I yell at you?"

Gerry said, "No, Al, I don't know why you yell at me all the time."

"Because you can take it."

Of course, the difference was that Arbour, Quinn and Sather also made their players feel respected.

Darryl and I have kind of patched it up over the past twenty years. I got to know him much better after I was done playing for him. Recently, I was on YouTube, watching a feature the L.A. Kings made called "In My Own Words," where I saw the Darryl Sutter I wish I'd known back when he coached us.

He was talking about how much it meant to him that he only played with one team, the Blackhawks, coming up through the system and becoming captain, and then retiring and then eventually becoming the coach.

He got emotional when he talked about how badly he'd wanted to play each and every game at the old Chicago Stadium, and then he said something that really hit me: "You just hope you can get players to see that and feel that."

If he had just shown us that guy, the guy I saw in the video, my last year in San Jose would have been very different, because his humanity was something I would have latched onto. It's what I was looking for. It's what all players are looking for.

Chapter 30

The Goalie
Who Cried Wolf

AS I TOLD YOU EARLIER, I had a history with Mike Vernon. I played against him in the provincial championships in 1978. He was playing for his South Calgary community team. I was playing for my Canadian Athletic Club team in Edmonton. We won the two-game series, but he was unreal in goal. I didn't know him back then.

Mike came onto my radar when we started playing against each other in the Western Hockey League. He was a remarkable talent. He had skill and mental toughness, and he was a workhorse. He played a ton of games. We'd bump into each other every once in a while over the years, maybe have a bit of a chat after the games, but we were never friends. And then, when I was traded to Los Angeles, we played the Calgary Flames a ton. At that time, our conversations would last a little longer.

When I talked about handshakes, I mentioned that when I played a team I had to hate them, but about ten to fifteen minutes after a game there was no hate anymore. I was really good at turning the switch on and off. That surprised people. Even away from the NHL, if I was playing any kind of sport, I'd use that hate. One year, some local guys in Medicine Hat recruited me to play summer ball hockey. It was really fun and good for fitness because there was lots of running involved. I played with NHL-level intensity. I was a real jerk, and I think my opponents scratched their heads over how I could play that way, and then, moments after the game, I was back to being just a normal, friendly guy. That's how it was with Mike. I hated him and the Flames during the game, but afterward, everything was cool.

In the 1990 playoffs, first round, we faced Mike and the Flames. They were the Stanley Cup champions from the year before. On April 14, Game Six, we beat them in double overtime on a really weird goal by my teammate, Mike Krushelnyski. I felt bad for Vernon afterward because he played a heck of a series and it's one of the strangest goals you'll ever see. You can Google it.

We were the underdog of all underdogs in that series with Calgary, but that all turned around when Krushelnyski won the faceoff in our zone, headed up ice, and gained the blue line with Tony Granato and winger Steve Kasper beside him. Tony took the pass and put what I thought was a pretty harmless shot on net because he was looking for a rebound.

Vernon made the save, but when Krushelnyski took a swing at the rebound, I thought, "That's got a chance of going in!" But Vernon made another save. This time, the puck bounced back to Steve Duchesne. As he was winding up, I was thinking, "Yes! This is it! This is it!" Steve let go a cannon and the rebound came out right in front. Krushelnyski was there again, but falling down face first on the ice with the Flames' Brian MacLellan riding horseback.

I remember watching Krushelnyski landing on his belly, and somehow freeing up his stick and sweeping the puck high into the air toward the net.

And of course we watch everything in slow motion now, but in real life that's kind of how it was, watching that puck flutter over Vernon's outstretched glove.

On his way out of the rink, Vernon was walking by our dressing room and he stopped in to visit with me. I was jubilant about the win, of course, but I didn't want to be a dick about it, so we went into the trainer's room away from everyone and talked. It was a really pleasant conversation, which struck me as weird, in a sense, because we'd just eliminated the Flames, who were highly favoured to repeat as champions. And oddly enough, that's where our friendship began. And then, when he was traded from Detroit to San Jose prior to the 1997–98 season to share goaltending duties with me, he quickly became one of my best friends.

Mike's got a really likeable personality and an infectious laugh. He and his wife, Jane, became super close with Donna and me. Mind you, when he started calling me Tutti-Frutti, I had my fingers crossed that that one wouldn't catch on. He's a know-it-all, by the way. He thinks he knows everything about everything. I'm sure everybody will back me on that one.

I not only liked him, I respected him. He was a two-time Stanley Cup winner—with Calgary in '89 and Detroit in '97. Jimmy Devellano, who drafted me to the Islanders, was part of the group that brought Mike to Detroit. Jimmy worked with Ken Holland and Scotty Bowman. Three brilliant hockey guys.

Mike was traded by the Flames in 1994 for defenceman Steve Chiasson. Detroit really needed an experienced goaltender at the time. Scotty made the pitch for Grant Fuhr, but Ken Holland felt that Vernon was better and Scotty went along with it. Obviously, it really worked out.

Mike was traded to San Jose right after winning the Cup and the Conn Smythe Trophy as MVP of the 1997 playoffs. I think there was a bit of a contract dispute, and Detroit was trying to move Chris Osgood into a more prominent role. Detroit traded Mike for two second-round picks, who turned out to be Maxim Linnik and Sheldon Keefe. Pretty great trade for us.

Mike was our team MVP, that's how great he was playing. He was unbelievable. Just amazing that year. His mental toughness was at the very top. I think the stats will show that if we ever got the lead in the second period, he held on to it and we'd win.

Mike tried to have as much fun as he possibly could, on and off the ice. I was his backup, and he took great joy in pulling my leg and keeping me on edge during a game. During the second or third period, he'd start wincing and stretching his neck or his back. He'd look over at me with a big frown, making eye contact that suggested he was feeling something wrong somewhere—like some injury was going to take him out of the game and force me in. When you're a backup and thinking you've got to go in even though you're not warmed up, well, that's unnerving. I'd squirm on the bench and try to prepare mentally. Then it would turn out he wasn't hurt at all, and he'd finish the game and have a good laugh about it.

Near the end of the season, we were playing in Toronto, and with about six minutes to go in the third period, he started doing his thing again—looking at me and motioning like I've got to get ready to come in. But this time he took it further. He started skating towards the bench. I rolled my eyes and waved him back. "Yeah, right. Screw it. You're not hurt."

He held the lead and we won 5–3, but much to my surprise, he limped into the dressing room afterward with a pulled groin. Darryl Sutter came up to us and said, "What the hell happened out there?" He looked at me and said, "Why the hell would you wave him back?"

We had a great relationship. There wasn't much of an age difference between us—I was only two years older—but I would say I was the one in the big brother role. When we were in playoffs with Dallas, we lost the first game and then we had a day off in between, so we had a late skate. I grabbed Mike after that and said, "Come on, Verny, let's go for lunch."

He said, "Yeah, okay, sure. I've got the perfect restaurant. It's great food."

So we got there and I saw it was a gentlemen's club, but as it turned out, it actually did have very good food. We finished eating and the manager told us, "Feel free to go sit out by the pool."

Mike looked around and said, "There's a pool here?"

It was about ninety degrees Fahrenheit in Dallas at that time, so they set us up under an umbrella in the middle of all these girls who were suntanning in bikinis. Mike leaned back and sighed, "Kelly, this is perfect!"

Well, the next thing you know, some of the girls came around and started talking to us. But all I could see was Donna's face when she asked me, "How was lunch?" So I hopped up and grabbed his arm—"Okay, Verny, we gotta go."

Mike looked at me like I'd just sat on his ice cream cone. "No, no! We can stay!"

"Nope, Verny. We're leaving right now. You've got a game to play tomorrow. You're not staying here!" I yanked him out of his chair and we took off.

DEAN HAD BROUGHT IN MARTY McSORLEY through a trade with the Rangers. When the Kings had their fire sale, Dean picked up another old Kings teammate, Tony Granato, too. I'd played with Marty for nearly a decade. Earlier, I mentioned Marty was always really strong in the dressing room. I think he was like that for two reasons. One, he grew up on a pig farm with ten kids, so he worked a man's job from the time he was very young. And two, he was a tremendous competitor. The times he went too far with some of the things he did or said, most of the veterans were like, "Meh, water off a duck's back." But the younger guys took it hard. Marty was a legend in the game at that point. Not just for winning Cups with Wayne, but because he was one of the toughest, most feared guys in the league.

In hockey, there are three stages—the up-and-coming, the plateau and the decline. Both Marty and I were getting older and our skills were diminishing. When that happens, you have to learn to accept the back seat. Doing that was a very difficult thing for a warrior like Marty, especially because he was struggling with injuries.

We were getting ready to go out for a game one time, and Marty was taking it to this young player in the dressing room, and he crossed the line. Sometimes he'd go after the guy's girlfriend or wife, saying things that were not acceptable. Whenever I walked out on the ice prior to the start of the game, my thoughts would be only about stopping the puck, right? But on this day, I couldn't get over the fact that Marty was being so hard on this young player. I was in the tunnel with the guys behind me when I turned and lifted up my mask. I yelled back at him over the heads of the entire team, "Hey Marty, try something fucking different today. Get the *other* team to hate you." Marty dialed it down a notch after that.

My second year with San Jose, 1997–98, I was thirty-seven years old and my game was slipping both physically and mentally. It was going down rather quickly for me. I felt my skills deteriorating. Even practices were hard. I was at the point where I had to be mentally ready, even facing the young guys. That should never be. When you're playing your top game in the National Hockey League, practice is physically demanding, but you don't have to be completely engaged to stop pucks because you're that good. Added to that, I had to admit to myself that the wins didn't seem as special anymore and the losses didn't hurt as much. This was tough for me because I loved the game so much.

On March 18, 1998, we played at home against Dallas, and although I played okay, I really doubted myself throughout the game. The next day, Dean Lombardi called me into his office. Again, because we could be honest with each other, we had a heart-to-heart conversation. He said, "You want my opinion on what I think when I watch you?"

I said, "Of course."

He said, "You look scared."

He absolutely nailed it. That was exactly how I felt going into every game. Scared because I might lose for the team and scared I might embarrass myself. I let out a sigh of relief when he told me that. I'd been going back and forth about whether I wanted to try to play one more year, and our conversation sealed the deal. I suddenly knew it was my last year. It's funny. You'd think I'd be bummed out, but I wasn't. Instead, I decided to relish the games I had left. Of course, nothing ever goes as planned, right?

Now, this was a rather embarrassing way to end my career, but I played only a few more games, and then I had a devastating injury. We were in St. Louis at the Kiel Center on March 30, 1998. Vernon was back home with his wife, Jane, who was having a baby. We were tied at 1–1 in the second period when Brett Hull took a one-timer from about fifteen feet in front of me. He unleashed that cannon he inherited from his dad, Bobby—about 105 miles per hour—and it caught me in the groin. I wore two cups for protection, but they were useless against this shot. My cherries hit my throat and I went down hard. The play was still alive, but the pain was beyond excruciating. I couldn't get up. You've heard the expression "shivering like a dog shitting razor blades?" Yeah, doesn't come close. They scored, and when I still hadn't moved, our trainer ran out. I was working hard to breathe. He helped me to my feet and I said, "I'm fine, I'll keep playing." Ten seconds later, St. Louis came across the blue line and scored again, and I was pulled and replaced by Jason Muzzatti. I sat on the bench, trying to breathe normally, and eventually went back in for Muzzatti. I let in two more and pulled myself.

Things started swelling up and I had to go to the hospital to make sure there were no ruptures or anything like that. I had an ultrasound, given to me by a male technician who happened to be on shift instead of the female tech he rotated with. Thank God. It was still very painful because the wand had to make contact.

I stepped gently for more than a week, thanks to a pair of black-and-blue navel oranges swinging between my legs. Even Darryl Sutter said he bit down hard every time he looked at me.

On May 2, 1998, in Game Six of the Western Conference quarter-finals, we lost in overtime to the Dallas Stars. We all skated out to congratulate Mike Vernon on such a great year and a great effort and then lined up for the handshakes. Most of the 18,000 fans were still up and cheering because it had been three years since the team had made the playoffs. I knew it was my last time in an NHL jersey. As I stood there, I opened up every one of my senses so I'd be able to relive the moment forever. I looked up into the steel spiderweb of the San Jose Arena rafters. There were no division championship flags yet, but it wouldn't be long. I scanned the crowd and took mental pictures, breathing in the smell of the jerseys, the beer, the popcorn and the burgers. As I skated off, I smiled to myself. Fifteen years. I felt like I was in a dream. A good dream. A great dream. An amazing dream.

Epilogue

MY HEROES WERE JACQUES PLANTE and Bernie Parent. I can't separate the two because they were both so impactful. Plante perfected the stand-up goaltending style of his generation, and Bernie was his protégé. Plante was a game changer in many ways. Everyone remembers him as the first NHL goalie to wear a mask for an extended period, but I really admired him because he was bold in his play and he stood up for himself. He was also really good at moving in and out of the net, forward and back and cutting off the angles. I think the most important thing I took from the way he played was that he handled the puck. Playing the puck became a huge factor in my game.

As far as positioning, my technique evolved from being a full stand-up, where I tried to emulate Plante and Parent, to recognizing that the game was changing and knowing that that style wasn't going to be quite as effective. I was still with the Islanders when I started going down and moving side to side like Glenn Hall. And then, when I moved to L.A., I had to adapt again and become even less rigid. At the insistence of Kings assistant coach Cap Raeder, I got better at sealing off my five-hole on breakaways. I was a bit stubborn about it at first, but I knew in the end he was right, so I became more of a butterfly guy.

First and foremost, what I look for in a goaltender—because once they get to the NHL, they are all so good—is a competitive spirit. I want to see him battle, especially when times aren't easy—when he's not doing very well, either in a game or a tough part of the season. That's one of the great qualities Henrik Lundqvist has. He's emotionally engaged, each and every game. Funnily enough, that can be his downfall too. His passionate reactions might be viewed negatively by some people in the dressing room.

Let me give you an example. In the 2014 final, as soon as Alec Martinez of the Kings scored the Cup-clinching goal against the Rangers, some of Lundqvist's teammates skated over to tap him on the pads. It was a nice, consoling gesture, but he skated away from them. He wanted to be alone. To me, that looked selfish. I know he was probably hurting or pissed and just trying to keep it together, but the picture he presented was that he was the only one who cared, or that he cared more than his teammates about the loss. I didn't like that.

Now, a guy who behaves in the opposite way is Jonathan Quick. I think he's open in the way he cares very much for his teammates, although I also think he's misunderstood as far as the way he competes is concerned.

This may sound funny, but to me, he's gracious. He's really figured out his role on the team and how he complements his

teammates. I interviewed him for *Hockey Night in Canada* at
the end of the 2013 season. The Kings had just won the Cup a
year earlier and would win it again the next year. The interview
took place while L.A. was playing Chicago in the conference
final, right before they lost.

I was impressed by how unselfish Quick is. I told him he
had a great reputation for making the big save at the right
time, and then I cited a few of them. I asked him, "What goes
on in your head? What are you thinking in the last five minutes while protecting a lead?" And his answer was not about
him or what technique he uses or anything like that. Instead,
he said what he thinks is "All right, I owe these guys. They
put us in a position where we can win." In other words, he
owes his team a save. Wow. That kind of attitude would really
resonate in the dressing room.

I think Quick is misunderstood because I don't think enough
people in the hockey world, particularly in the media, know
him well enough. I'm lucky because being a former goalie on
the same team, I share a sort of bond with him, so he always
makes time for me. We've had a lot of good chats. But he's not a
big personality. He keeps his head down, does his job and gives
away a lot of credit. A true team guy.

Quick and Lundqvist don't just have different personalities,
they are completely different in how they view goaltending
and how they play the position. For the majority of his career,
Lundqvist played extremely deep in his net, really close to the
goal line. He relied on his reflexes and his athleticism, knowing

he could react better to a shot if he was deeper because that would give him a greater chance to see the puck.

At the other end of the spectrum, Jonathan Quick is a very aggressive guy. If he's not at the top of the crease, he can be found even farther out than that. Some people think he's too aggressive. I think it's situational, so to me, he reads the play well. It's true, there are occasions when if you are that aggressive you will be picked apart because you're exposed, but it's all about feel, and that's what I like about Quick's style. He reads the play, he commits to it, and as a result, he's successful.

Now, because of that, Jonathan Quick has to really trust his defencemen and be aware of what they're doing. Because if he doesn't, and he plays that aggressively, he'll be picked apart. Quick's style doesn't work for every team. It works for the Los Angeles Kings because they understand him and he understands them.

Nobody could blame Lundqvist for the Rangers' elimination by Ottawa in the second round of the 2017 playoffs. I think he gave the series his all, but as another example of how he can get too ramped up, there was an incident in the first period of Game Five, with just over two minutes to go, where Lundqvist was getting too, too emotional. I think he might have been voicing his displeasure at his own centre, Derek Stepan, during the play.

I watched Stepan go to the bench on a change, and then the whistle blew and Stepan, who was on the far end of the bench, was standing up and yelling something at Lundqvist. And then the whistle blew again and Stepan came back on the ice and skated towards Lundqvist. He was very animated, and you could read his lips. He was saying, "Relax. Relax." And to his credit, Lundqvist got it together and scaled it down for the rest of the game. But as I said, his passion and emotion are two of his major qualities, too. I mean, the Rangers beat Montreal in the first round in 2017 because he was so totally engaged. He willed it to happen.

Corey Crawford of the Chicago Blackhawks has some of the same qualities. Crawford is a fighter and he doesn't get enough recognition for it, but he's very good technically. Corey always finds a way to get the best out of himself.

In 2015, Chicago won its third Stanley Cup in six years. In the first round, they played Nashville. Nashville scored three times in the first period of Game One, and Joel Quenneville pulled Crawford and played Scott Darling, the backup, for the remainder of the game, which the Hawks won in double OT. In Game Six, Darling was pulled in the first period and Quenneville put Crawford back in. I watched Crawford stand up, ready to go. You could see this look of pure focus and concentration on his face. Just before he pulled his mask on, I could see him cursing with resolve.

I love that kind of competitive spirit. Crawford went in and played lights-out and took the Hawks all the way to the Cup. Now, I've never asked Joel Quennveille about this, but I believe that he knew that if he played Darling in those games, it would spark Crawford, just like Darryl Sutter knew he could spark Jonathan Quick in February of 2017, when the Los Angeles

Kings were chasing a playoff spot, by telling the media, "Quick needs to be better."

The Crawford–Darling, Sutter–Quick situations kind of reminded me of what was going on between Barry Melrose and me when I was in a slump and he played Robb Stauber. Although, I don't think Crawford or Quick have ever gone through a stretch like I did. They will, because it happens to almost everybody.

Most goalies go through slumps—it's the nature of the position. You have success, and then you find yourself treading water and sinking. When I hear the media going overboard about a young hotshot—he's on top of the world and fans are chanting his name in the building—I always think to myself, "Just wait. One day, that chanting will be nothing but boos raining down." I've seen it in every rink.

Look at long-time Pittsburgh goalie Marc-André Fleury, now with the Vegas Golden Knights. At the start of the 2017 playoffs, I read an article in the *Toronto Sun* where his general manager, Jim Rutherford, called him the best team player in sports. But I remembered a time when they wanted him out of there.

Pittsburgh won the Stanley Cup in 2009, and then Fleury followed up with some miserable playoff performances. While he struggled, he was willing to work with a sports psychologist. In the 2016 playoffs, he watched a very talented young guy, Matt Murray, come in and win the Stanley Cup. I'm sure it was tough for him. But he's such a competitive, likeable person that all of us former NHL goalies were pulling for him. He's the epitome of a great teammate.

Fleury wasn't supposed to be the Penguins' number one goalie for the 2017 playoffs, but Murray got hurt in the warm-up before the first playoff game. Fleury stepped in and totally stole the first round from the Columbus Blue Jackets and had a huge part in beating Washington in the second round, and that's all because of attitude. He played until the third round of the Eastern Conference final, and then Murray took over again.

I thought Fleury made such a classy move when he was handed the Stanley Cup on the ice after the Penguins' victory that year. He went for the usual skate with the Cup, and then, knowing fully that he wouldn't be with the team after the expansion draft in June, the first thing he did was hand the Cup to his goaltending partner, Matt Murray.

I believe that in the history of the game, goaltending has never been better. I say this for a number of reasons. There is so much talent out there right now, the equipment has never been better, and the technical approach to the position has advanced. I would have loved to play the way they do now, but we didn't want to get hurt by going down on our knees all the time. It was painful in those little pads we used to wear. These guys today don't have to contend with pain, or at least the way that we did.

I know this is going to be a controversial thing to say, but in my era goaltenders were the weak link for most teams. Just look at some of the bad goals we let in. You don't see goals like that anymore. Nobody comes down the wing anymore and just fires a slapshot the way Mike Bossy or Mike Gartner did. The puck wouldn't go in today. Why not? Because today, every goal-tender plays a variation of the same style. I would guess that only about one in forty-five straight-on shots in the NHL go in. You rarely beat goalies with straight-on shots today.

And in the old days, guys used to be able to pass it one way, then pass it the other way, which left the goalie out of position and the net open, but today's goalies beat the pass, and then beat the pass again, and they're still in position. They make the save, and rather than scrambling and diving and having to fig-ure out what leg to stick out to make the next save, they use back-leg recovery to spring up and get back into position.

The goalie's job today is to be in the middle of the net. The middle of the net is where he has the best chance to make the save. So if the puck goes across the ice, he simply gets up with his back leg. Say he pulls power from the right side, he will push himself to the left. We used to do whatever we could to get across to make a save. There wasn't a whole lot of rhyme or reason to it. The idea was "If I can make the save, then I'm good." Today, it's "If I can be in position, I will make the save."

In the eighties and nineties there was a ton of talent in net—legendary names like Patrick Roy, Ed Belfour, Curtis Joseph, Mike Richter, John Vanbiesbrouck, Bill Ranford, Mike Vernon, Grant Fuhr, Dominik Hasek, Martin Brodeur, Félix Potvin and Ron Hextall. Andy Moog was one of my favour-ites to watch. So was Arturs Irbe. The list is so extensive. Chris Osgood, Pete Peeters and Kirk McLean also come to mind. And the interesting thing is, each of us played a completely different game. The goaltenders of the eighties and nineties had to be ridiculously good athletes to be able to develop their own style and make some of the saves they made by relying on reflexes and reading plays.

Take Mike Vernon and Patrick Roy—they were virtually playing different games. Vernon was standing up and using angles, focusing on using his limbs to stop pucks. Mike was an incredibly good goalie and a winner, but so was Patrick Roy, who, like Jean-Sébastien Giguère, was a student of François Allaire, the man who refined the butterfly, a technique that every goalie uses today.

Almost everything that goalies do today comes from François Allaire. He's the one who started with back-leg recovery, which led to inside edge pushes—instead of getting up for the next save, stay down with the load on your back leg and push across, rotating the butterfly and making a save again.

Marc-André Fleury was huge with back-leg recovery around the same time as Giguère. Remember, he was the big star in the World Junior Championship—he had the big yellow pads and got a lot of attention. He was using cutting-edge techniques that the NHL guys weren't onto yet. The butterfly, and then back-leg recovery from the butterfly have been the biggest changes in goaltending. Glenn Hall was the innovator of the butterfly, and then Allaire coached both Roy and Giguère, who made it popular.

Before that, as Mike Vernon did in the eighties and nineties, a goalie would stand there and make as many saves as he could.

He'd be really difficult to score on with a straight-on shot, but now basically everything is movement. Goalies don't have to scramble into position to make a save, because they are already in position for every save. The idea now is that it's all based on movement rather than save technique.

That's the biggest thing that's changed in the game and put everyone on the same page—movement before the saves. Moving from one place to the next in the net with efficiency, understanding path of direction, and moving through the paint to get to a certain position. Making the save is really the simplest part now, and every save is essentially made with a variation on the butterfly. Whether you're extended to one side, on the post, or on the shoulder in a "lean" position. And finally, after the save, there is structure as well.

I was talking with NHL goaltending coach Eli Wilson recently and he said, "The way the position is played today, the detail, the technique behind it, it's like a map. You can follow it and become really good. The goalies in earlier years were super talents with no map on how to execute. The way we teach now makes it way easier to be a good goalie."

It's hard to even make a list of the best goalies today because so much of their success is based on their team and circumstance. I've always felt there's a difference between being the best and winning. There's Roberto Luongo, who's not going away. He's still good every night. Craig Anderson in Ottawa beats guys left, right and centre. Lundqvist's former backup, Cam Talbot—now the starter in Edmonton—is coming into his own. He's as good as any on any given night in the league. Pekka Rinne has come back again in 2016–17 after struggling. He's a dominant goalie.

Braden Holtby of Washington really grabs my attention because he's so consistent. He's learned how to provide a high level of goaltending every single night. That's what most coaches and managers look for. Highs and lows are okay, but no big valleys in between.

But I think Carey Price has had maybe the biggest impact on the position of goaltending since Giguère and Roy. He's the role model for young kids now. You actually see it. If you go to a game outside the NHL, you see the guys copying what Carey does. I love his talent level. I love his demeanour. I love how he approaches the game. Before I knew much about him, I remember watching him in Sochi at the Olympics. He was in a really difficult position because Canada wasn't scoring very much, and he wasn't getting a lot of action himself, but he was still able to make huge saves at the right time. I thought, "He just doesn't ever seem to get rattled. And I don't know if below the surface he's like that duck—calm on top of the water but paddling like crazy underneath."

Now that I've watched him more, I see that he's like a Tai Chi master—he only expends the effort needed. A lot of goalies try to be fast, to beat plays and be on top of it, and they do it with this crazy effort that makes them scramble. Carey has this calmness and smoothness about him that doesn't make him slow. In reality, it makes him unbelievably fast. Early on, in his younger days, people felt he wasn't working very hard because of all the self-control that he had.

This is just an example, but look at Jonathan Quick. He's super-fast. He scrambles around the net, moving quickly from one side to the next, up and down. Carey does all that and more, but with no wasted effort. And by all accounts, he's super coachable.

A lot of people think being coachable means there is good communication between him and his coach, but it really doesn't. Coachable means that when the coach says, "Do this," the player can do it.

Eli Wilson is Carey's coach, and—full disclosure—I'm on the board of Eli's foundation for his goalie schools. Eli has a brilliant mind and eye for the game. He's written a great book called *Hockey Goaltending: The Definitive Guide to Elite Goaltending.* Eli came up with the idea of lead-leg recovery coming off the post position. That's when you're down on the post position, and you get up off the lead leg. When the goalie is on the post in a lean position—which means he's down on the ice, leaning on the post and the puck's in the corner—say there's going to be a pass from the corner and then a high slap. The goalie is going to recover on his lead leg and get to the top of the paint in a hurry.

Most goalies that Eli has introduced the concept to—and these are pros—would stumble for a while, not quite understand it right away. The first time Eli showed Carey how to recover off the post, it was like he'd been doing it for four years. There was no flaw in his execution whatsoever. It was done to perfection.

But I suppose the thing I'm drawn to more than anything about Carey is his community involvement. He's got a really great heart. He helps people from all walks of life. Two summers ago, he was involved in Eli Wilson's really cool one-day camp in Kelowna, British Columbia, for kids from across the country. They were flown in and got outfitted from head to toe with free equipment. I was invited, and I was with them the entire day, morning until night. It was amazing to see how Carey treated the kids.

At the start of this book, I talked about how I put my idols, like Jean Béliveau and Bobby Orr, on a pedestal. Part of it was the mystery of what went on on the bench or behind the dressing-room doors. The hockey rink was its own little world. Well, that doesn't exist anymore. The game has changed, and we are in much different times where you have interviews with coaches on the bench in the middle of the game, and players are multimillionaires who have zero privacy. They can't do anything without being noticed.

I'm not saying it's better or worse, just different. The locker room is different, the personalities are different, the money's different, the influence of agents is different, the business part is different. But watching Carey with those kids almost made me emotional, because I saw for myself that the heart of hockey will never change. Players still understand how important it is to do the right thing.

Acknowledgements

We lost my dad, Steve, just before I started this book, but I still feel him by my side whenever I take on something big, and so thanks, Dad, for always watching out for me. I want to thank my brother, Ken, and mom, Pauline, for cheering me on through thick and thin. They were the ones in the stands, but I am their biggest fan.

Special thanks go out to my teammates on every team I played for, from peewee to the pros, from the Medicine Hat Tigers to the Indianapolis Checkers, through the New York Islanders, Los Angeles Kings and San Jose Sharks to the *Hockey Night in Canada* panel and Calgary Flames broadcast team. Leaders like Denis Potvin, Bob Nystrom, Wayne Gretzky, Luc Robitaille and Ron MacLean inspire and raise the bar for all of us.

I would like to thank my friend and teammate Kirstie McLellan Day, without whom my own personal journey and stories would never have been told my way.

Kirstie and I would like to thank the following people for their friendship and help in writing this book: Kirstie's content team—her husband and partner, contributing writer and editor Larry Day; chief researcher and right hand Kaitlyn Kanygin; hockey expert and fact checker Ron Wight; Julie Sinclair on the details; Steve McLellan, our number one transcriber; as well as Len Glickman from Cassels Brock Lawyers. Kirstie also wants to thank her family for supporting her through the long hours it takes to make a book like this happen—Buddy, Kristin, Téa, Jaxon, Griffin, Charlie, Lundy, Geordie and Paul, and her folks, Bud and Joan McLellan.

From HarperCollins, Jim Gifford, our editor, for his mentorship, constant support and sage advice; Lloyd Davis for his keen eye; Jeremy Rawlings and Alison Woodbury for their legal advice; Noelle Zitzer and Patricia MacDonald for editorial assistance; Leo MacDonald, senior VP of sales and marketing; Michael Guy-Haddock, senior sales director; Irina Pintea and Colleen Simpson, publicity; Iris Tupholme, senior VP and executive publisher; and CEO Craig Swinwood.

We'd also like to thank historian Radomir Bilash, Doug Bodger, photo expert Tom Braid, Pat Conacher, Jimmy Devellano, Gerald Diduck, Eric Duhatschek, Lloyd and Carol Friedland, Greg Gilbert, Todd Gill, Tony Granato, Wayne Gretzky, Darren Haynes, Glenn Healy, Donna Hrudey, Ken Hrudey, Pauline Hrudey, Troy Loney, Andrea Malysh of the Canadian First World War Internment Recognition Fund, Ron and Cari MacLean, NHL Alumni and BreakAway Program's Wendy McCreary, Bruce McNall, Barry Melrose, legal historian Mark Minenko, Scott Moore, Ken Morrow, Larry Murphy, Bernie Nicholls, Bob Nystrom, Terry O'Reilly, Luc Robitaille, Doug Smeaton, Brent Sutter, Bill Torrey, Bryan Trottier, Andy Van Hellemond, Mike Vernon, Tom Webster and Eli Wilson.

Index

Smeaton, Doug, 24
Smith, Billy, 10, 13, 35, 36, 43–44, 64,
66–69, 78–79, 159
Smith, Craig, 91
Solheim, Ken, 17
sports psychologists, 163, 224
Springsteen, Bruce, 210–11
Stallone, Sylvester, 118
Stasiuk, Vic, 23–24, 32
Stauber, Robb, 158, 177, 228, 294
as starting goalie, 160, 161, 175
trade to Buffalo, 229
Stepan, Derek, 292–93
steroids, 47–48, 256
Stewart, Monte, 173–74
stick blades
curved, 183–86
goaltender's focus on, 82–83, 251
Storr, Jamie, 228
Sudafed, 256
Suter, Gary, 141, 154
Suter, Brent, 18, 40, 42, 56, 84, 136–38
Suter, Brian, 137
Suter, Connie, 102
Suter, Darryl, 158, 287
criticism of players, 269–70
handling of Sharks rookies, 272, 275–77
handling of Sharks veterans, 265–69
as Kings coach, 293–94
softer side of, 277–78
work ethic, 241
Suter, Duane, 74, 84
Sweeney, Don, 231
Sydor, Darryl, 155
Sykora, Michal, 257

Talbot, Cam, 298–99
Tardif, Patrice, 247
Taylor, Beth, 144
Taylor, Dave, 130, 144, 222
Terreri, Chris, 253–55, 257
Thomas, Wayne, 249–50
Thornton, Joe, 270
"three-shower prank," 131–32
Tikkanen, Esa, 147
Tonelli, John, 44, 45
Toronto Maple Leafs, 178–82

Torrey, Bill, 8, 137
management of team budget, 44–46
promotion of Hrudey to Islanders, 34–35
and trade of Hrudey to L.A., 107–9
Tremblay, Mario, 259
Trottier, Bryan, 11–12, 45, 63, 77–78, 84,
87, 214
Trottier, Monty, 34
Trotz, Barry, 70–71
Tsujiura, Steve, 18
Tsuygurov, Denis, 229–30
Tufts, Ray, 255

Ultimate Orange, 48

Vachon, Rogie, 113, 128, 232
Van Halen, Eddie, 211
Van Hellemond, Andy, 87, 90, 92
Vanbiesbrouck, John, 74
Vanbiesbrouck, Rosalyn, 74
Vancouver Canucks, 177–78
Vernon, Jane, 281–82, 287
Vernon, Mike, 23, 112, 279–84, 287, 297
Vopat, Roman, 247

Waite, Jimmy, 158
Washington Capitals, 36–37, 81–95
Watters, Tim, 155
Webster, Tom, 128–34, 137, 141–42,
145–49, 206
Wickenheiser, Doug, 60
Willis, Bruce, 210–11
Wilson, Eli, 298, 300–301
Winnipeg Jets, 55

Yaremco, Mary. *See* Karpo, Mary
(grandmother)
Yzerman, Steve, 120

Zhitnik, Alexei, 155, 229
Zultek, Matt, 247